IMAGES
of America

MARTIN COUNTY REVISITED

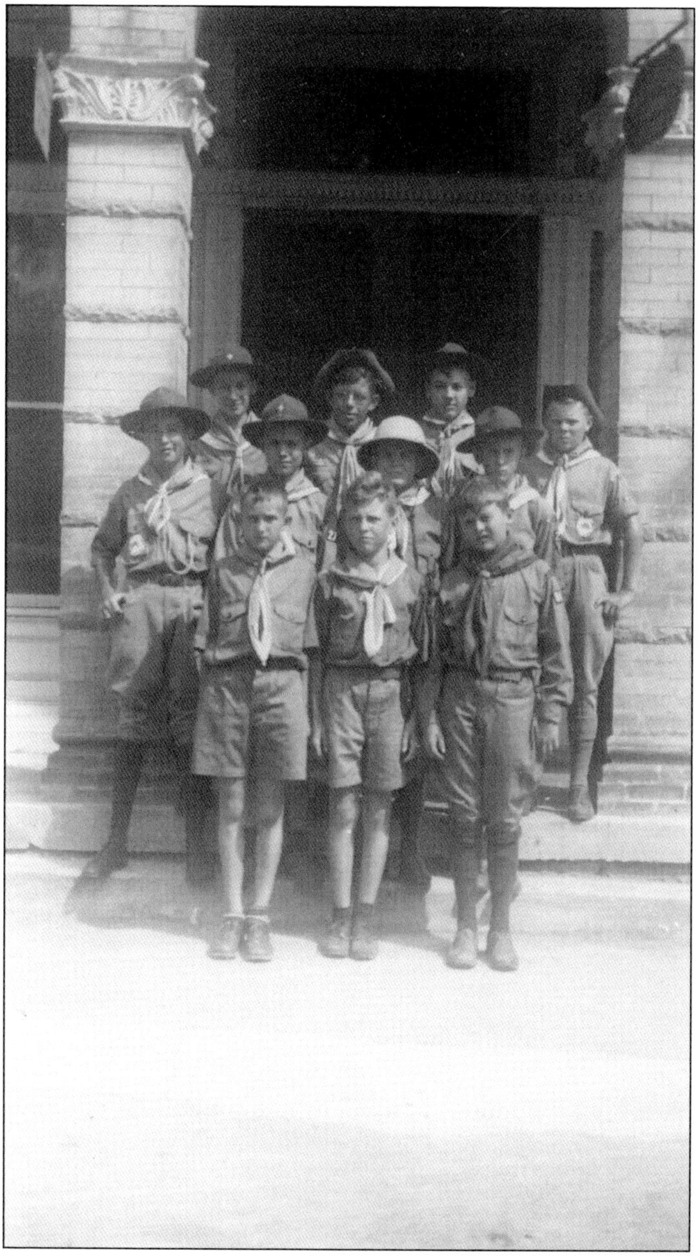

WILLIAMSTON BOY SCOUTS, C. 1940. In 1932, Boy Scout organizations in Williamston, Greenville, and Washington, North Carolina, merged with others in the eastern section of North Carolina to form the East Carolina Council of Boy Scouts. (Courtesy of Martin County Historical Society.)

ON THE COVER: A marching band moves west along Main Street in the 1952 Williamston Harvest Festival parade. A highly promoted event, the Williamston Harvest Festival began as an annual event in 1947 in celebration of the harvests connected with tobacco and peanuts and their great economic impact to the area. (Courtesy of the J.Y. Joyner Library, East Carolina Manuscript Collection.)

IMAGES
of America

MARTIN COUNTY REVISITED

Fred W. Harrison Jr.

ARCADIA
PUBLISHING

ISBN 978-1-4671-2052-4

Published by Arcadia Publishing
Charleston, South Carolina

Printed in the United States of America

Library of Congress Control Number: 2013937019

For all general information, please contact Arcadia Publishing:
Telephone 843-853-2070
Fax 843-853-0044
E-mail sales@arcadiapublishing.com
For customer service and orders:
Toll-Free 1-888-313-2665

Visit us on the Internet at www.arcadiapublishing.com

To my dear and loving parents,
Fred W. Harrison Sr. and Ann Holliday Harrison

Contents

ACKNOWLEDGMENTS

Many thanks go out to all who have either encouraged or assisted me in some way with this project. My great regret is that time did not allow for a more exhaustive search for images that I know would have made the volume all the more valuable. As they say, the show most go on, and I can only hope that others gain inspiration from this modest effort to continue preservation of Martin County's visual record.

Much credit and thanks are extended to the Martin County Historical Society for its stewardship of many valuable images contained within this volume. The society's continued perseverance in maintaining a local history archive for nearly 30 years now, with only the aid of volunteers, is commendable. Without the benefit of that archive, this volume may have developed little beyond its initial consideration.

I am very appreciative of the North Carolina Museum of History for providing copies of some previously unpublished photographs of Jamesville, North Carolina, dating to 1888. Although Jamesville is the second-oldest town in Martin County, there is little physical evidence today that indicates its rich past associated with the Roanoke River and a once notable lumber and shingle industry.

Included herein are images by several well-known 20th-century Martin County photographers and studios. They are Eugene Rice of Williamston, Royal Photographic Studio of Williamston (owned by the Tetterton family), B.W. Parker, and Irving L. Smith Sr. of Robersonville. Their respective artistic abilities in capturing the essence of Martin County cannot be overstated.

In addition to those mentioned above, other organizations assisting this effort include J.Y. Joyner Library's special collections division, providing images from, in particular, the East Carolina Manuscript Collection and the Verona Joyner Langford North Carolina Collection. Longtime mentor and friend Maury York was gracious in providing permissions to publish negatives located in the *Daily Reflector* collection and several unrelated holdings. Also, I thank John Lawrence with the Verona Joyner Langford North Carolina Collection for procuring for that collection, at my request, a number of rare Civil War depictions relevant to Martin County.

Further thanks go to the *News and Observer*; North Carolina Division of Archives and History; the Williamston *Enterprise & Weekly Herald*; individual contributors Ila Parker, Elizabeth Roberson, Elizabeth Brandon, Rita Mizell, Gail Everett, Gene and Jean Rogers, the late Irving Smith Jr., Judy Critcher, Jesse Silverthorne, Martha McDonald, Madge R. Partin (Robersonville Public Library), and Beverly Mills; and supporters Cynthia James and Fred and Ann Harrison.

Finally, I thank Patsy Roberson Miller, who put into my possession her entire personal collection of photographs, knowing better than I that I might put them to use someday for the greater benefit of Martin County history. I hope she is pleased.

INTRODUCTION

Few places in North Carolina boast a more diverse and interesting history than Martin County. From its earliest period, Martin has been somewhat of a microcosm of the drama and events that have played out on the national stage. First documented by Ralph Lame's expedition up the Roanoke River in the 1580s as a result of Sir Walter Raleigh's first attempt to settle a colony in the New World, the area now known as Martin County would eventually form the entrance to North Carolina's first proprietary precinct, Albemarle County, in the late 1600s. By the 18th century, it had become home to families like the Smithwicks, whose speculative land ventures fostered a diverse array of new immigrants who would in turn see to Martin's improved status as a county in its own right in 1774.

It is surprising to many today to learn that one of Martin County's early citizens was the first individual elected as president of the United States—prior to ratification of the Constitution. As far-fetched as it may sound, the fact is that Samuel Johnston was elected by Congress under the nation's first form of government, the Articles of Confederation. He refused the post, citing the need to attend more to personal affairs neglected during the Revolutionary War, but continued active involvement in state and national affairs until his death in 1815. His home, The Hermitage, stood in the vicinity of the present-day Roanoke Landing Shopping Center in Williamston.

Speaking of the county's shire town, another notable character to grace Martin County for a short while in the 1790s was Eliza Bowen. The New York socialite, more notoriously known as Madame Jumel, died in 1865, and a famed court case over her will revealed a rather adventurous past and residence in a rented home in Williamston.

After completion of the Roanoke River Bridge and causeway in 1922, Williamston developed as a stop along the East Coast's first interstate highway—the Ocean Highway, or US 17—during the 1930s and 1940s. By the early 1950s, downtown establishments like the George Reynolds Hotel closed in favor of the automobile-friendly convenience of motels and trendier restaurants like the Town and Country Restaurant, which opened its doors in 1955.

Parades of various sorts have long been part of Williamston's history. Some of the most memorable and best promoted may have been those attached to the Williamston Harvest Festivals of the late 1940s and 1950s.

A small but special chapter in this volume highlights a long history of family reunions held by the Benjamin Harvey Roberson family. While the tradition of annual family reunions in Martin County is not unique to this family, it is remarkable that they saw fit so early on to maintain a historical record of their gatherings. Benjamin Harvey Roberson descendants comprise one of several branches making up Martin County's overall Roberson family, which traces its beginning in the area to Henry (early spelling Robason) Roberson (1747–1818). The town of Robersonville is named for the sons of Henry Roberson, and their offspring continue to flourish there today.

Martin County saw great destruction in the Civil War as battles at Little Creek and Rawls's Mill made the area the talk of national and international newspapers.

The 1925 Needleman Case, the 1963 civil rights episode, baseball, tobacco, peanuts, and Williamston's growing importance as a major highway hub mark highlights of activity that saw the county through much of the 20th century.

Today, Martin County stands tall on more than two centuries of history. A peek through just a few pages of her past reveals a land full of down-home heritage and unending hospitality.

One

People and Places to Remember

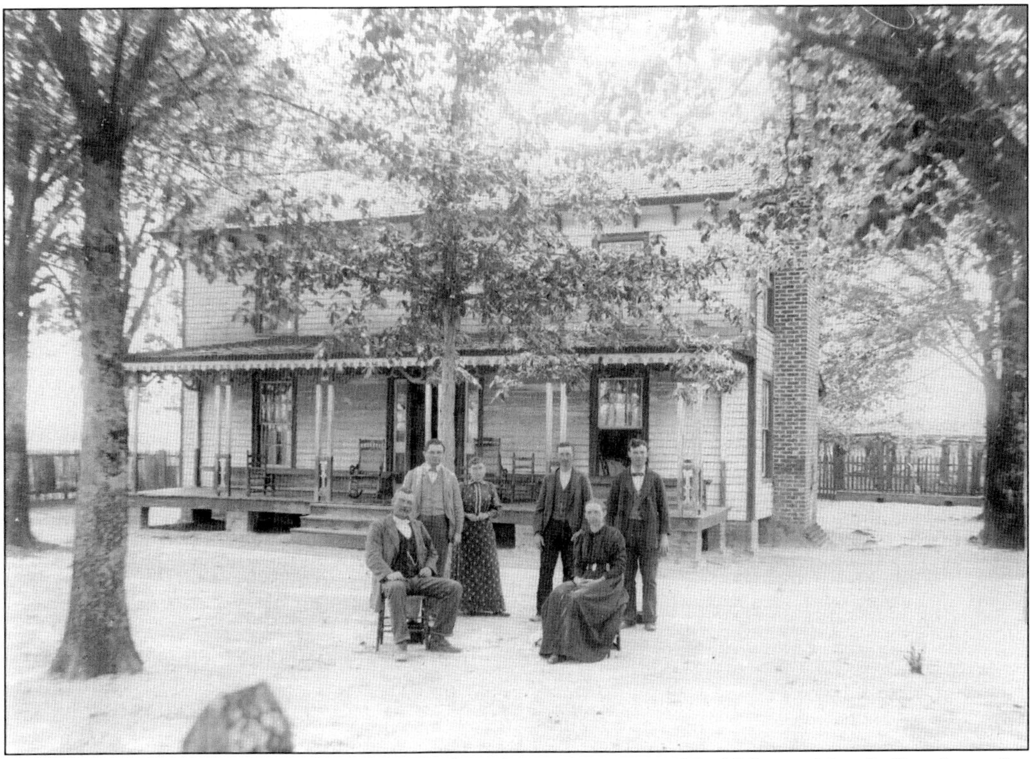

John E. Roberson Family, 1898. Located in the community of Gold Point, North Carolina, the John E. Roberson home was acquired in the 20th century by the Vanderford family. John E. and Sarah Coburn Roberson were parents of J.H. Roberson and grandparents of Vance L. Roberson of Robersonville. (Courtesy of Patsy R. Miller.)

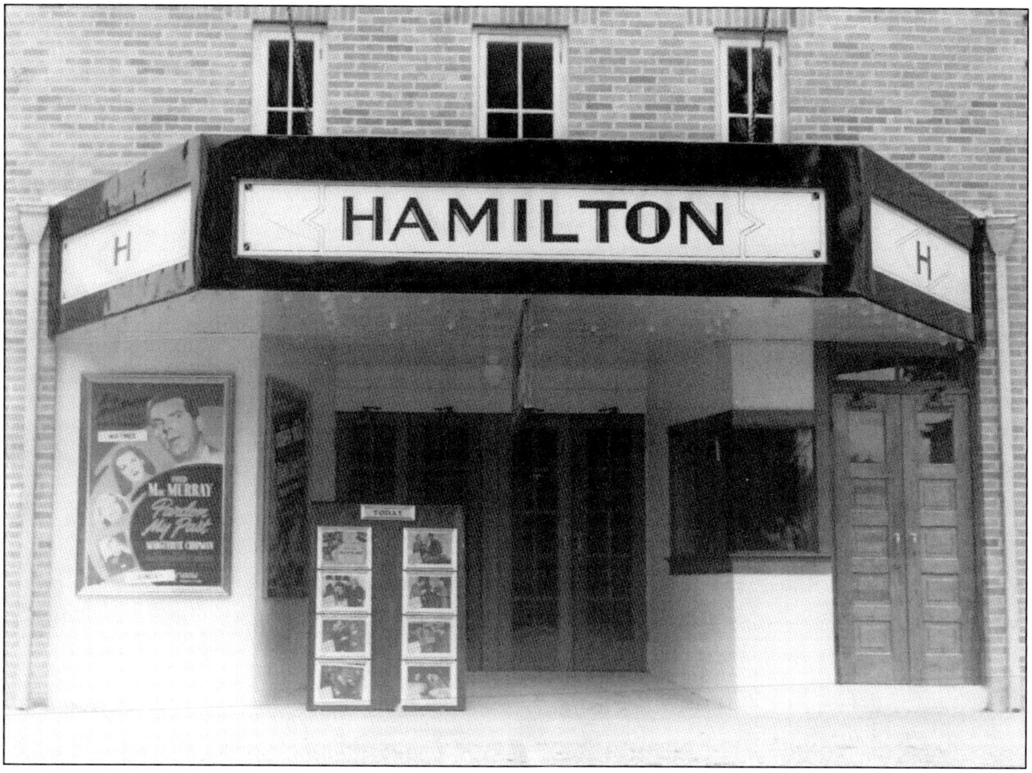

HAMILTON MOVIE THEATER, C. 1945. This business served Hamilton, North Carolina, and the surrounding area throughout the 1940s and early 1950s. (Courtesy of Martin County Historical Society.)

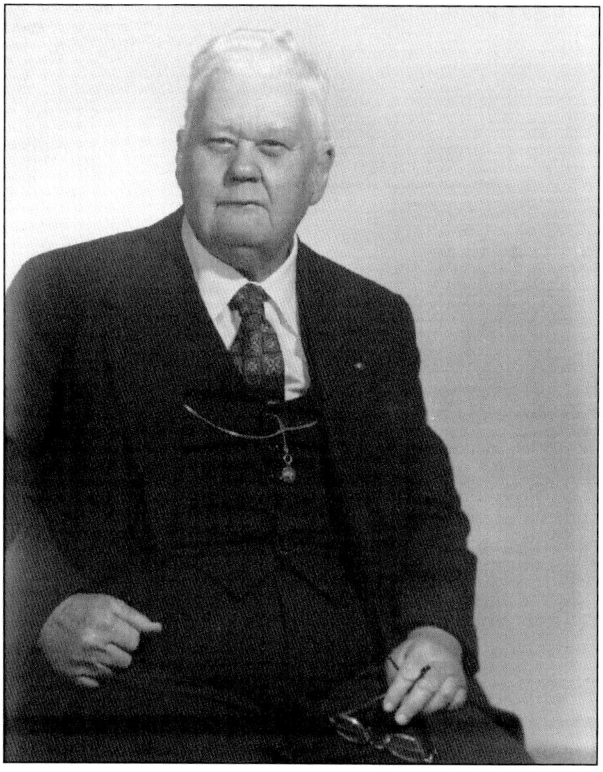

ROBERT BURTON NELSON, C. 1960. Nelson, a Robersonville native and North Carolina's only officially designated highway promoter, graduated from North Carolina State College in 1928 with a degree in engineering. In 1947, he became interested in advising and coordinating the development of new and existing highways across the state. A portion of the road in front of his home on Academy Street in Robersonville was designated as the Robert Burton Nelson Highway compliments of former North Carolina governor James E. Holshouser. (Courtesy of Jesse Silverthorne.)

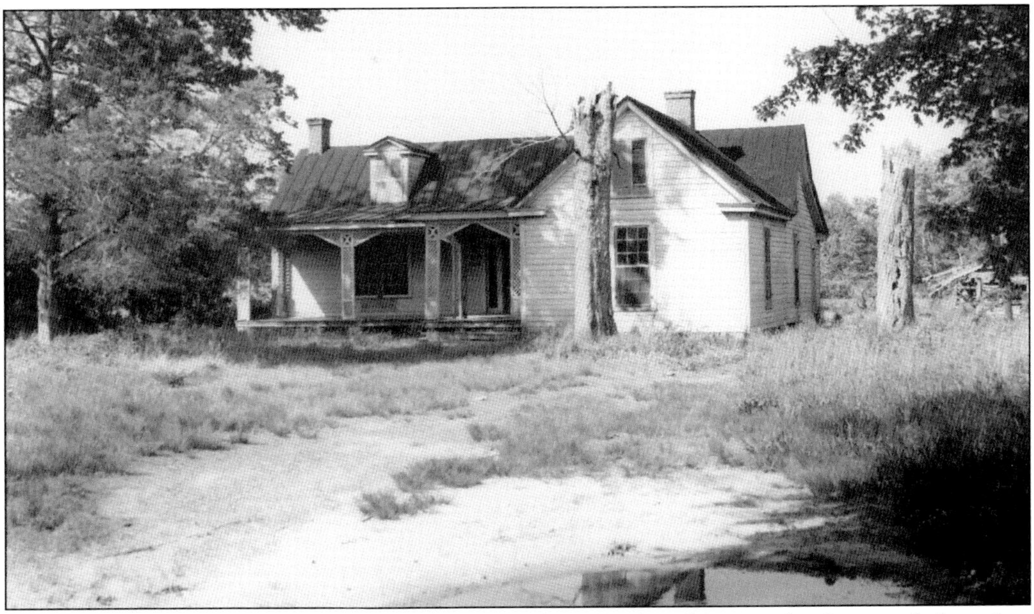

Dr. S.W. Watts Home, 1960. Located on Hamilton's Railroad Street, this home is believed to have been built just prior to the Civil War. It has since been demolished. (Courtesy of Martin County Historical Society.)

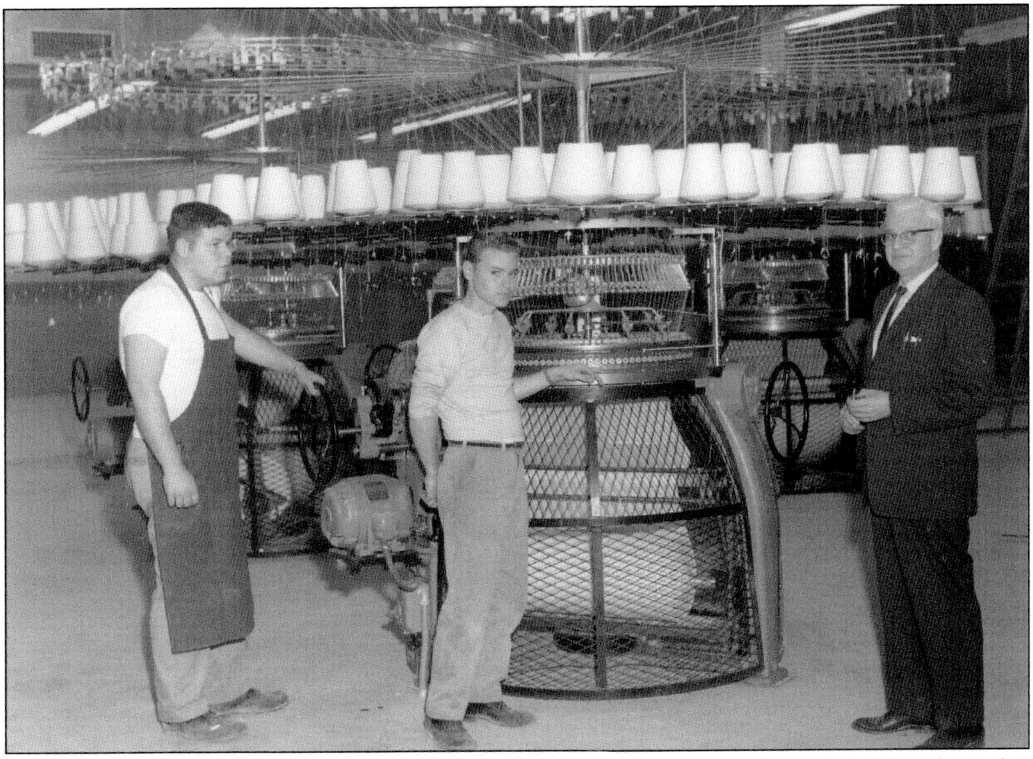

Beaunit Mills, February 15, 1962. Located on a 47-acre site outside the town of Hamilton, this company began operating in January 1962 with the purpose of manufacturing knitted synthetic yarn. (Courtesy of Martin County Historical Society.)

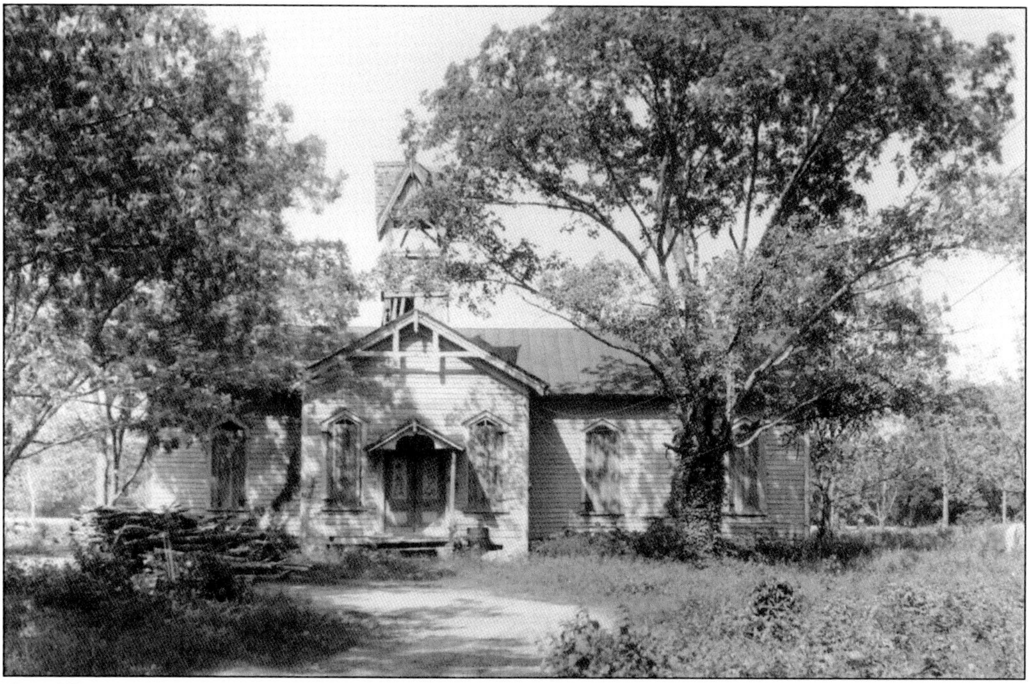

Old Hamilton Academy, April 1967. Built sometime in the late 1800s, this school was used until 1924. R.B. Salisbury is credited with building the structure and later selling it to the local school board. It has since been demolished. (Courtesy of Martin County Historical Society.)

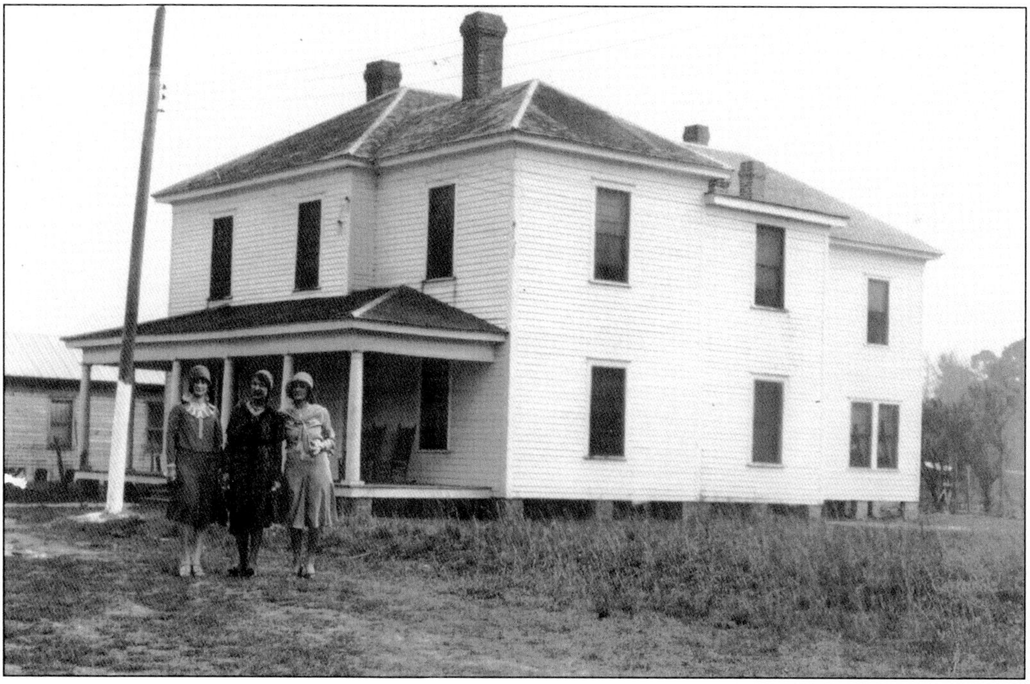

Oak City Teacherage, c. 1929. During the early 20th century, before paved roads and widespread automobile travel, the need for teacher accommodations was prevalent in nearly every community in Martin County. (Courtesy of Martin County Historical Society.)

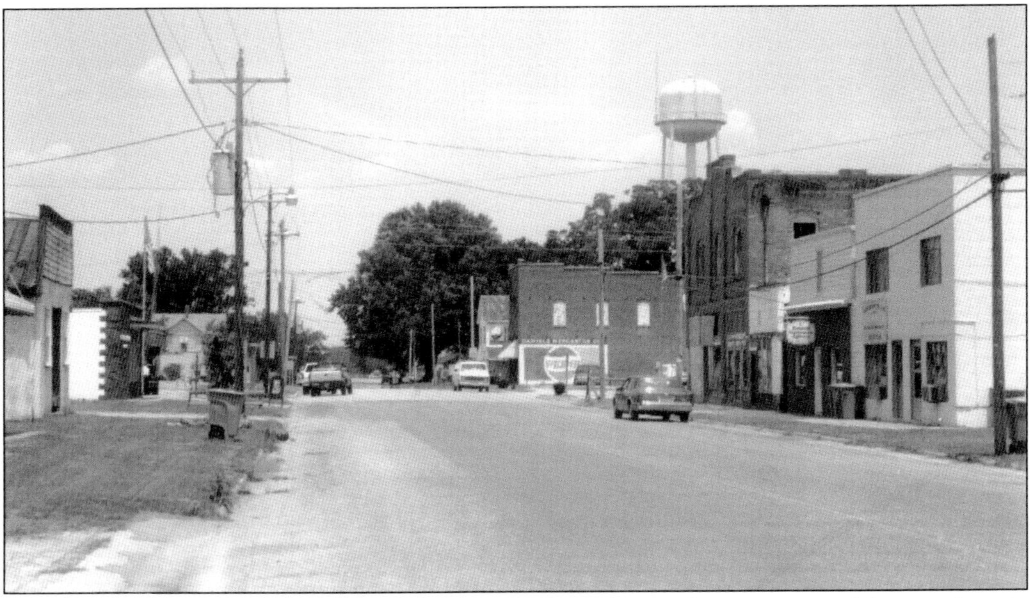

Downtown Oak City, c. 1990. This view scans along the northeast section of the town's main corridor. A once thriving center along the railroad in western Martin County, the town has sadly lost many of its early commercial buildings in recent years. Brick structures seen here have since been torn down. (Courtesy of Martin County Historical Society.)

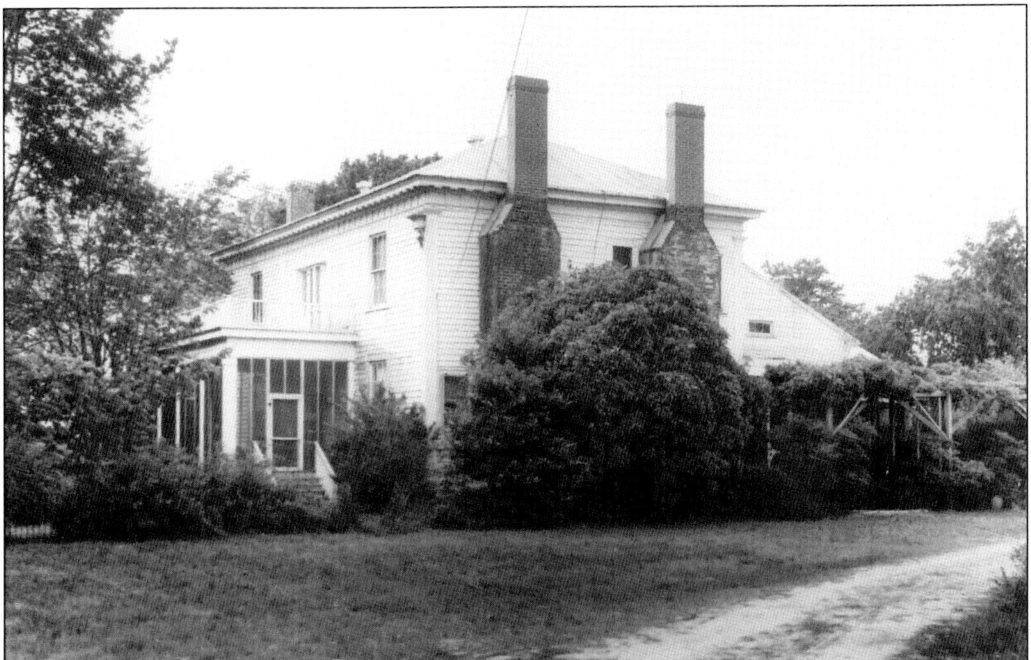

Swamplawn Plantation (Jones-Everett House), c. 1960. Constructed in 1857 by well-known North Carolina builder Albert G. Jones, this house was first occupied by wealthy planter Thomas Jones. The Justus Everett family bought the home in the 1880s. In 1925, when R.O. Everett entertained the graduating class of Oak City High School on the home's front lawn, then governor Angus Mclean attended and gave a speech. (Courtesy of Martin County Historical Society.)

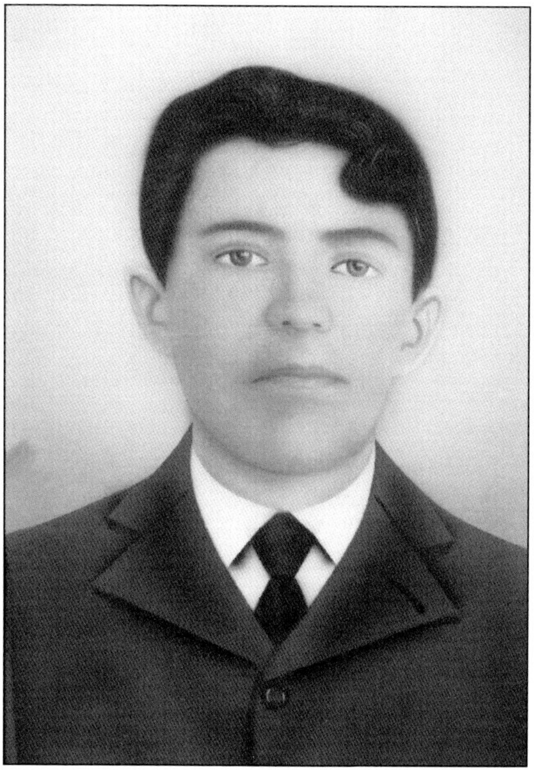

Robert Dawson "Bob" Jones (1882–1960), c. 1902. Williams Township resident and farmer Jones was born in Pitt County and moved with his parents, Dan J. and Martha T. Jones, to Martin County during his childhood. He was married to Martha Ann Perry Jones. (Courtesy of Martha J. McDonald.)

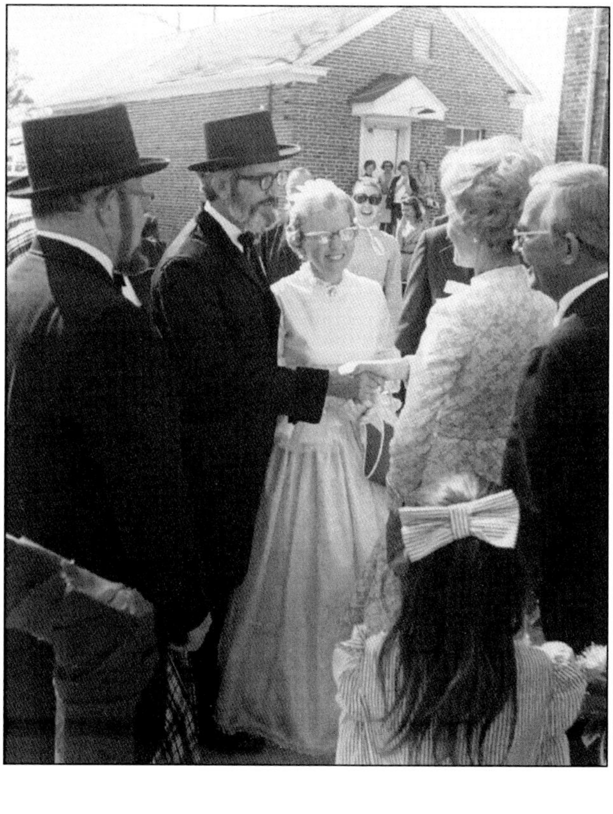

Pat Nixon's Robersonville Visit, April 1972. First Lady Pat Nixon (second from right) is greeted by Robersonville dignitaries, from far left to right, Donnie Hardison and Mayor Wilson and Mary Wynne during her visit to the town's centennial celebration. The man on the far right is believed to be a government official, while the young girl is unidentified. (Courtesy of Madge R. Partin, Robersonville Public Library.)

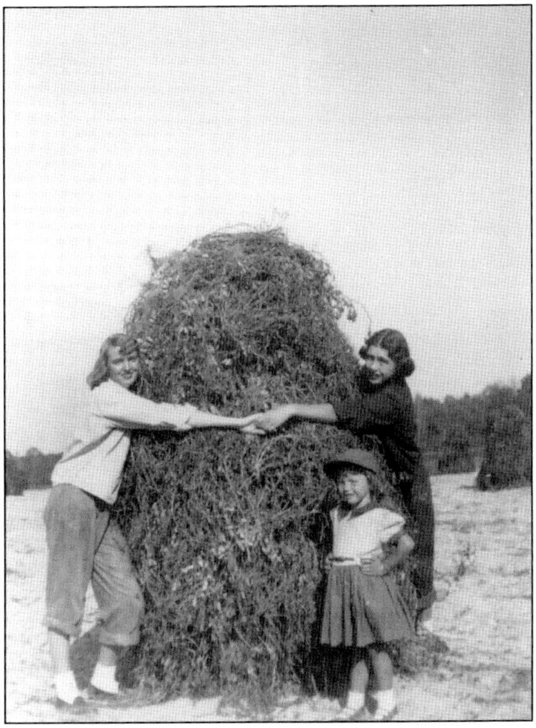

PEANUT HARVEST, C. AUTUMN 1953. Polly Williams (left), Nell Holliday (center), and Ann Holliday gather around one of numerous peanut stacks in a field outside Williamston. (Courtesy of Ann H. Harrison.)

ROBERSONVILLE MAIN STREET GATHERING, C. 1940. R.H. Taylor from Gold Point, North Carolina, is identified on the horse at center. (Courtesy of Irving L. Smith Jr.)

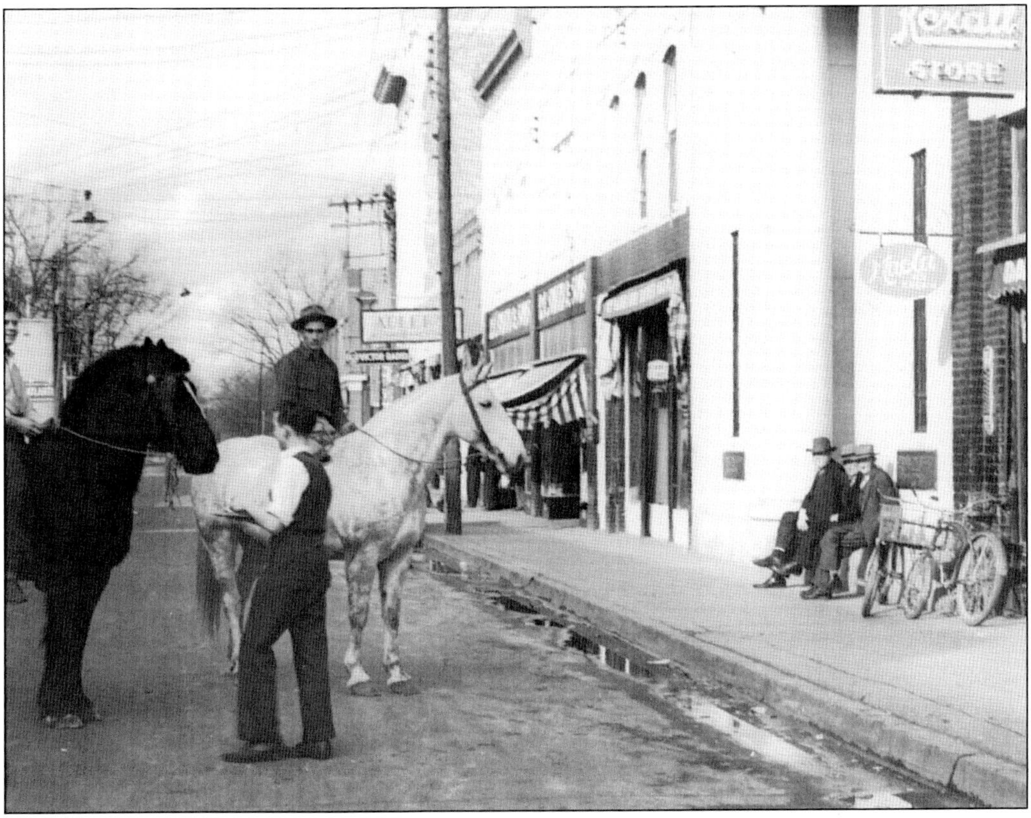

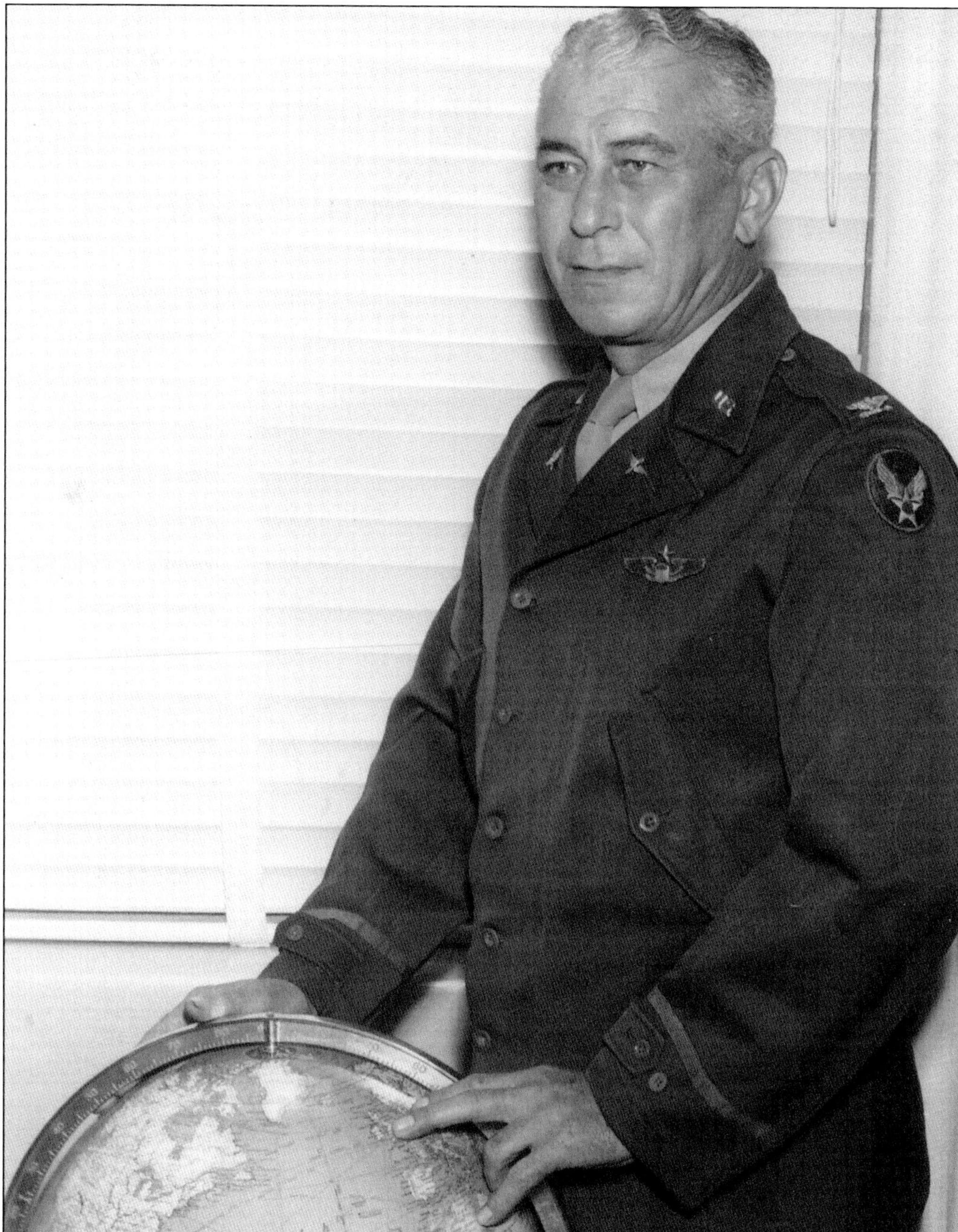

Gen. Frank Armstrong, December 1953. Armstrong was a highly acclaimed military figure, and his exploits during World War II later became the subject of a best-selling novel and the hit movie *Twelve O'Clock High*. Armstrong was born in Hamilton, North Carolina, lived for a time with his grandparents J.A. and Annie Deborah Long Hobbs in Williamston, and spent the remainder of his formative years in Hobgood, North Carolina. He married Vernell "Fluffy" Lloyd on March 15, 1929, and they had one son, Frank A. "Dutch" Armstrong III. Dutch and his wife, Vera, had one daughter, Lloyd Armstrong. (Courtesy of Martin County Historical Society.)

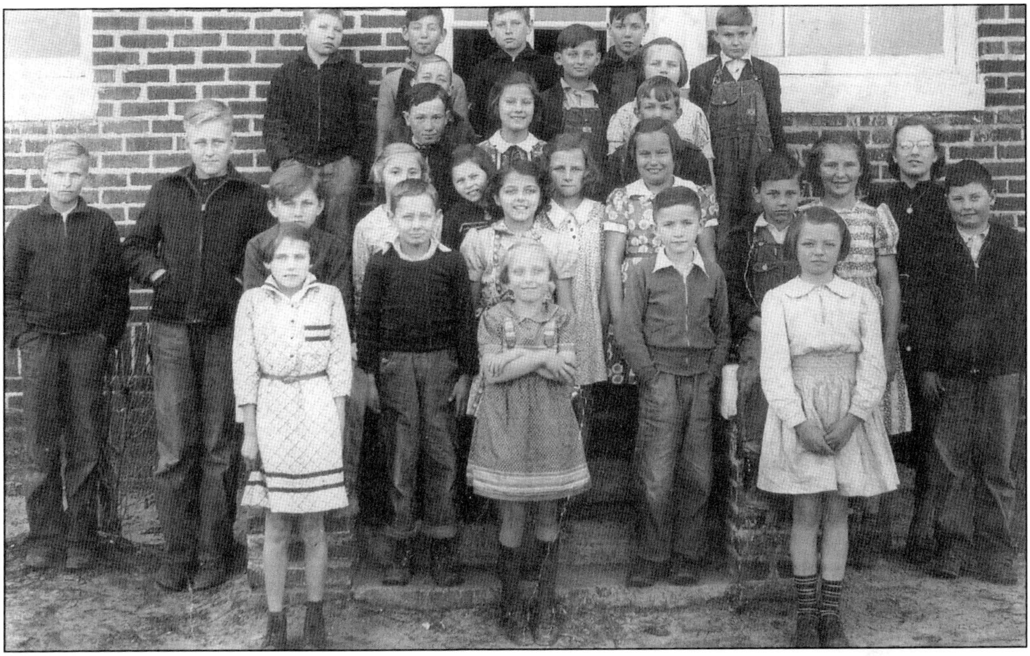

Bear Grass Grammar School Students, c. 1937–1938. The Bear Grass School was constructed in 1926 and replaced an earlier structure across the road that was destroyed by fire. (Courtesy of R. Eugene Rogers.)

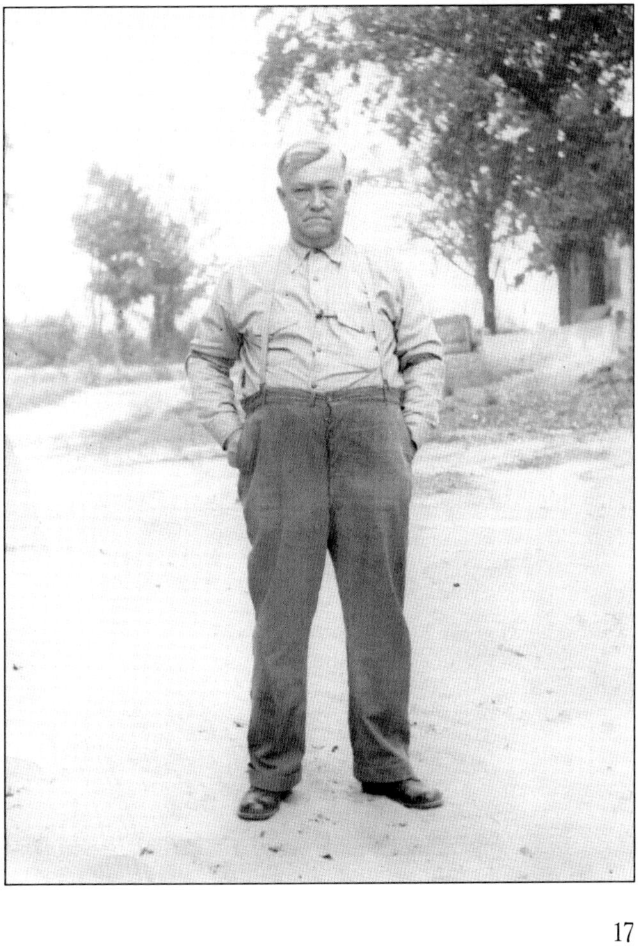

James Samuel "Sam" Jones, c. 1940. Sam Jones, brother of Bob Jones, came to Williamston from Pitt County with his family as a child. A farmer by trade, Sam was married to Charlotte Andrews Jones. (Courtesy of the author.)

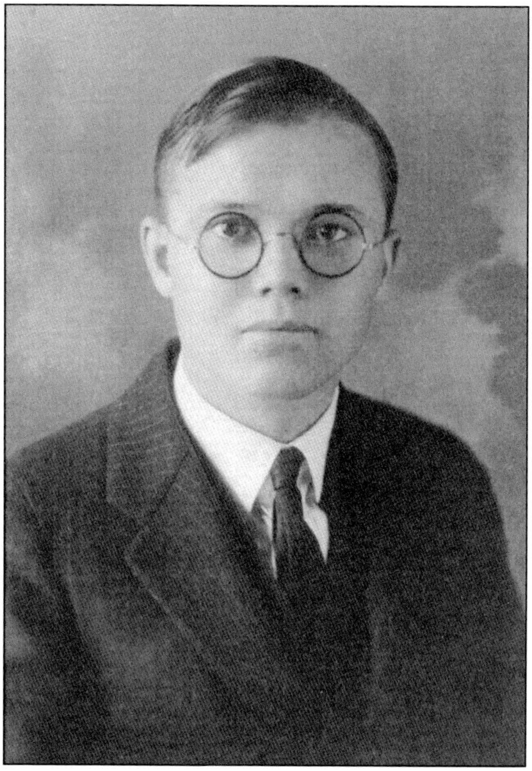

FRANCIS M. MANNING, c. 1925. Having great interest in local history, Manning generously used his newspaper, the *Enterprise*, to record and make publicly available a treasure trove of historical data about Martin County. The Martin County Historical Society's Francis Manning History Room is named in his honor. (Courtesy of Martin County Historical Society.)

WILLIAM CHRISTIAN MANNING HOME, c. 1925. Located on the southwest corner of North Haughton and Church Streets in Williamston, this home fell victim to fire sometime before 1950. (Courtesy of Martin County Historical Society.)

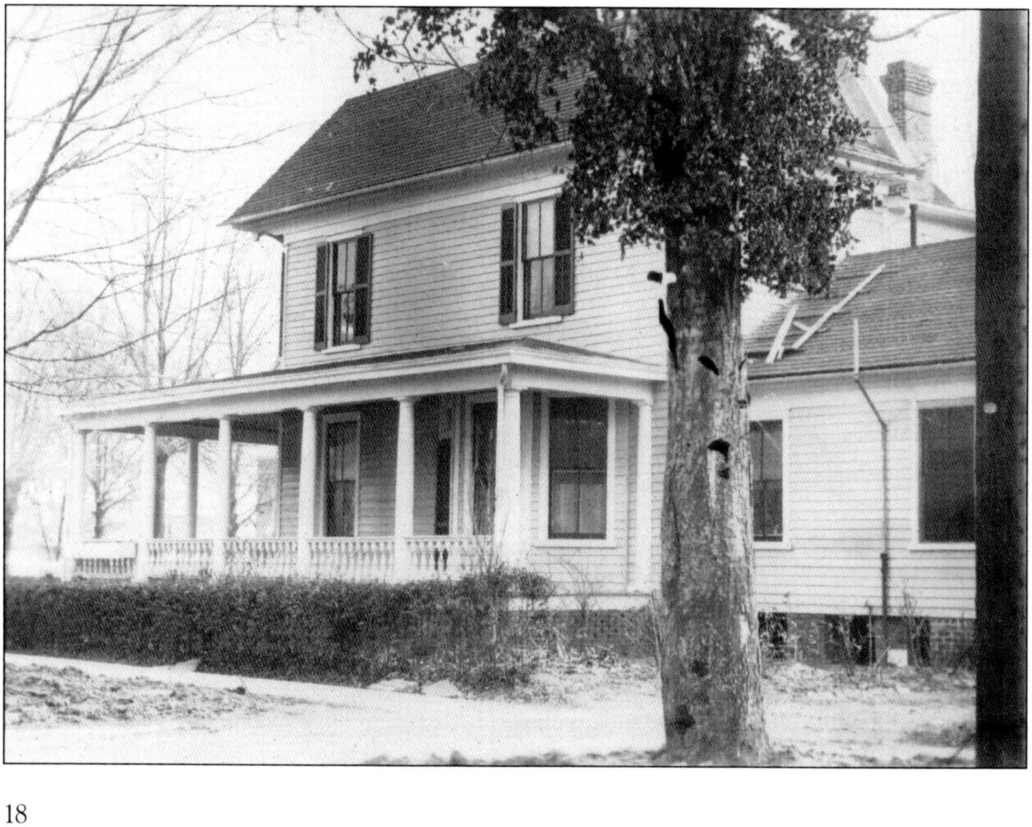

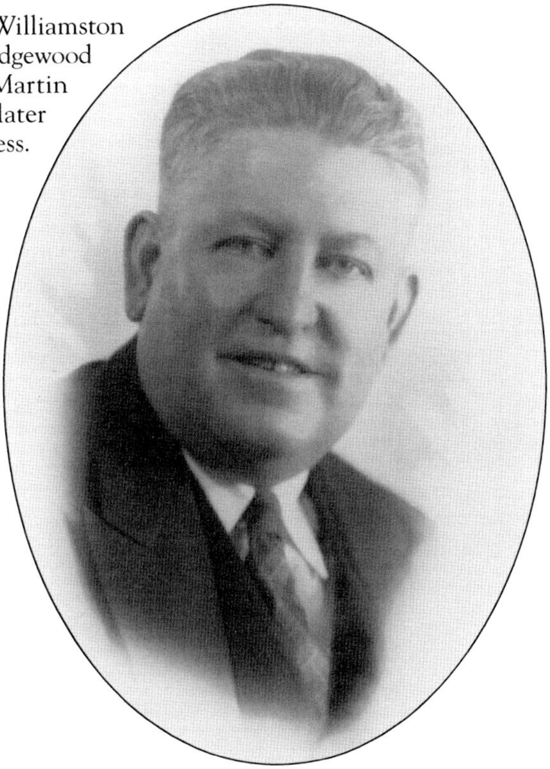

FRANK WEAVER (1896–1967), C. 1940. A Williamston farmer and dairyman, Weaver managed the Edgewood Dairy, which was located on the Wheeler Martin farm on the western edge of town. In his later years, he also ran a popular landscaping business. (Courtesy of Rita W. Mizell.)

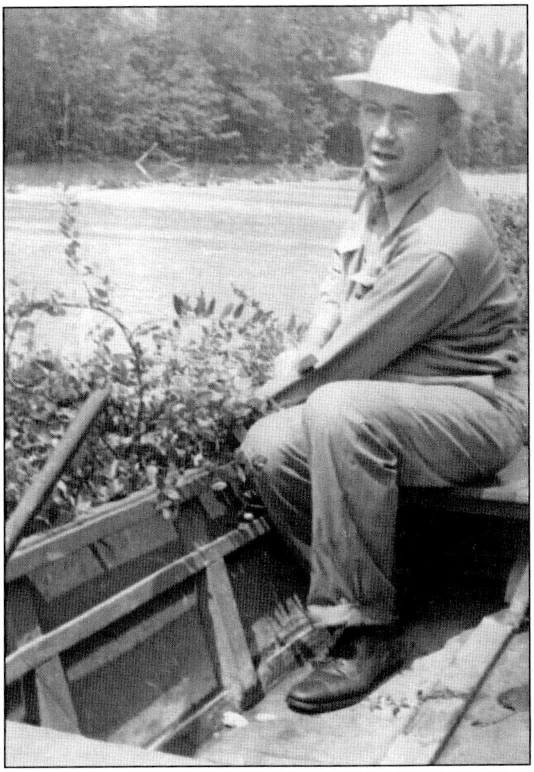

THOMAS B. BRANDON SR. Brandon, who served as Martin County agricultural extension agent from 1924 to 1957, is pictured here out on the river assessing damage during the August 1940 flood. (Courtesy of Martin County Historical Society.)

FIRST METHODIST CHURCH

WILLIAMSTON, NORTH CAROLINA.

Corner Church and Watts Streets

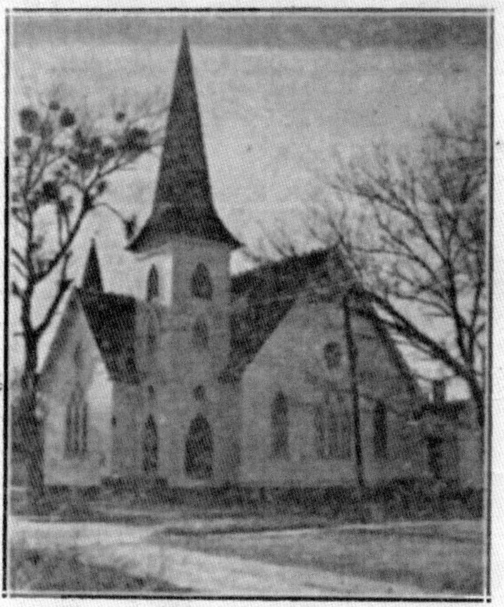

BERNARD T. HURLEY, Pastor

Parsonage: 114 E. Church Street Phone: 219-J

SCHEDULE OF SERVICES

Church School	9:45 A. M.
Worship Services	11 A. M. and 7:30 (8:00) P. M.
Epworth League	6:30 (7:00) P. M.
Prayer Service, Wednesday	7:30 (8:00) P. M.
Choir Rehearsal, Wednesday	7:30 (8:00) P. M.
W. S. C. S., Monday after Third Sunday	3:30 P. M.
Woman's Circle, Monday after First Sunday	3:30 P. M.
W. S. Guild, Monday after Second Sunday	8:00 P. M.
Board of Stewards	Wednesday Night after First Sunday

WILLIAMSTON METHODIST CHURCH. Established in 1828, Williamston Methodist was the first religious body to locate within the town limits of Williamston. A program for the church's Easter services, dated April 5, 1942, is seen here. (Courtesy of the author.)

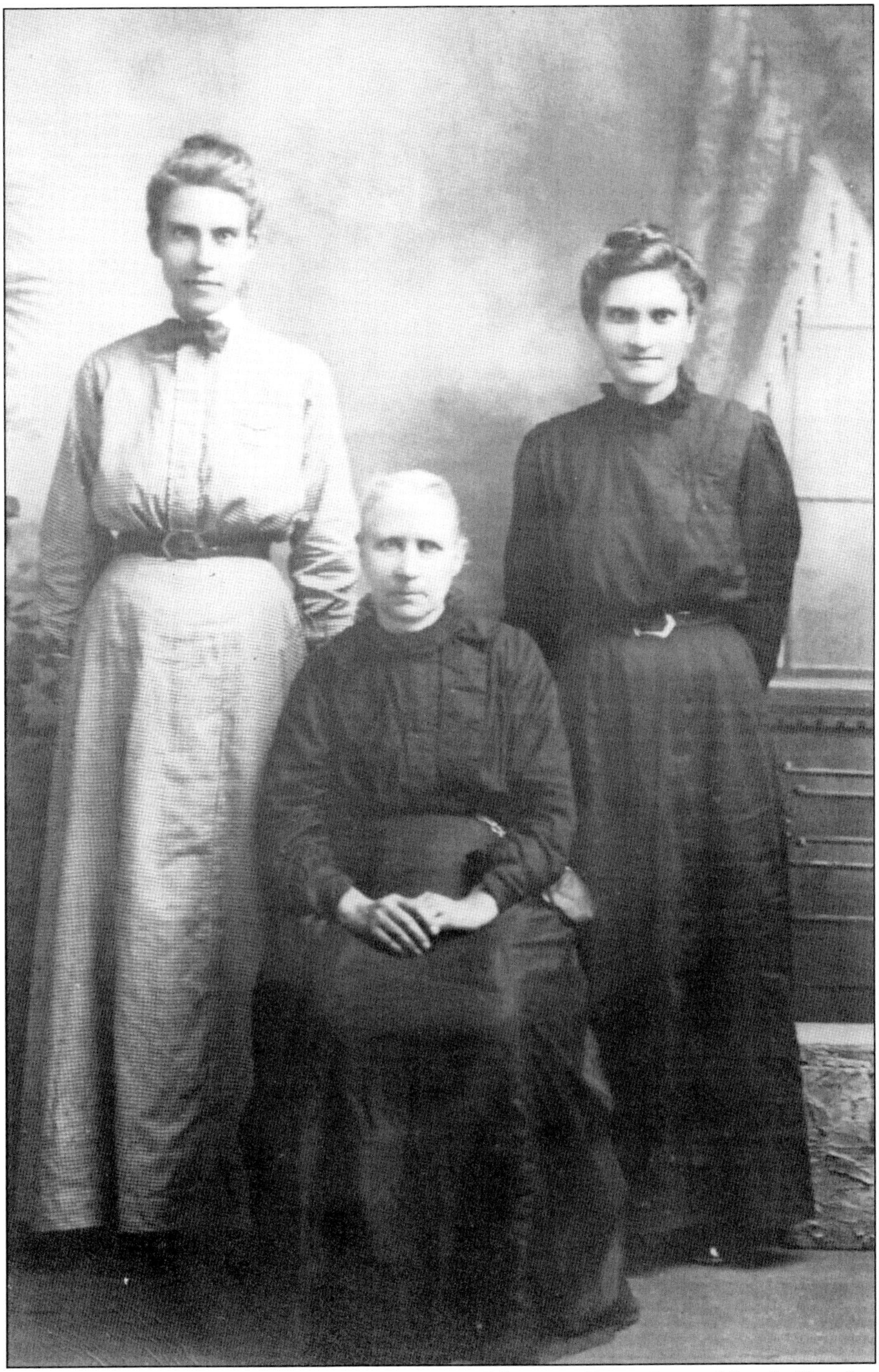

Family of Eli Thomas Rogerson, 1912. Pictured here in Bear Grass, North Carolina, are, from left to right, Rogerson's daughter Ernest R. Ward (1876–1958); wife, Caroline M. Cherry Rogerson (1848–1937); and daughter Harriet R. Harrison (1879–1951). Eli Thomas's first cousin Reuben Henry Rogerson is remembered for establishing the first general mercantile store in the township. (Courtesy of the author.)

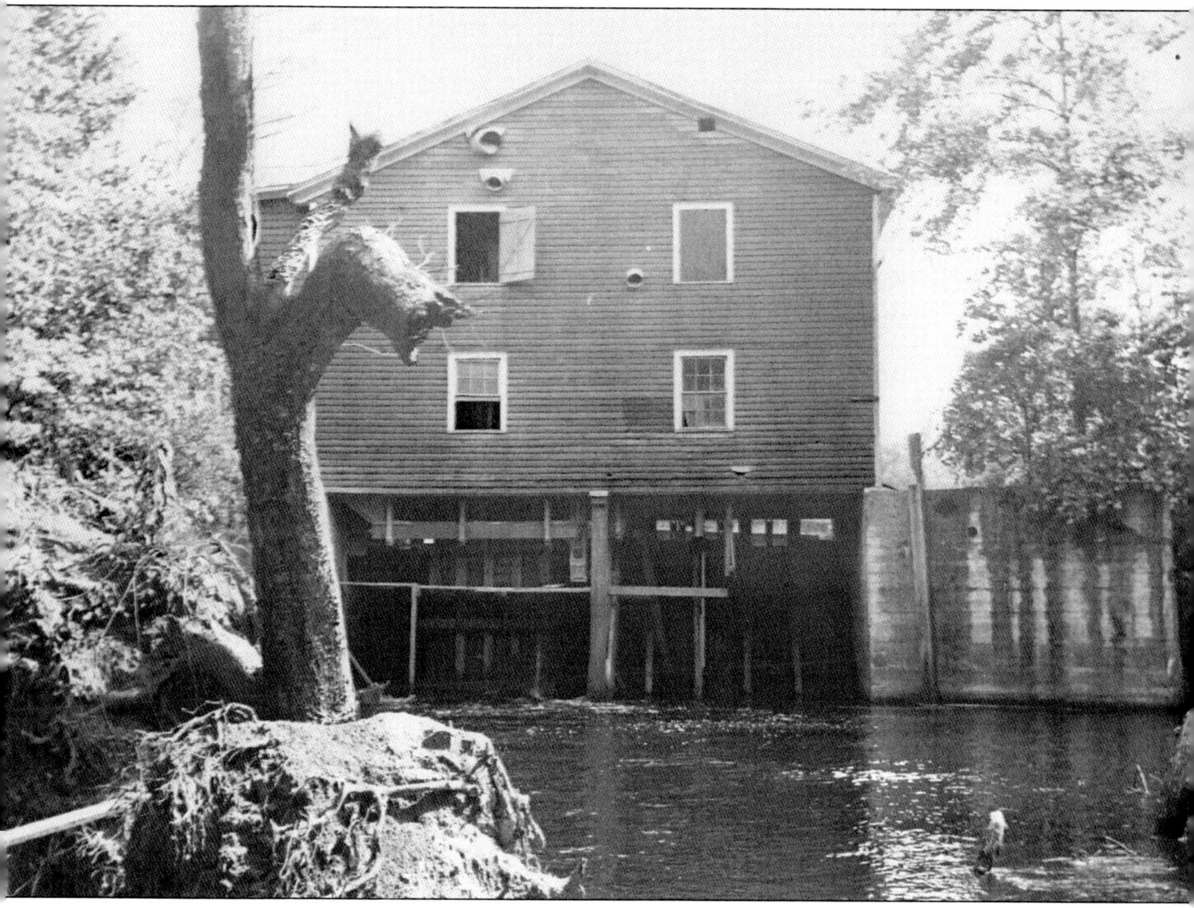

MOBLEY'S MILL, C. 1945. Also known as Everett's Mill, this gristmill operation, located on Highway 125 in the Williamston Area, was purchased from Warren E. Everett by W.O. Abbitt in 1933. It burned on June 6, 1952, and was replaced with a modern facility. (Courtesy of Martin County Historical Society.)

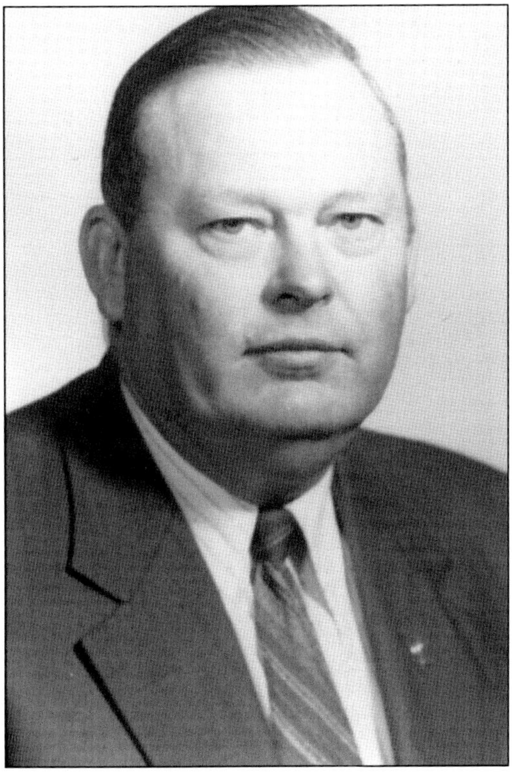

TIM MALONE, C. 1965. A former county commissioner, businessman, and promoter of tourism in Martin County, Malone (and his wife, Keathley) opened Green Acres Family Campground outside of Williamston in 1966. Quickly developing a national reputation, the campground was heavily visited—as was Williamston in general—during the March 7, 1970, solar eclipse. The campground was only four miles from the center line of the eclipse. (Courtesy of Martin County Historical Society.)

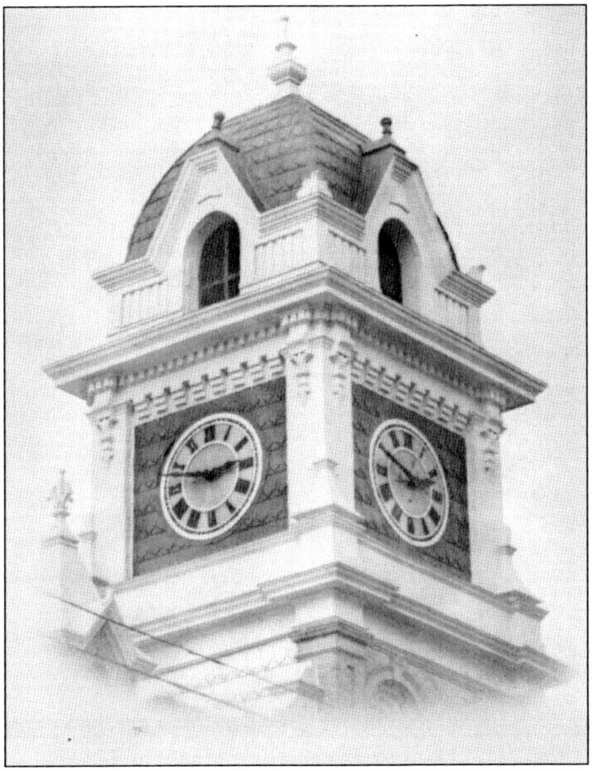

WILLIAMSTON CITY HALL CLOCK TOWER, 1957. Williamston's most noteworthy landmark for the first half of the 20th century was destroyed by fire in December 1958. This image is included in the local high school yearbook, *Slewarkee*, for 1958. (Courtesy of the author.)

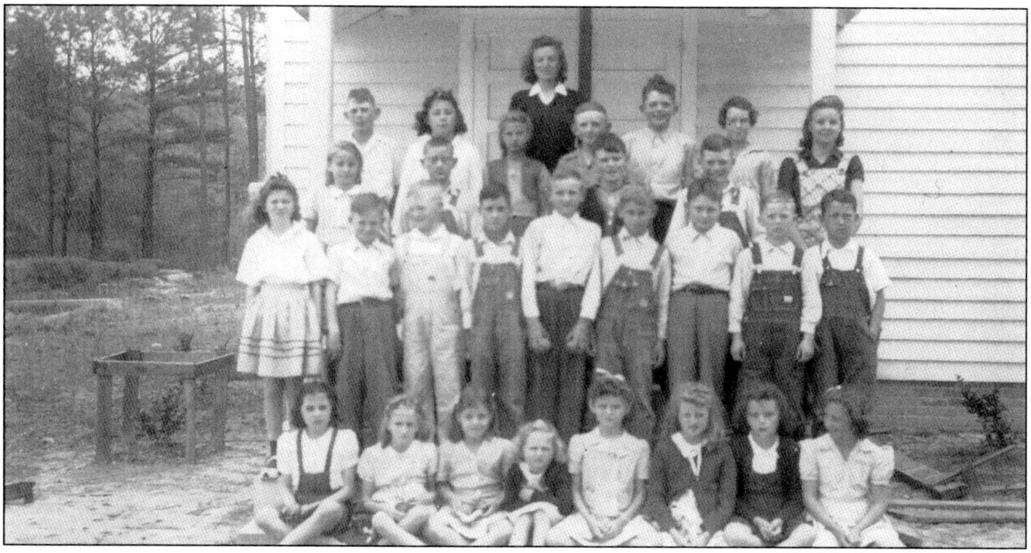

Farm Life School, Griffins Township, 1942. Mildred Ward's third-grade class is pictured here. (Courtesy of Jean G. Rogers.)

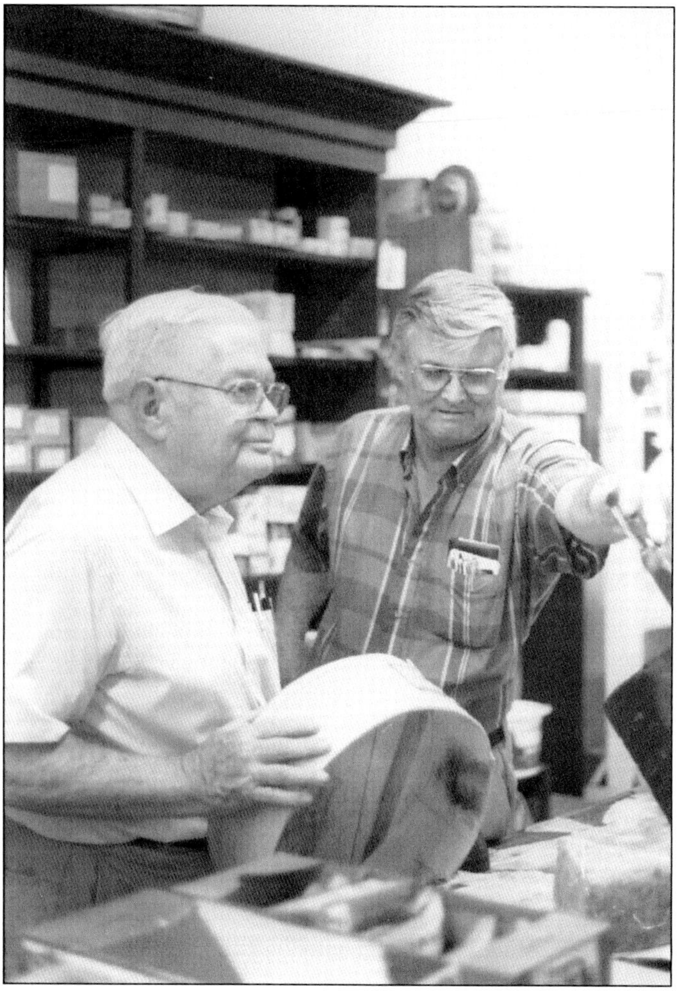

Martin Supply Co., c. 1995. Billy Griffin (left) and Eddie Hardison share space at the counter of this well-known farm-supply business on Williamston's Washington Street. The original stockholders for the company, chartered on January 3, 1940, were E.M. Trahey, W.W. Tice, and Wheeler Martin. (Courtesy of Patsy R. Miller.)

JANICE HARDISON FAULKNER, c. 1960. A Martin County native, Faulkner began her career as a member of the faculty at East Carolina University in the late 1950s and later assumed direction of that institution's regional development institute. She was a highly successful and noted organizer, and former governor Jim Hunt appointed her secretary of the North Carolina Department of Revenue in 1993, secretary of state in 1996, and commissioner of the North Carolina Division of Motor Vehicles in 1997. (Courtesy of the J.Y. Joyner Library, Verona Joyner Langford North Carolina Collection.)

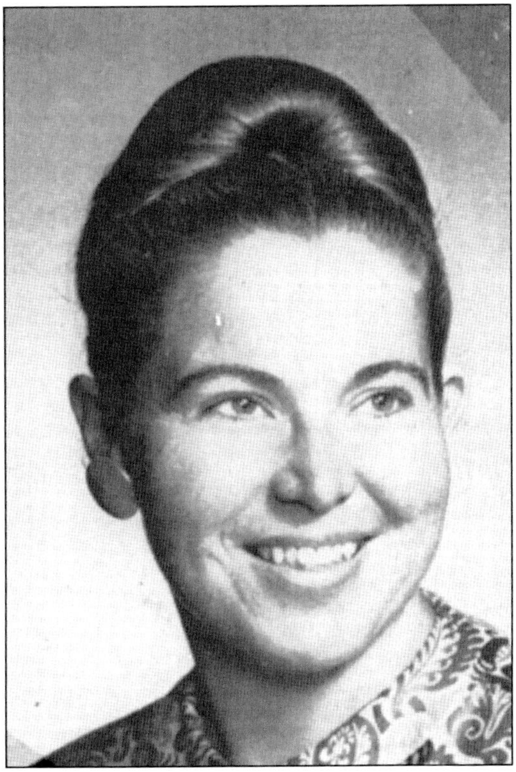

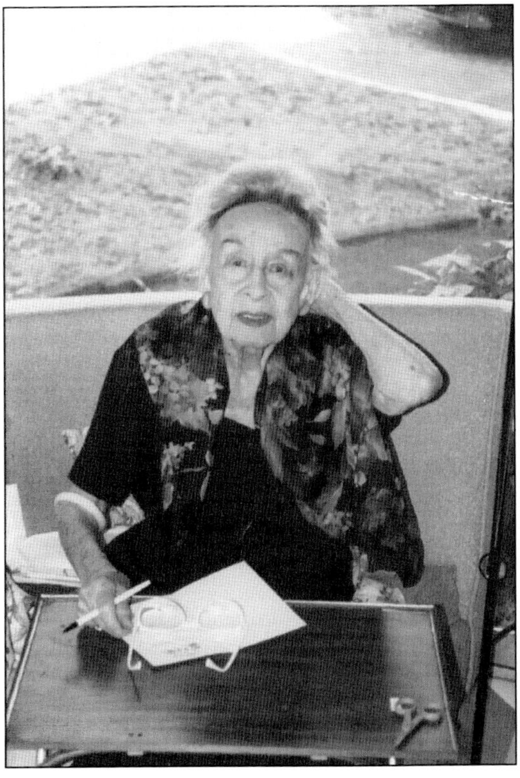

GERTRUDE NORTON "GERTIE" CARSTARPHEN (1903–2004), c. 1995. A longtime Williamston retailer, Carstarphen, along with Rita Everett, originally managed the Wear-Right Shop, a fine ladies' apparel store, before its transformation into the House of Fashion in the late 1950s. Carstarphen's husband, Bill, died in 1958; his own family's history as retailers in Williamston reaching back to 1872. Gertie Carstaphen continued to operate her popular shop into her 90s. (Courtesy of Patsy R. Miller.)

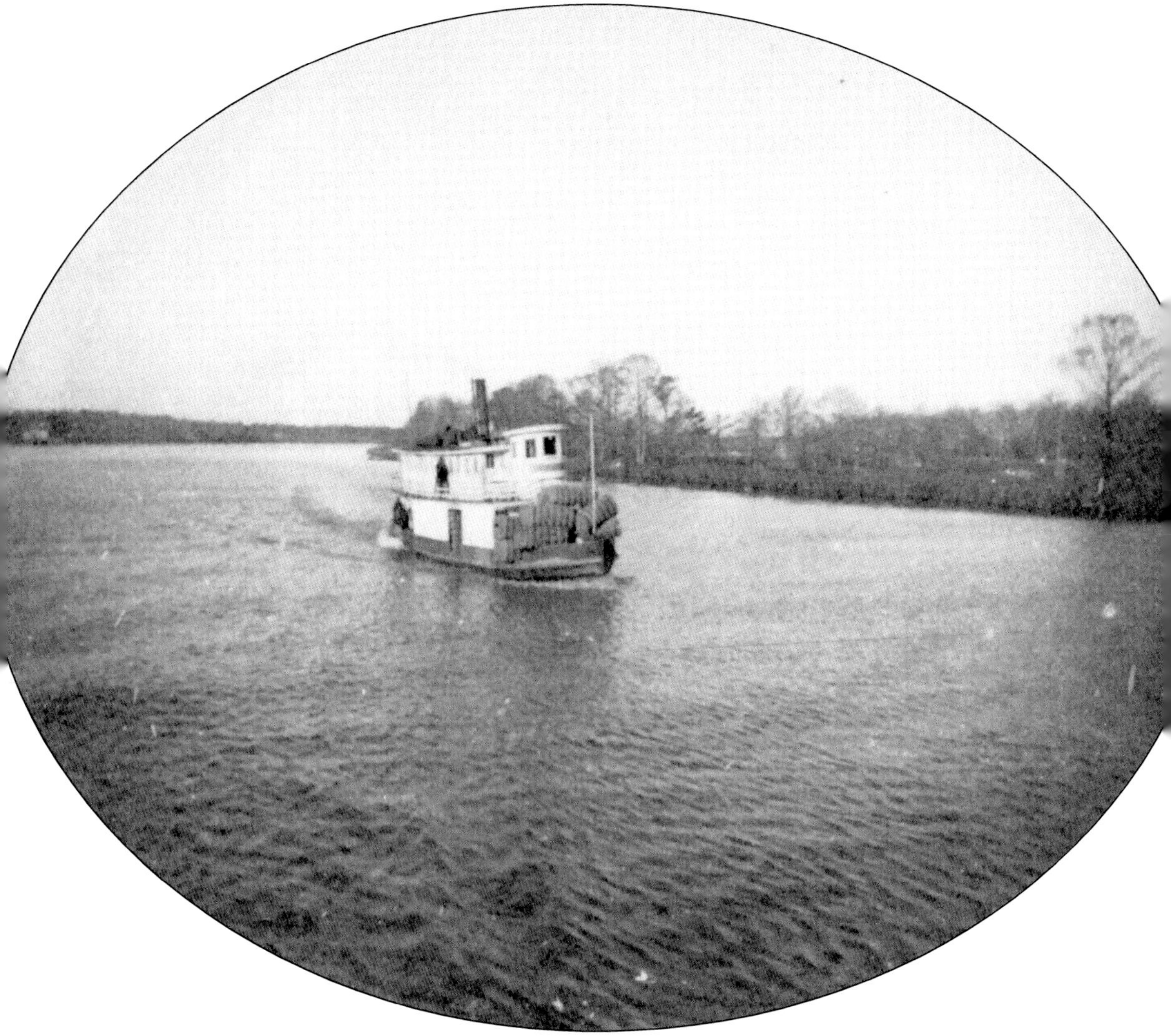

The *Bertie*. Dated December 22, 1888, this rarely viewed photograph is one of eight related images donated to the North Carolina Museum of History in 1950. Described in notation by its creator as the steamboat *Bertie* going down the Roanoke River at Jamesville, North Carolina, it was most likely taken by an official with the Jamesville & Washington Railroad and Lumber Company. (Courtesy of the North Carolina Museum of History.)

Two

ROANOKE RIVER HERITAGE

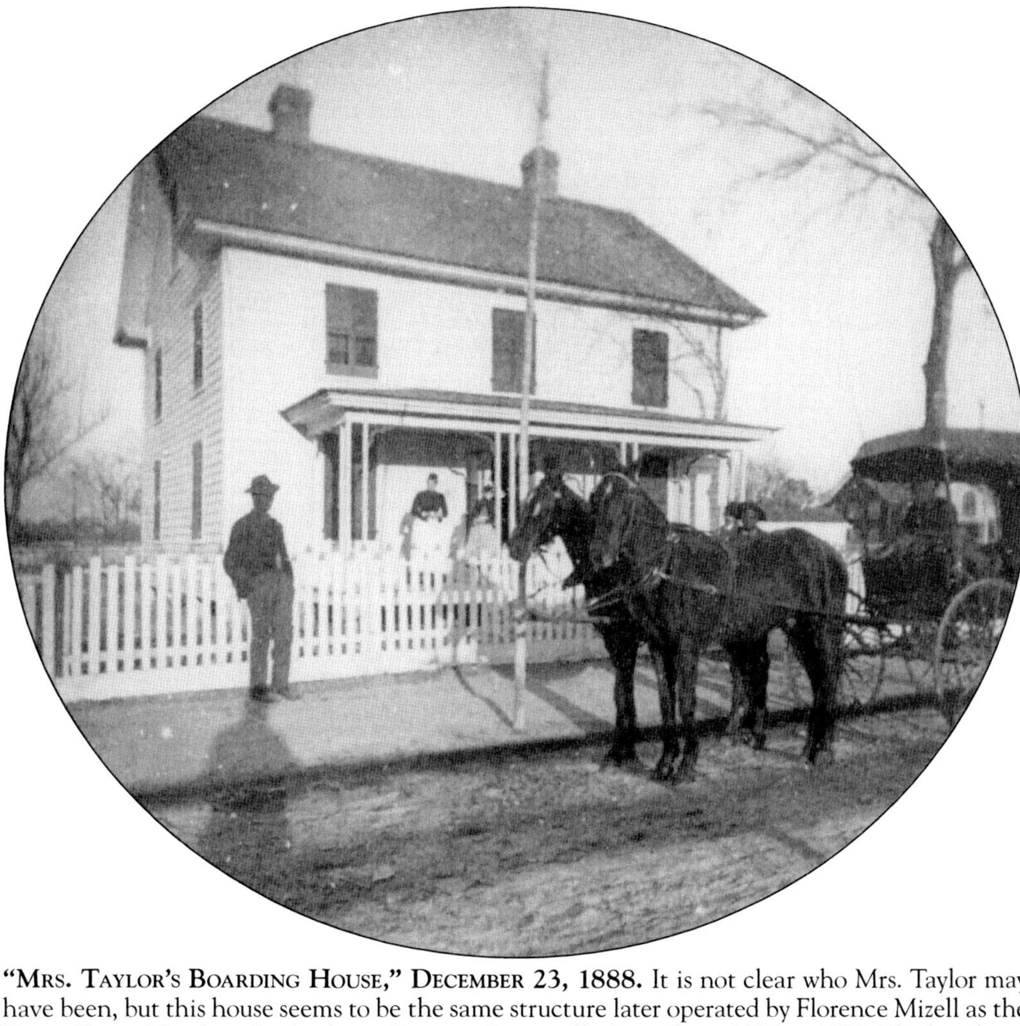

"MRS. TAYLOR'S BOARDING HOUSE," DECEMBER 23, 1888. It is not clear who Mrs. Taylor may have been, but this house seems to be the same structure later operated by Florence Mizell as the Kemp House Hotel on St. Andrews Street in Jamesville from about 1890 to 1907. The hotel was later turned into a private residence for W.B. and Ella Gaylord in the 20th century and remains a dwelling as of 2013. (Courtesy of the North Carolina Museum of History.)

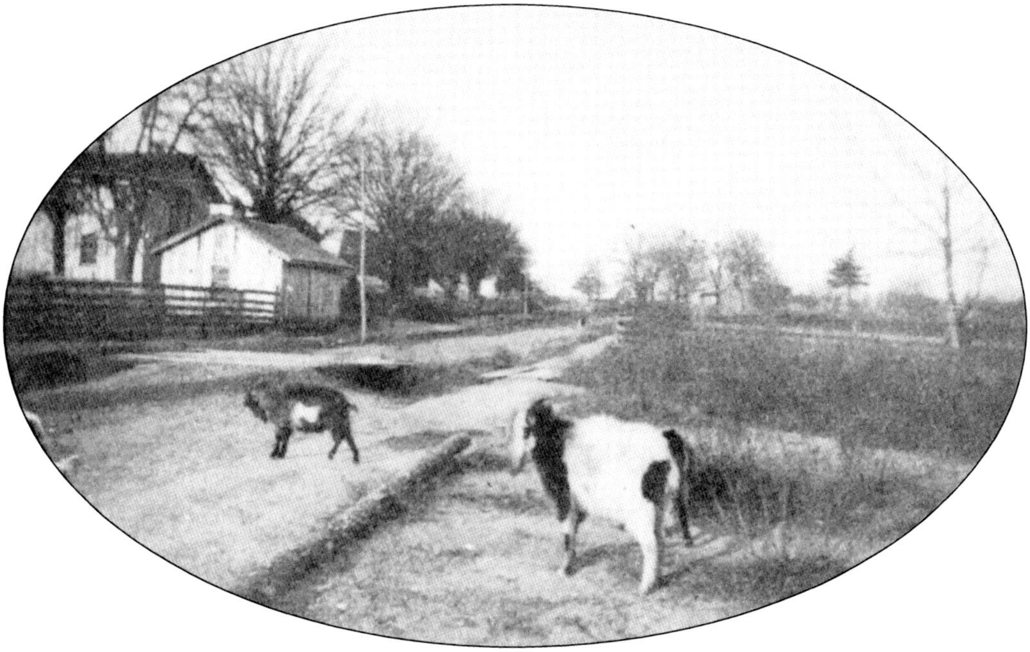

Street Scene, December 23, 1888. This image harkens back to a time when livestock roamed freely throughout town. First incorporated in 1785 as James Town on lands belonging to Luke Mizell and William Mackay, the community was renamed Jamesville in 1855 and is the second-oldest town in Martin County. (Courtesy of the North Carolina Museum of History.)

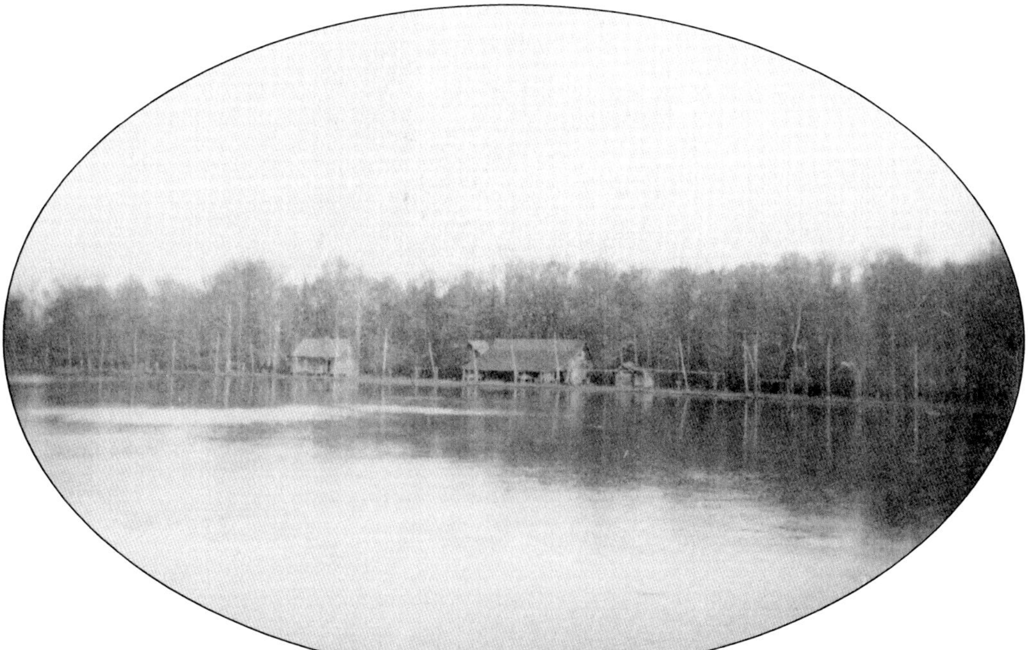

Roanoke River Fisheries, December 22, 1888. For many years, the herring and shad fisheries located near the river wharf in Jamesville provided an important seasonal industry for the town and surrounding community. (Courtesy of the North Carolina Museum of History.)

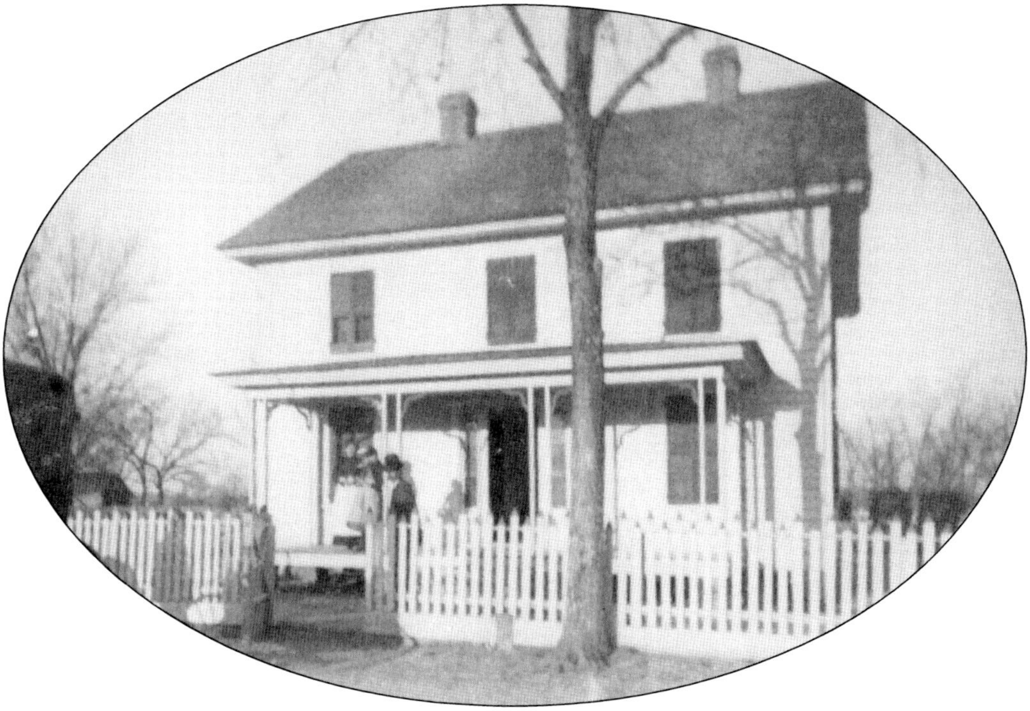

Another View of Mrs. Taylor's. The oldest house (built in the early 19th century) still standing in Jamesville as of 2013 is that now referred to as the Burras House, built in the early 19th century. (Courtesy of the North Carolina Museum of History.)

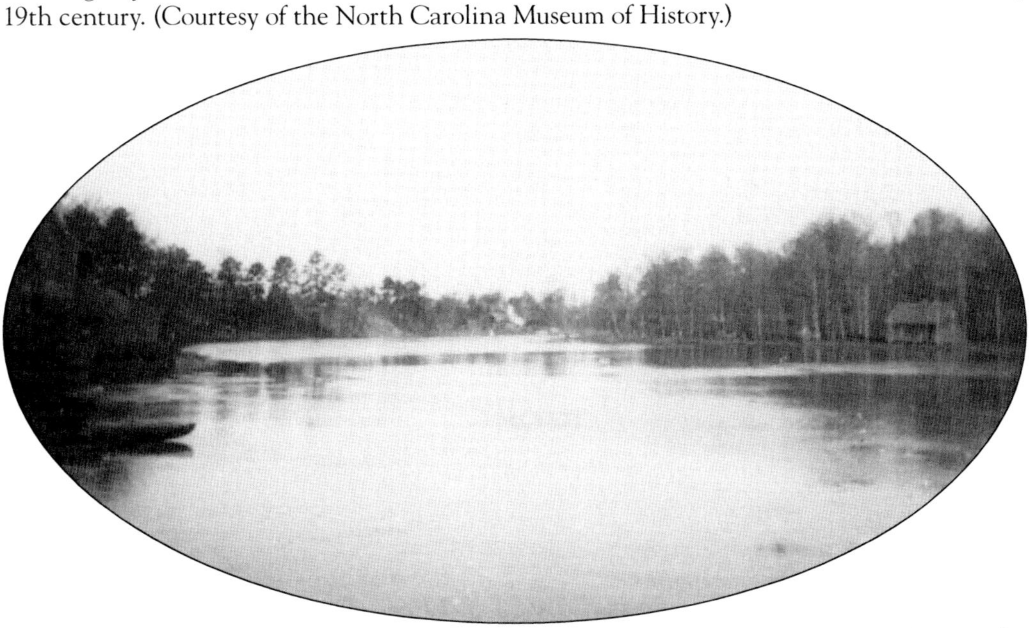

Roanoke River at Jamesville, December 22, 1888. On the river, immediately west of Jamesville, is a landing still known today as Astoria. It was here that the main mill complex of the Dennis Simmons Lumber Company once stood. Established about 1853, this business was quite successful and expanded greatly in the 20th century to include plants in the towns of Kenly and Middlesex in Wilson County, North Carolina. (Courtesy of the North Carolina Museum of History.)

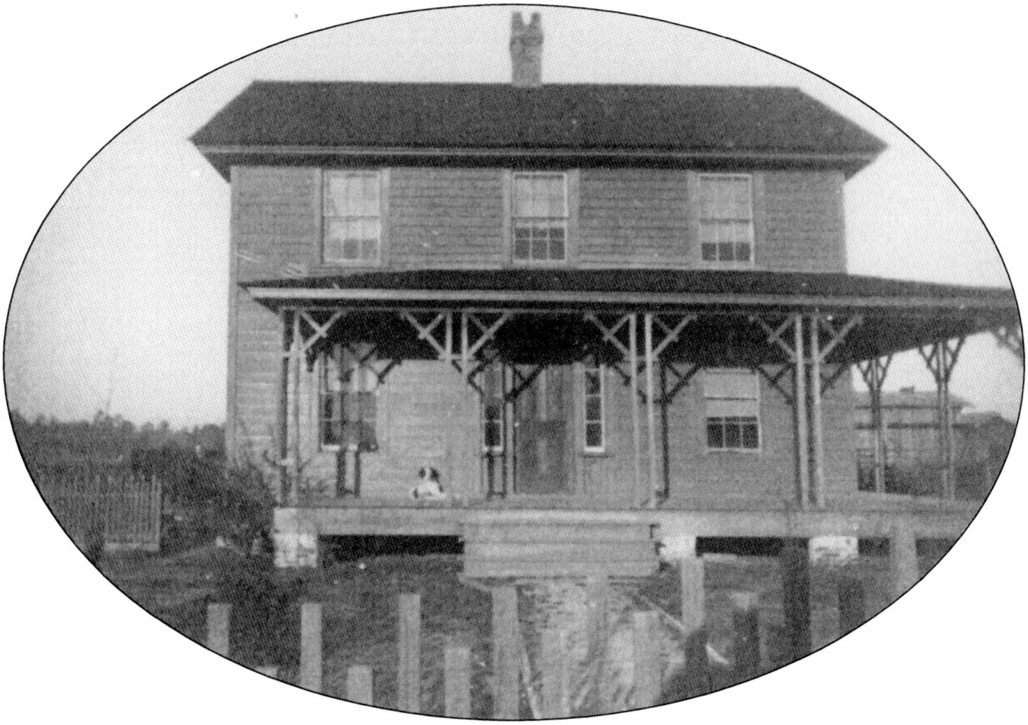

Unidentified Jamesville House, December 23, 1888. In late November 1862, Jamesville was virtually burned to the ground in the aftermath of Union general John G. Foster's raid through Martin County. Modest homes like the one pictured were perhaps the norm for many area families during Reconstruction. (Courtesy of the North Carolina Museum of History.)

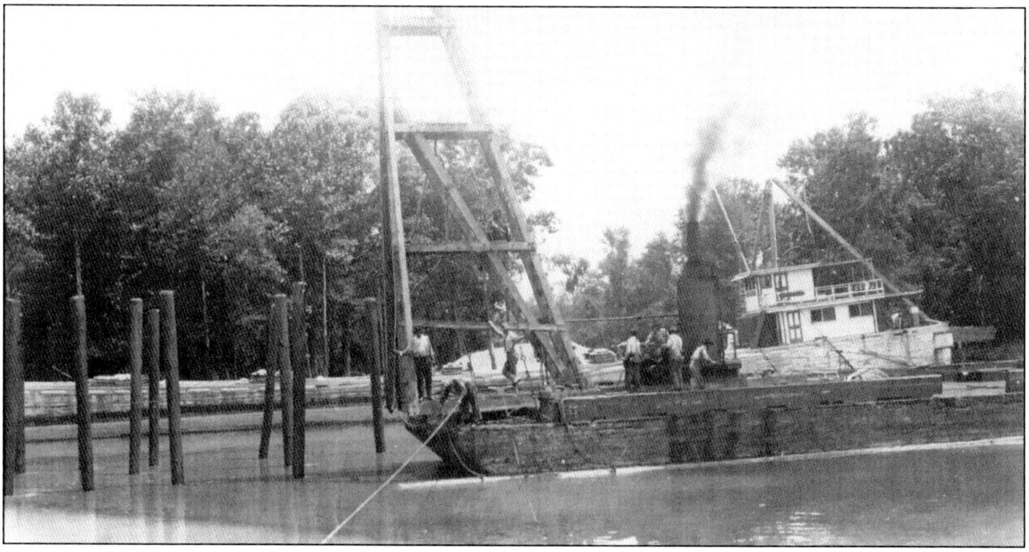

Roanoke River Bridge Construction, 1921. The construction at Williamston of the Roanoke River Bridge and causeway leading into Bertie County, North Carolina, marked an important milestone for modern travel and communication in Martin County. This photograph, dated June 24, 1921, is one of many from what appears to be an engineer's personal diary of structural work connected with the project. (Courtesy of the author.)

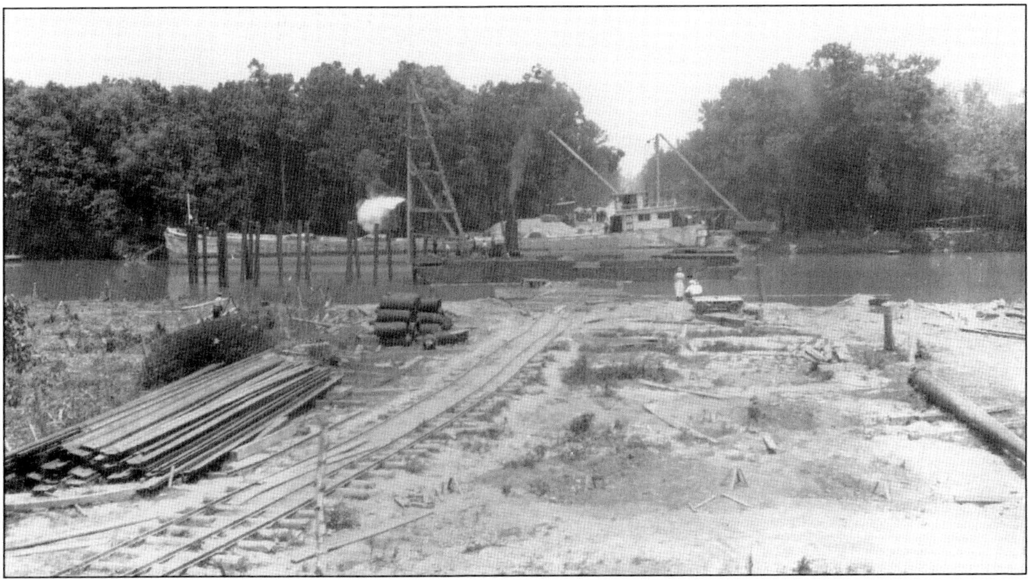

Roanoke River Bridge Project, June 24, 1921. This general view is taken from the Williamston side of the river. Note the temporary railway for hauling materials. (Courtesy of the author.)

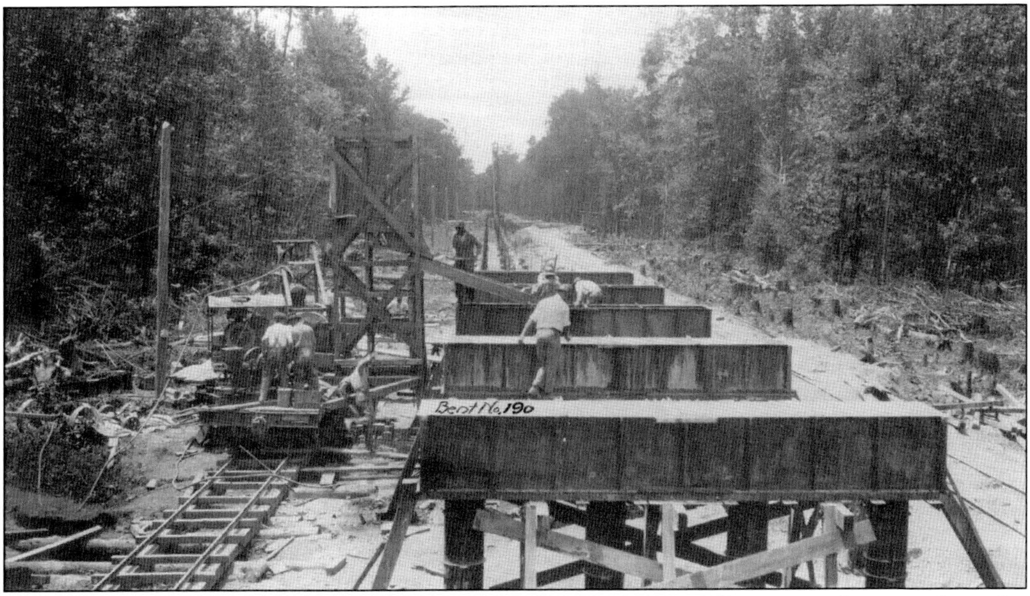

Construction of the Roanoke River Bridge, July 19, 1921. This image shows work on the Roanoke River Bridge project as it was being undertaken in the lowland area across the river in Bertie County. The bridge and causeway were completed in 1922. (Courtesy of the author.)

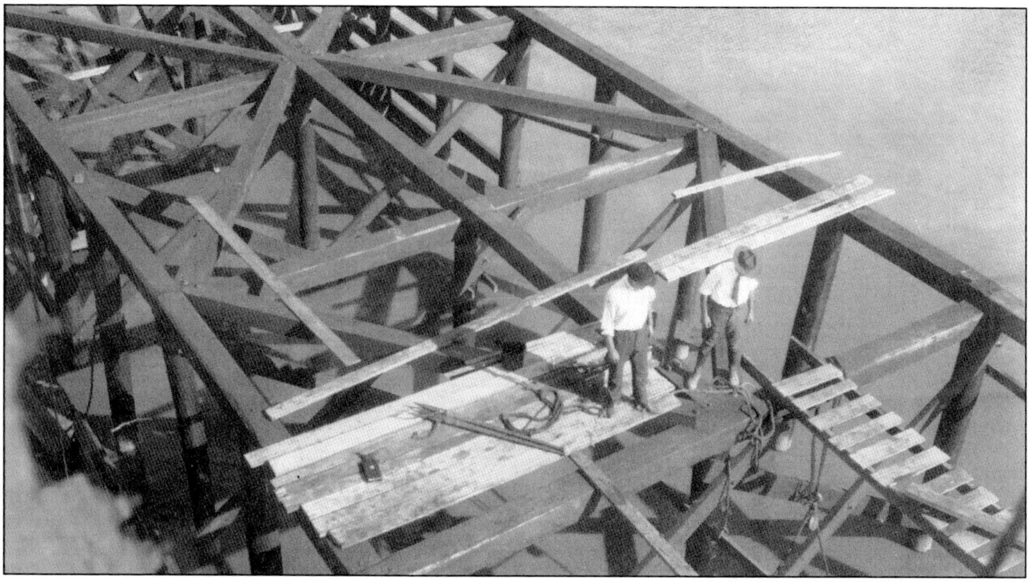

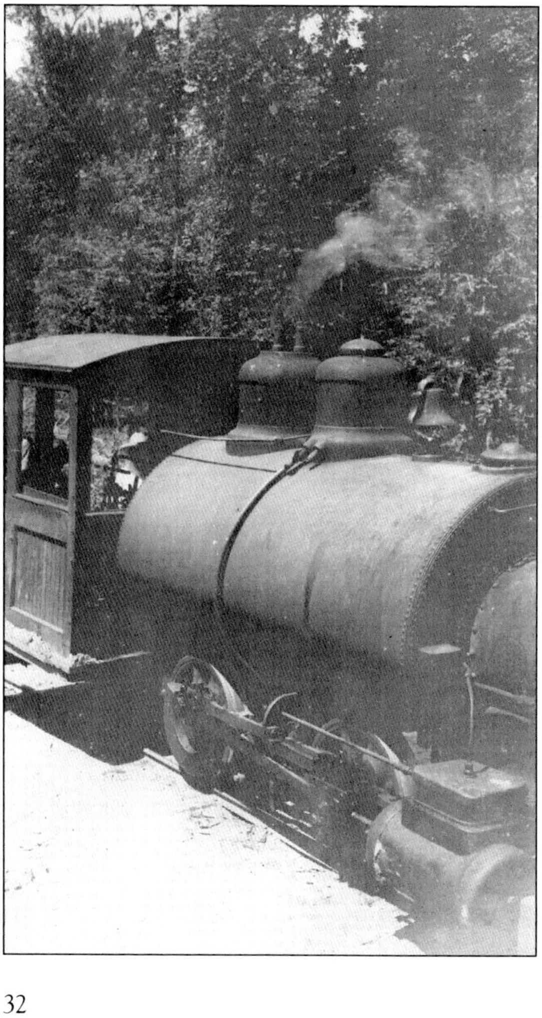

Roanoke River Bridge Construction, August 4, 1921. In 1990, a high-rise, four-lane span replaced all previous vestiges of the 1920s bridge. (Courtesy of the author.)

Locomotive Used in Bridge Construction, c. 1921. The project necessitated a temporary rail service for hauling materials. (Courtesy of the author.)

SCHOONER AT WILLIAMSTON WHARF, 1935. This image shows one—if not the last—of the old-time schooners docked at the Williamston Wharf. At one time, the Williamston port was one of the busiest of its kind in northeastern North Carolina. As late as 1936, over 213,000 tons of freight, valued in the millions of dollars, was being handled through this center. (Courtesy Martin County Historical Society.)

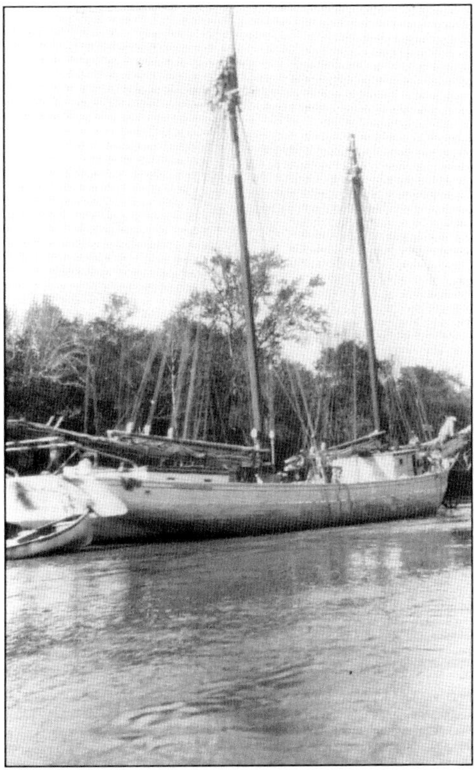

GREAT FLOOD AFTERMATH, AUGUST 1940. Onlookers standing near the open draw of the Roanoke River Bridge in Williamston assess the enormity of the great flood of August 1940. A large portion of Williamston's industrial district and at least one neighborhood sitting below the "river hill" were extensively flooded. (Courtesy of Irving L. Smith Jr.)

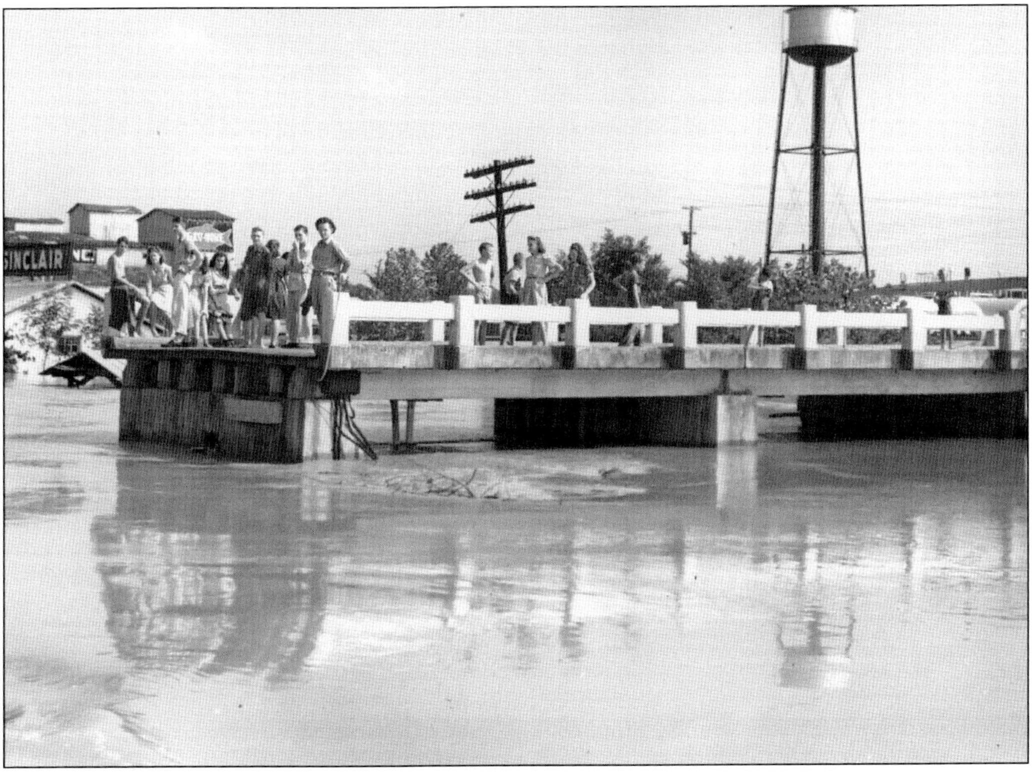

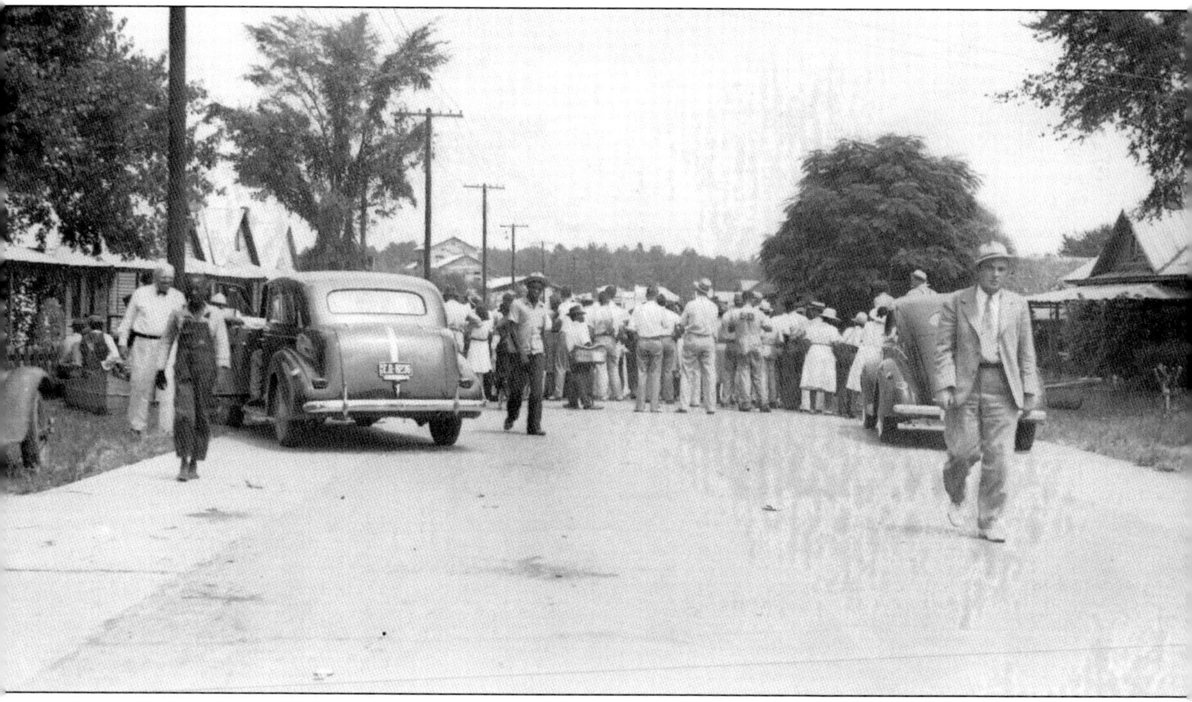

CROWD VIEWING FLOOD. The event brought many visitors from surrounding communities eager to see the extent of the flooding. The people pictured here are on East Main Street. (Courtesy of Martin County Historical Society.)

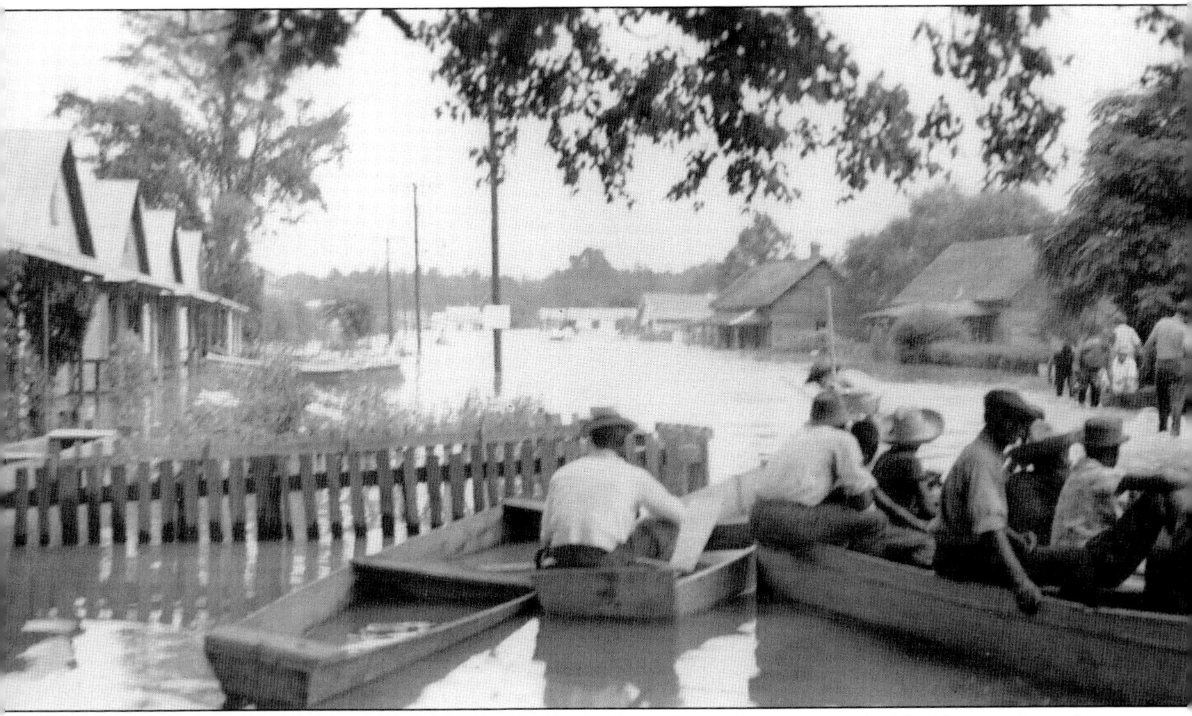

FLOODWATERS OVERTAKE EAST MAIN STREET. A number of people, young and old alike, navigated boat tours through the devastated areas. (Courtesy of Martin County Historical Society.)

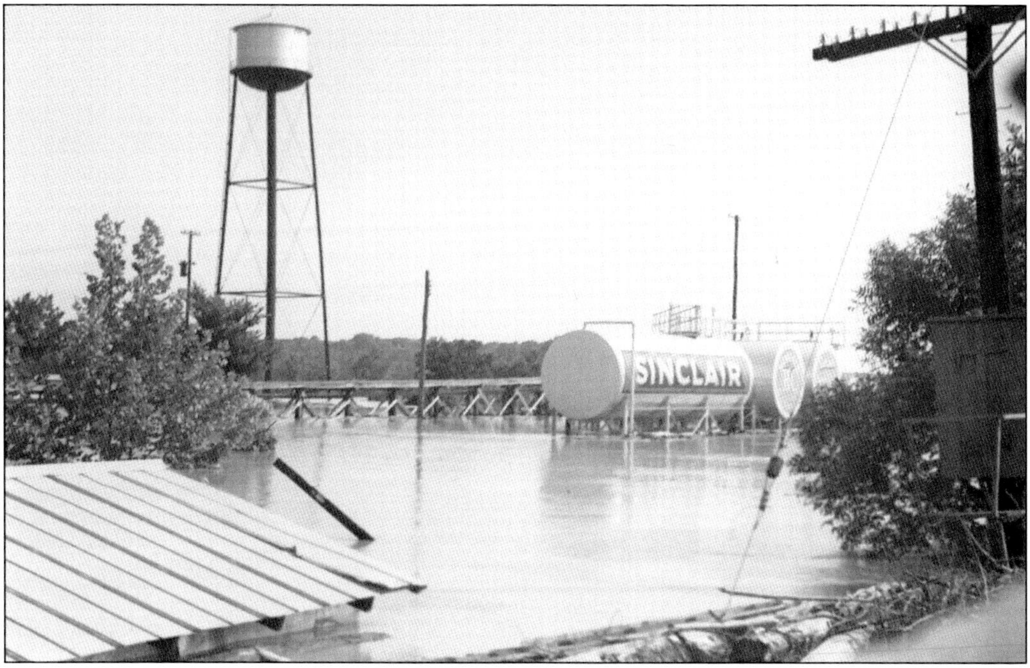

Flood Scene Near Oil-Distribution Center. In 1945, the Roanoke River Basin Association was established by North Carolina and Virginia authorities to promote solutions to curb the extent of damages like those experienced in the 1940 flood event. In 1953, Kerr Dam was completed for the purposes of flood control and hydropower in the Roanoke River basin. (Courtesy of Irving L. Smith Jr.)

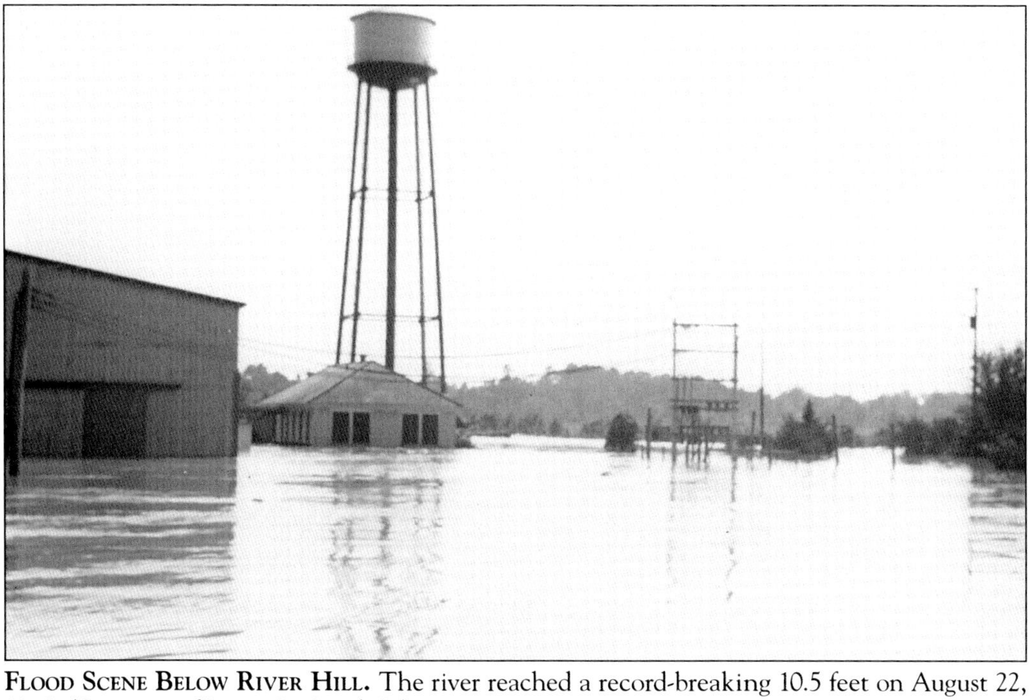

Flood Scene Below River Hill. The river reached a record-breaking 10.5 feet on August 22, 1940. (Courtesy of Irving L. Smith Jr.)

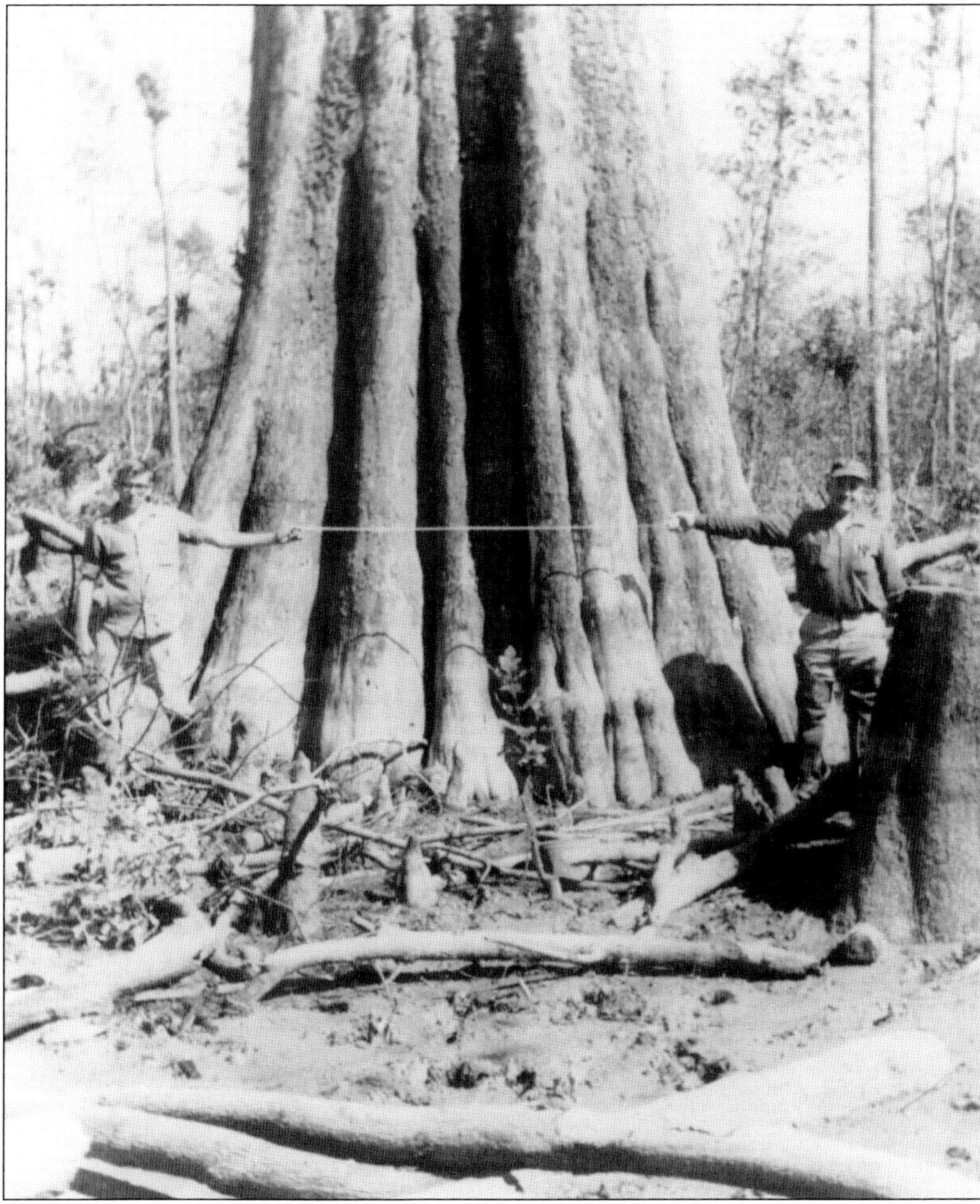

CHAMPION CYPRESS TREE. In June 1979, the North Carolina Forest Service investigated what was then thought to be one of the largest trees east of the Mississippi. The giant specimen of cypress, located about seven miles northeast of the town of Jamesville, measured over 35 feet in circumference and over 11 feet in diameter. Believed to be around 2,000 years old, the tree towered 133 feet over the lowlands of an island in the Roanoke River. Pictured here in (or possibly before) 1969 are Tommy Bedwell (left) and Tilmon Coltrain (right) with an eight-foot tape. (Courtesy of Martin County Historical Society.)

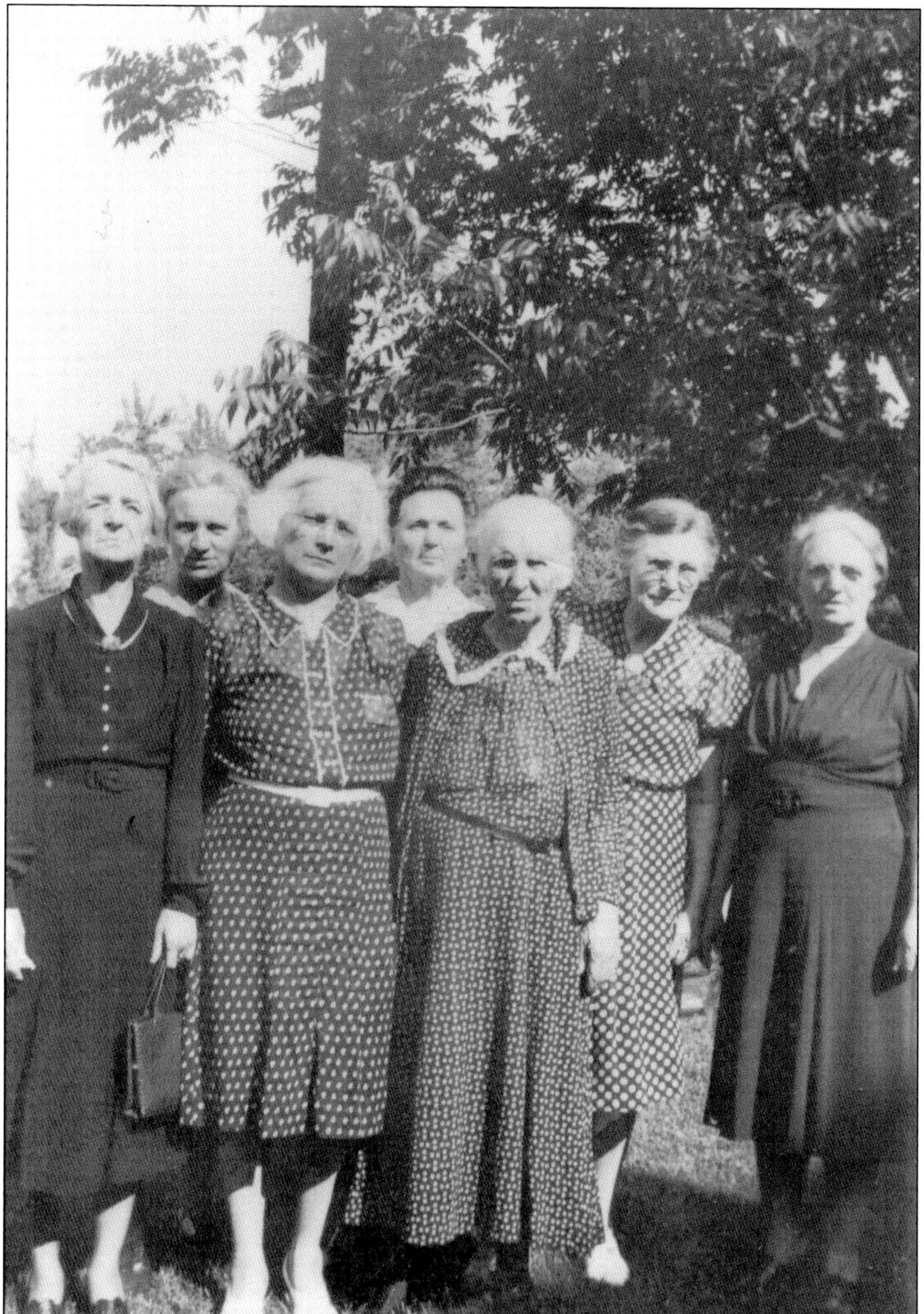

CHLOE ROBERSON AND DAUGHTERS, JUNE 1940. Chloe Frances (Coburn) Roberson (1856–1944), the widow of Benjamin Harvey Roberson (1852–1925) stands with her daughters for a family portrait at the B.H. Roberson annual family reunion in Robersonville, North Carolina, on June 9, 1940. Pictured, from left to right, are Ida Crofton, Fannybel Wilson, Vivian Roberson, Alida Roberson, Chloe Roberson, Emma Liza Mumford, and Jane Arminta Everett. Benjamin Harvey Roberson was a merchant in the community of Gold Point before moving his family to Robersonville in the 1920s. (Courtesy of Judith A. Critcher.)

Three

Roberson Family Reunions

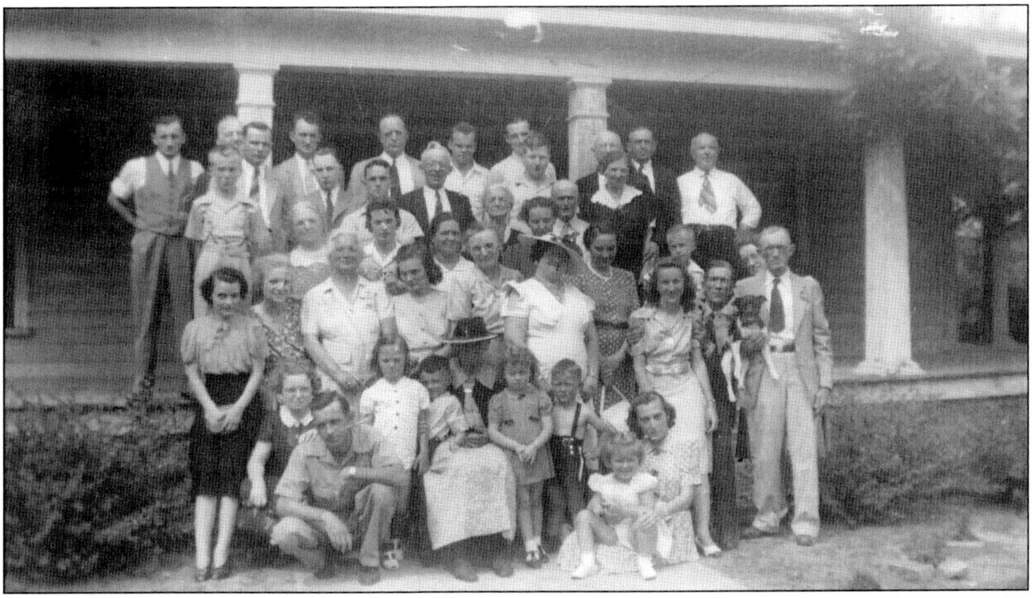

Roberson Family Reunion, June 1941. One of a number of Roberson families living in the Robersonville area, the Benjamin Harvey Roberson family maintained a long tradition of gathering annually in June each year to renew and strengthen family ties. Faithful member Lucy Crofton Ayers initiated a family scrapbook in the 1930s to document many of these celebrations, which continued nearly into the last quarter of the 20th century. (Courtesy of Judith A. Critcher.)

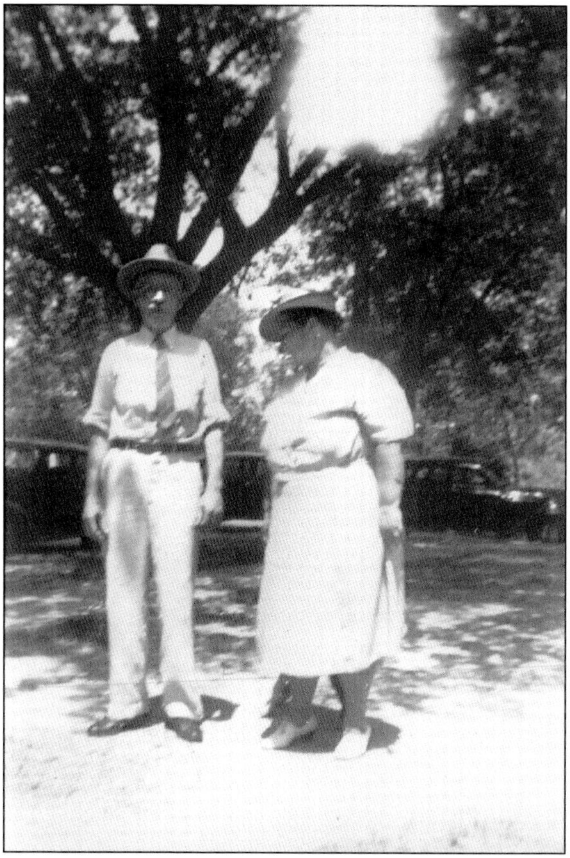

PITT AND ANNE PHILLIPS ROBERSON, 1943. Pitt Roberson held the position of family historian for many years. (Courtesy of Judith A. Critcher.)

REUNION AT WILSON HOME. On June 9, 1940, the reunion was staged on the front lawn of the home of Charles Leon and Fannybel Roberson Wilson on North Main Street in Robersonville. Built in 1931, the home was—and still is—considered one of the town's most beautiful architectural treasures. (Courtesy of Judith A. Critcher.)

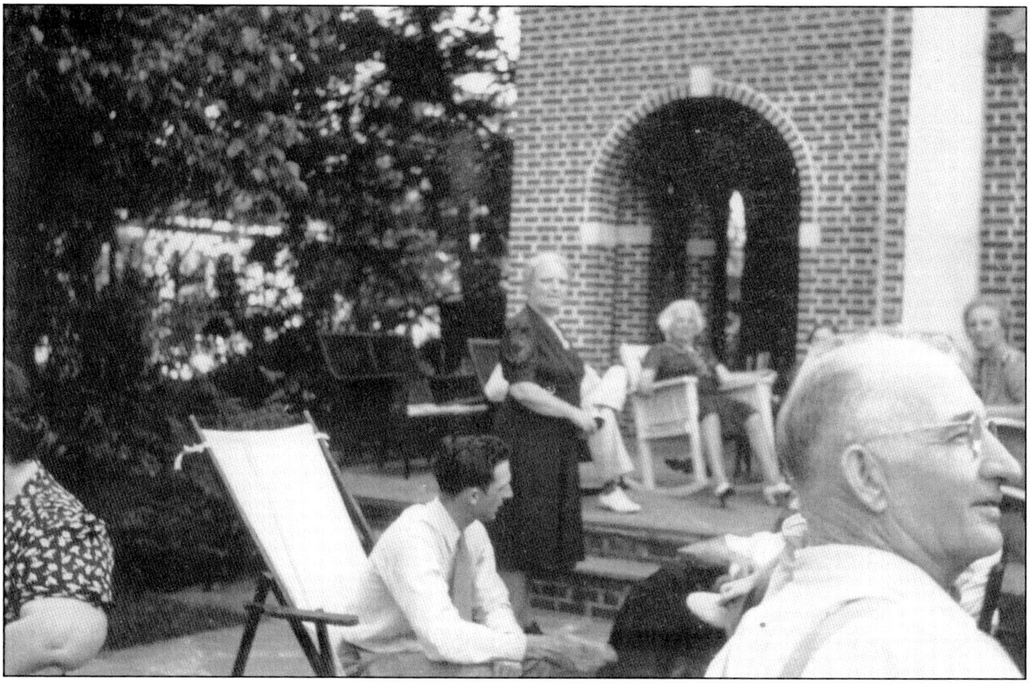

HARVEY AND LENA PARKER ROBERSON. The couple poses for the camera with sons Dixie (left) and Rodney (right) at the 1941 reunion. (Courtesy of Judith A. Critcher.)

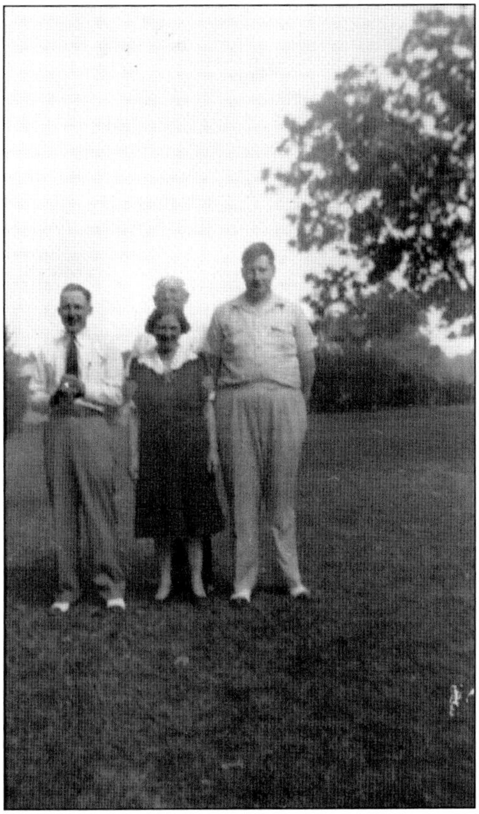

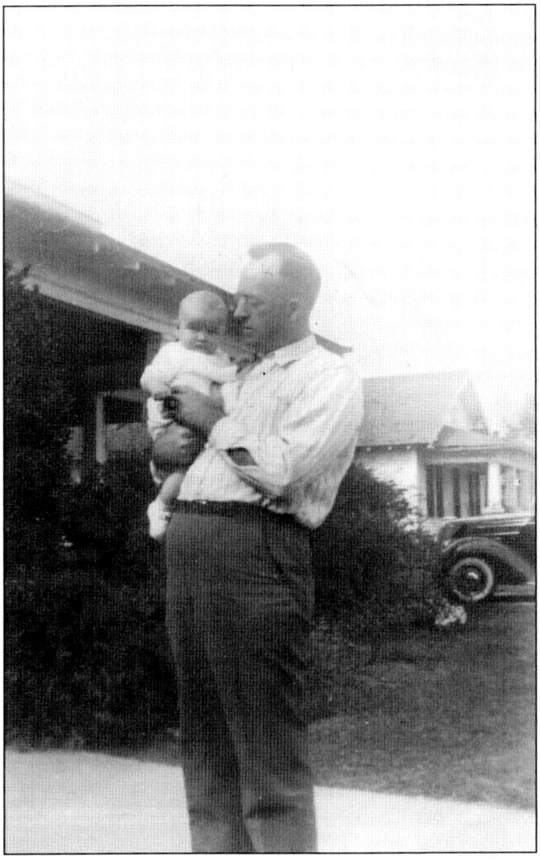

W.B. EVERETT AND DAUGHTER, C. 1939. William Benjamin Everett is pictured here with his infant daughter Elizabeth Ann at their home on South Main Street in Robersonville. The William Benjamin Everett family included two other children—Mary and William B. Jr. (Courtesy of Judith A. Critcher.)

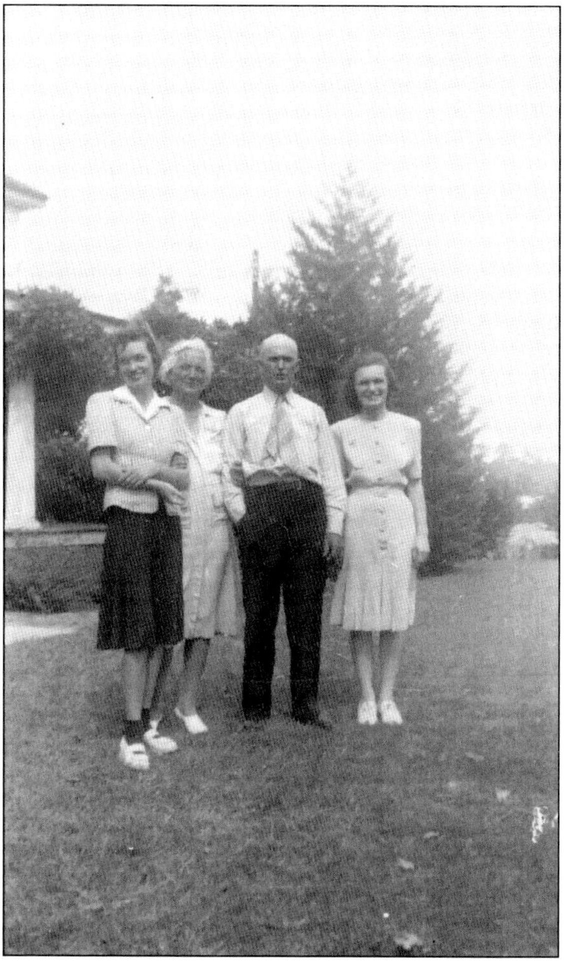

C. ABRAM ROBERSON FAMILY. C. Abram and Vivian Roberson are pictured with daughters Emeline (left) and Chloe Vivian. The family hosted the reunion at their home in June 1941. (Courtesy of Judith A. Critcher.)

C. ABRAM ROBERSON HOME, JUNE 1941. A lunch consisting of barbecue chicken, tomato salad, pickles, breads, ice cream, and cake was served, according to a local newspaper article. Abram "Abe " Roberson (1890–1963), a successful farmer, had been the first male to graduate from what later became Robersonville High School and was a member of the University of North Carolina class of 1912. (Courtesy of Judith A. Critcher.)

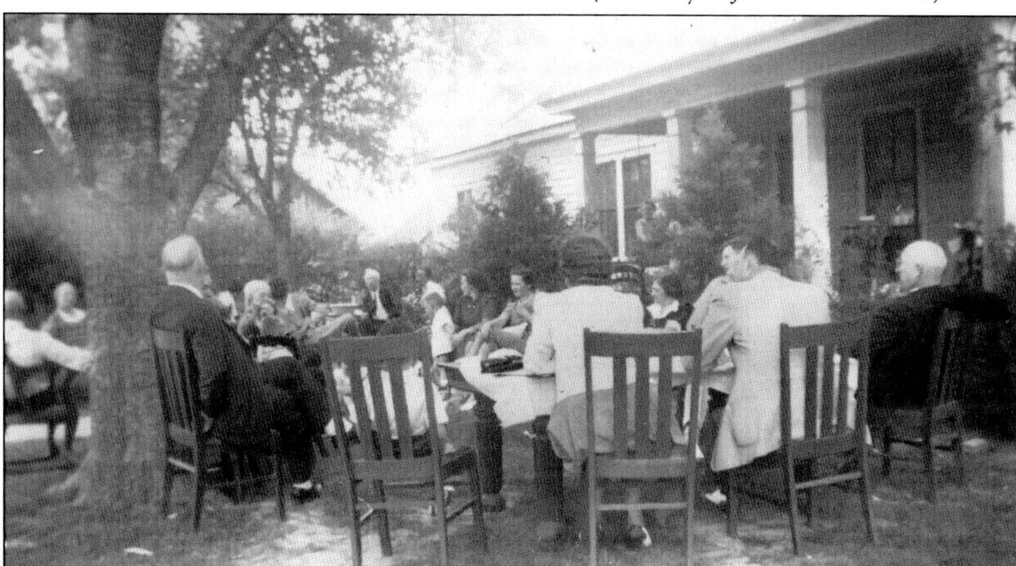

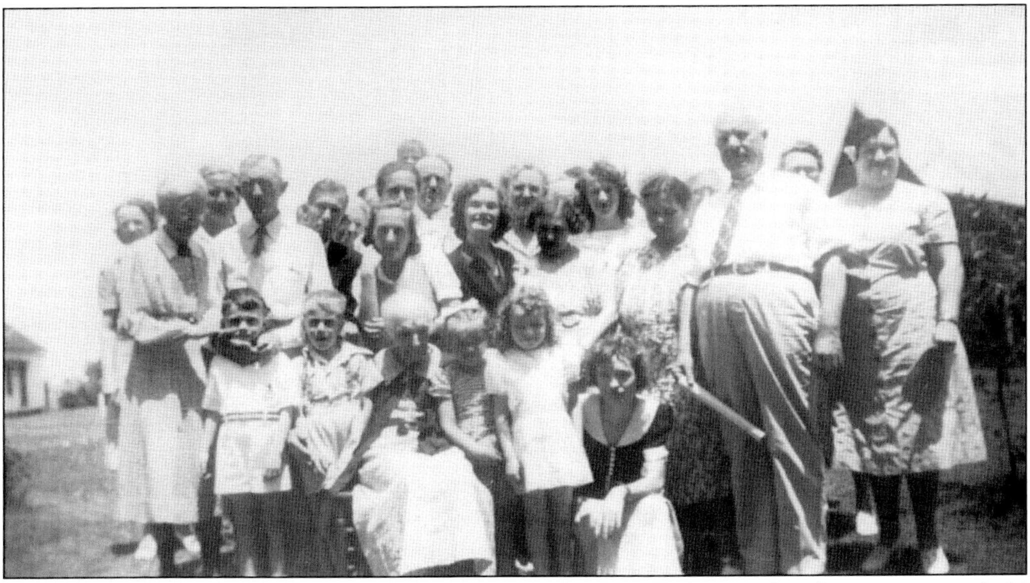

Reunion at H. Lister Everett Home. In 1942, the B.H. Roberson family reunion was held at the country home of H. Lister Everett on Highway 903 between the town of Gold Point and Spring Green Primitive Baptist Church. (Courtesy of Judith A. Critcher.)

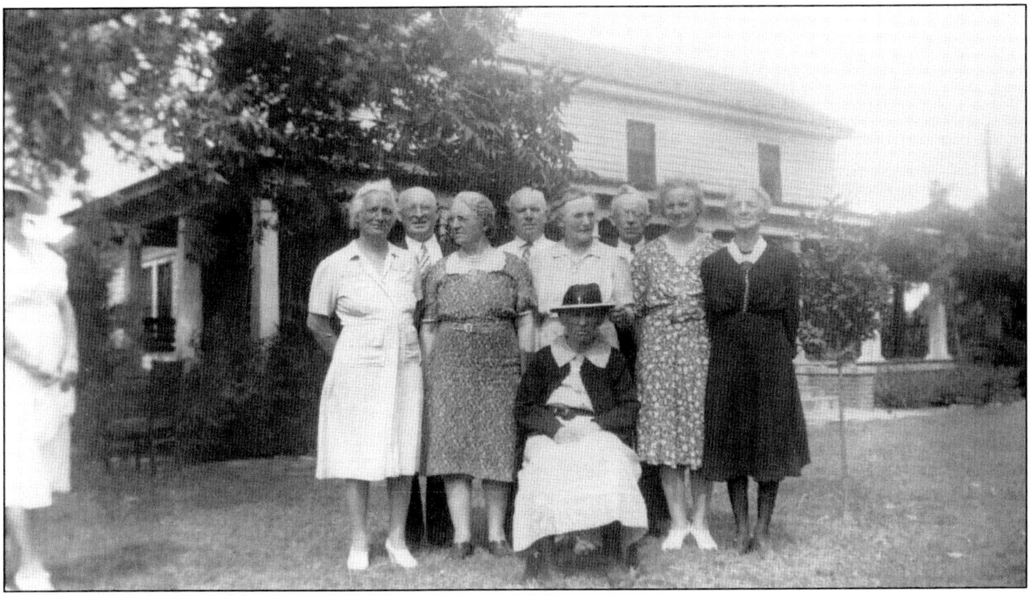

Chloe Roberson and Children, June 1941. Chloe Frances Coburn Roberson (seated) poses for a family portrait with her children in front of the C. Abram Roberson home. They are, from left to right, (front row) Vivian Roberson, Jane Arminta Everett, Emma Liza Mumford, Fannybel Wilson, and Ida Crofton; (back row) Harvey Roberson, William Ander Roberson, and Ashley Pitt Roberson. (Courtesy of Judith A. Critcher.)

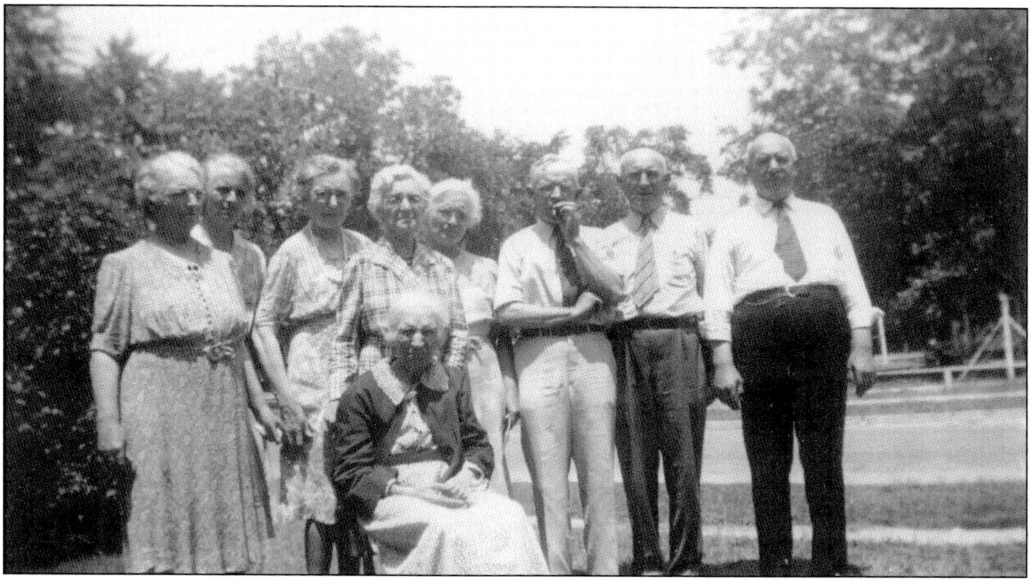

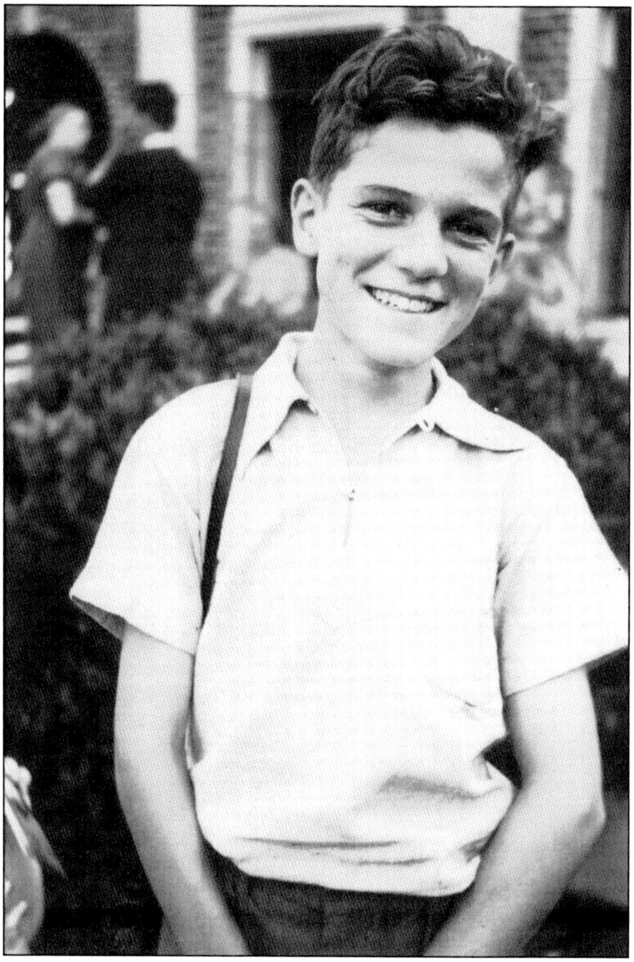

Attendees at the June 1943 Reunion. Chloe C. Roberson is pictured with her children—from left to right, Jane Arminta Everett, Fannybel Wilson, Emma Liza Mumford, Ida Crofton, Vivian Roberson, Ashley Pitt Roberson, Harvey Roberson, and William Ander Roberson—on the lawn adjoining her home and that of Mr. and Mrs. C.L. Wilson on North Main Street in Robersonville. (Courtesy of Judith A. Critcher.)

Charles Leon Wilson Jr. (1926–2012). Son of C.L. Sr. and Fannybel Roberson Wilson, young Charles is seen here at the 1940 Roberson family reunion. In later life, he married Doris Little of Robersonville, had four children, and was engaged in his father's building supply business and farming operations. (Courtesy of Judith A. Critcher.)

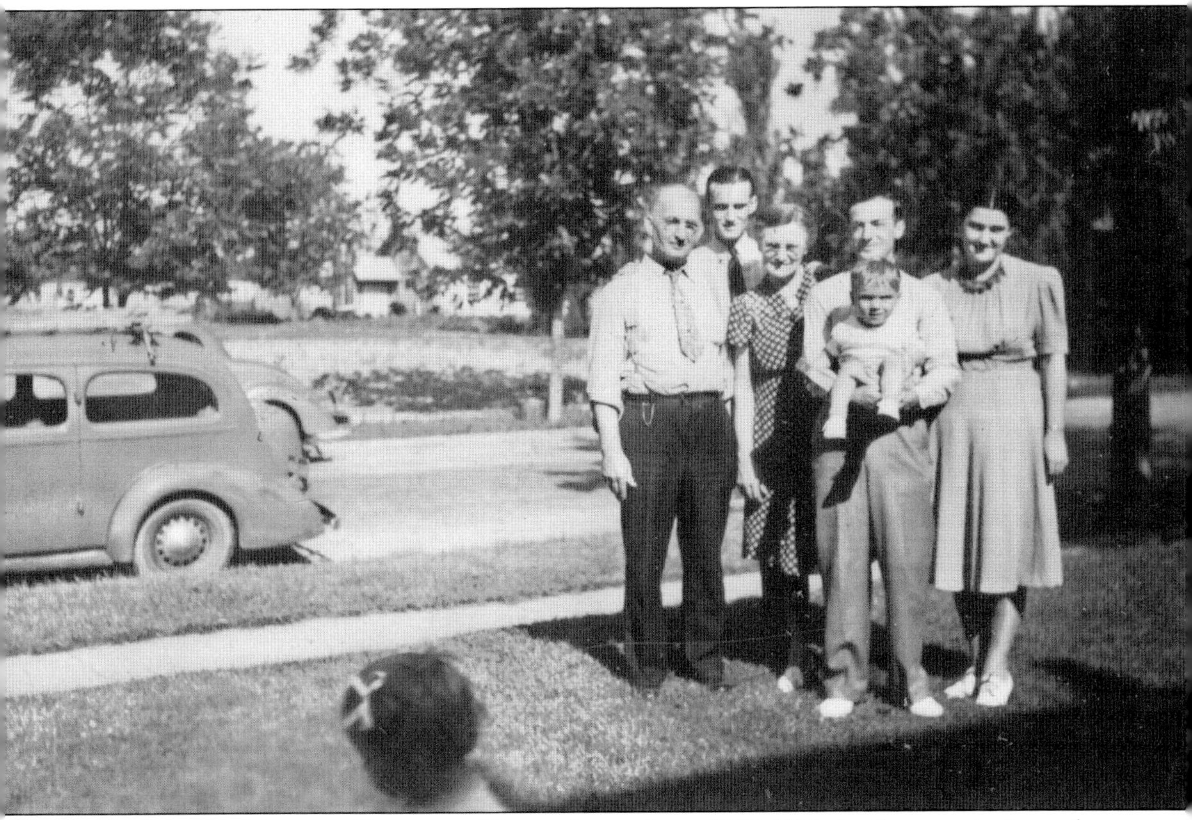

Heber Gardner Mumford Family on Wilson Lawn, June 1940. This family group is pictured on the front lawn of the C.L. Wilson home in Robersonville. During this period, North Main Street was developing as a residential area. (Courtesy of Judith A. Critcher.)

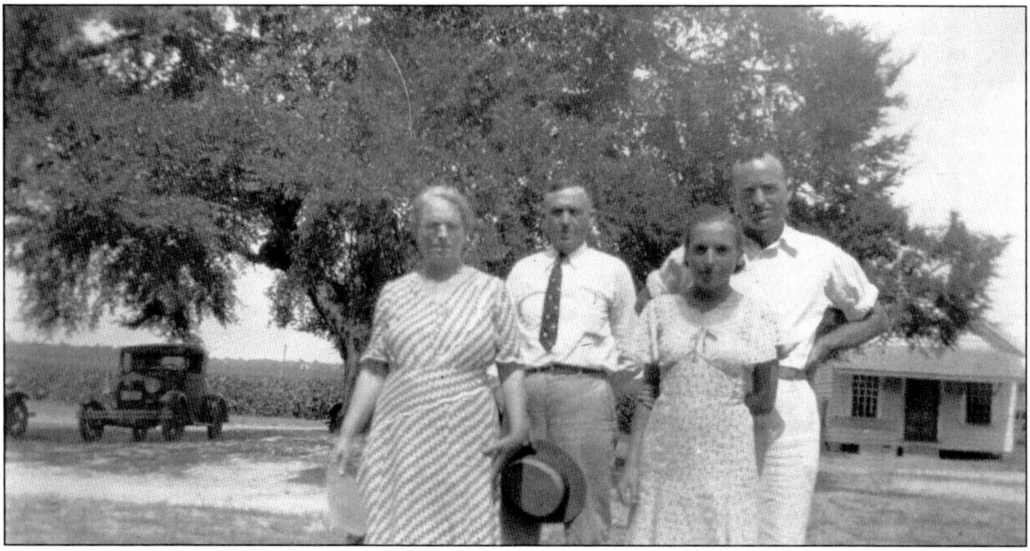

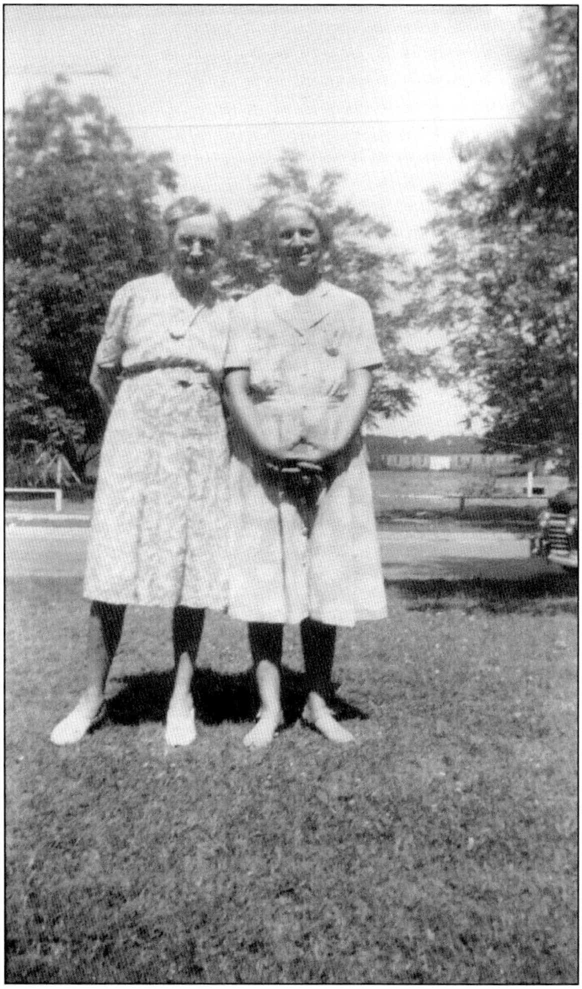

EVERETTS IN JUNE 1942. Pictured here are, from left to right, Jane Everett, H.L. Everett, Janie Yates Everett, and W.B. Everett. Janie was born on August 1, 1918, and she and William were married around the time this image was made. (Courtesy of Judith A. Critcher.)

EMMA LIZA MUMFORD (LEFT) AND FANNYBEL WILSON, 1943. These sisters pose for the camera on the lawn of the C.L. Wilson home in Robersonville. (Courtesy of Judith A. Critcher.)

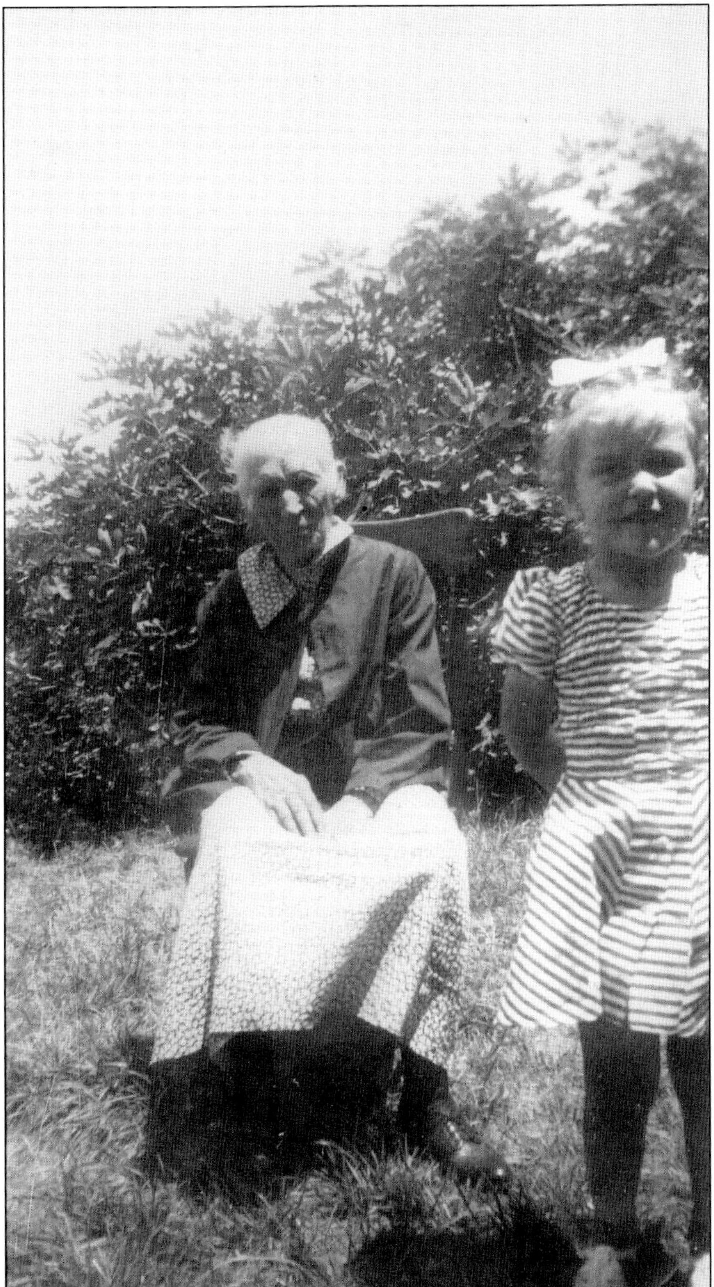

CHLOE ROBERSON AND ELIZABETH ANN EVERETT, 1942. Chloe and Benjamin Harvey Roberson had nine children during their marriage—John Henry (who married Daisy Johnson), Mary Ida (who married George Arthur Crofton), William Ander (who married Bertha Purvis), Jane Arminta "Mint" (who married Howard Lister Everett), Emma Liza (who married Heber Gardner Mumford), Harvey (who married Lena Parker), Vivian (who married Charles Abram Roberson), Ashley Pitt (who married Annie Laurie Phillips) and youngest child Fannybel (who married Charles Leon Wilson Sr.). Chloe is pictured here with her great-granddaughter Elizabeth Ann Everett. (Courtesy of Judith A. Critcher.)

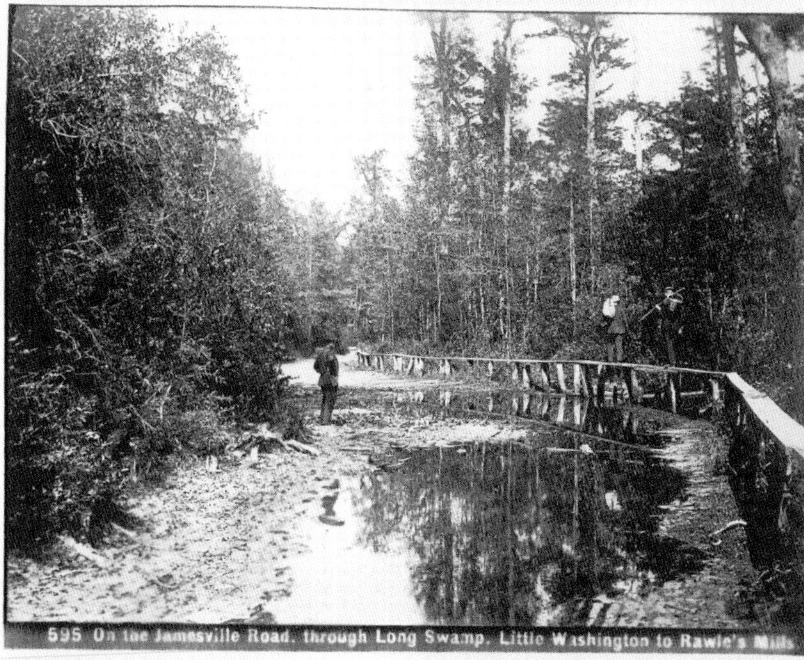

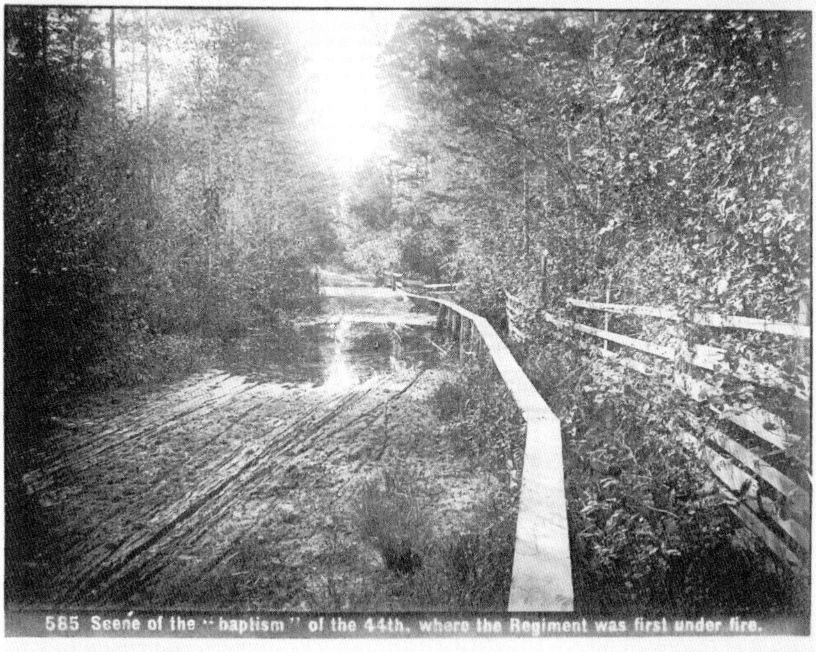

Civil War Battleground. These rare 1884 photographs were taken by Boston photographer William Garrison Reed and reproduced in a limited number of special issues of the 1887 regimental history *Record of the Service of the Forty-fourth Massachusetts*. Made 20 years after the conflict in Martin County, they record the scene of action experienced by the 44th as it advanced on Little Creek (Smithwick Creek) and Rawls's Mill in Martin County, North Carolina, on November 2, 1862. (Courtesy of the J.Y. Joyner Library, Verona Joyner Langford North Carolina Collection.)

Four

War and Controversy

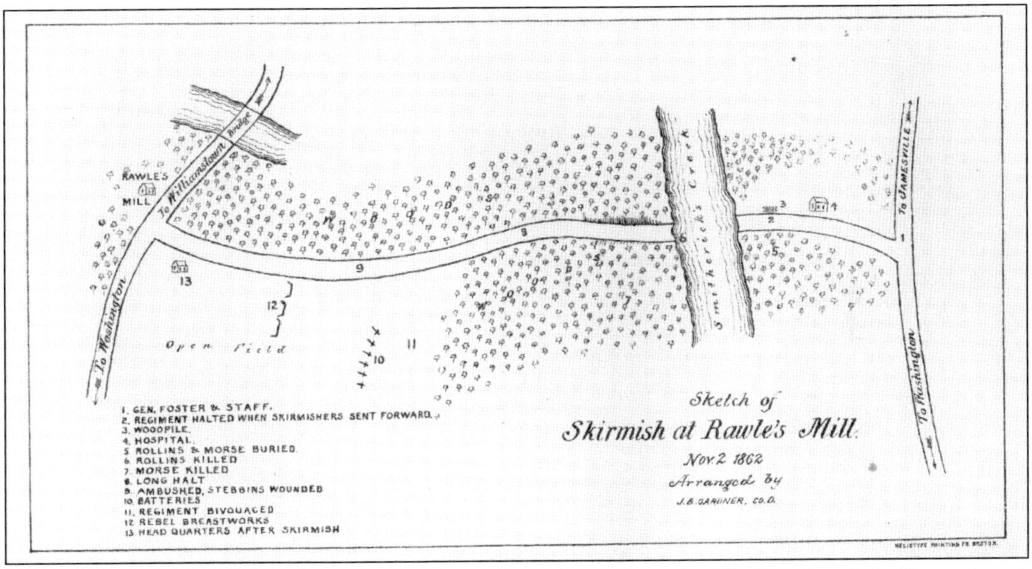

Map of Rawls's Mill Battle. A map from the volume *Record of the Service of the Forty-Fourth Massachusetts Volunteer Militia in North Carolina, August 1862 to May 1863* (1887) records the Battle of "Rawle's" Mill on November 2, 1862. Of two parallel roads leading from Washington to Williamston, General Foster's army used the eastern approach, going through what is now the Farm Life Community, or Griffins Township. The map shows locations along what is presently thought to be Mill Inn Road leading into current US Highway 17 and the Reedy Swamp Bridge. The old mill house was located on the left, just before the bridge as one goes toward Williamston. Little Creek was apparently a tributary leading into Reedy Swamp and crossed Old Mill Road approximately a mile or less before the Highway 17 intersection. (Courtesy of the J.Y. Joyner Library, Verona Joyner Langford North Carolina Collection.)

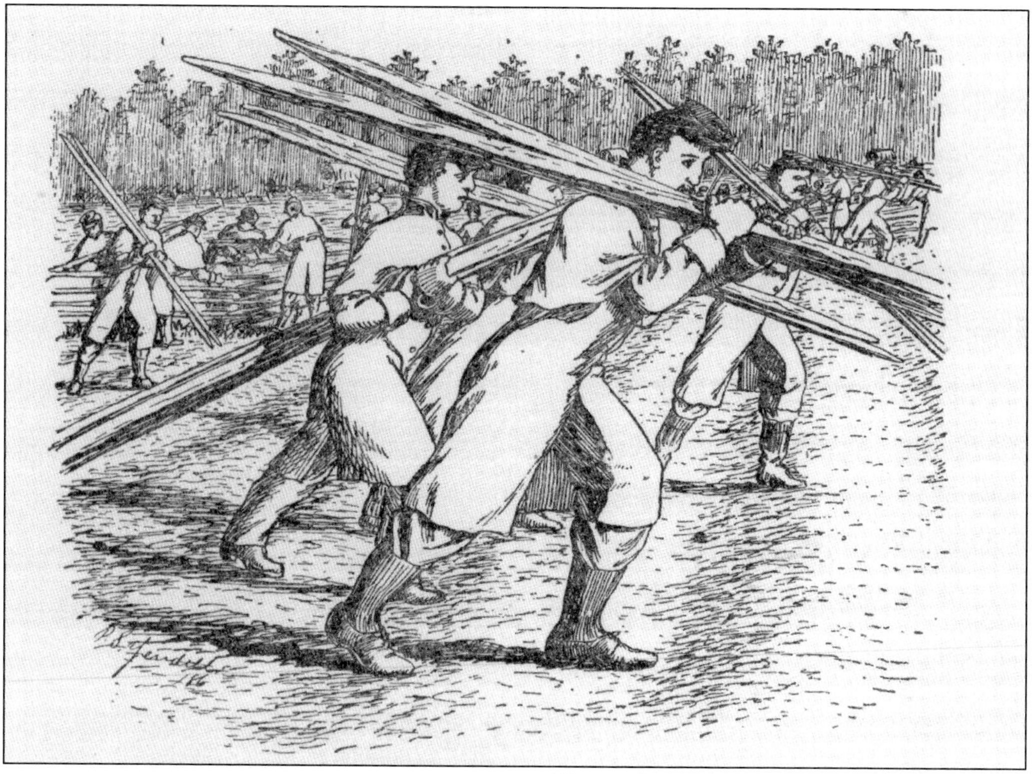

Union Soldiers in Martin County. In this image taken from the volume *Record of the Service of the Forty-fourth Massachusetts Volunteer Militia in North Carolina, August 1862 to May 1863* (1887), soldiers are shown removing fence posts for firewood. (Courtesy of the J.Y. Joyner Library, Verona Joyner Langford North Carolina Collection.)

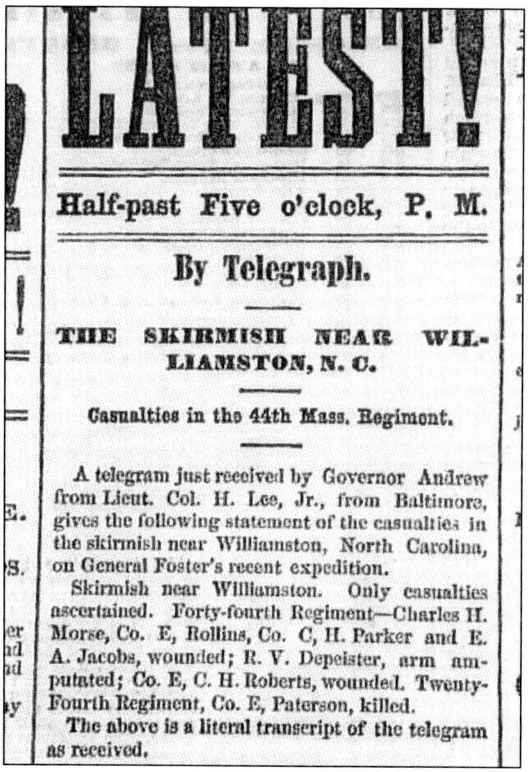

LATEST!

Half-past Five o'clock, P. M.

By Telegraph.

THE SKIRMISH NEAR WILLIAMSTON, N. C.

Casualties in the 44th Mass. Regiment.

A telegram just received by Governor Andrew from Lieut. Col. H. Lee, Jr., from Baltimore, gives the following statement of the casualties in the skirmish near Williamston, North Carolina, on General Foster's recent expedition.

Skirmish near Williamston. Only casualties ascertained. Forty-fourth Regiment—Charles H. Morse, Co. E, Rollins, Co. C, H. Parker and E. A. Jacobs, wounded; R. V. Depeister, arm amputated; Co. E, C. H. Roberts, wounded. Twenty-Fourth Regiment, Co. E, Paterson, killed.

The above is a literal transcript of the telegram as received.

Boston Evening Transcript, November 11, 1862. The article here records Union casualties connected with the Rawls's Mill skirmish near Williamston. (Courtesy of the author.)

ANOTHER VIEW OF RAWLS'S MILL INCIDENT. This rare, hand-drawn map of the Battle of Rawle's Mill in Martin County was first published in Jasper Weyth's 1878 volume, *Leaves from a Diary Written While Serving in Co. E, 44 Mass.* (Courtesy of the J.Y. Joyner Library, Verona Joyner Langford North Carolina Collection.)

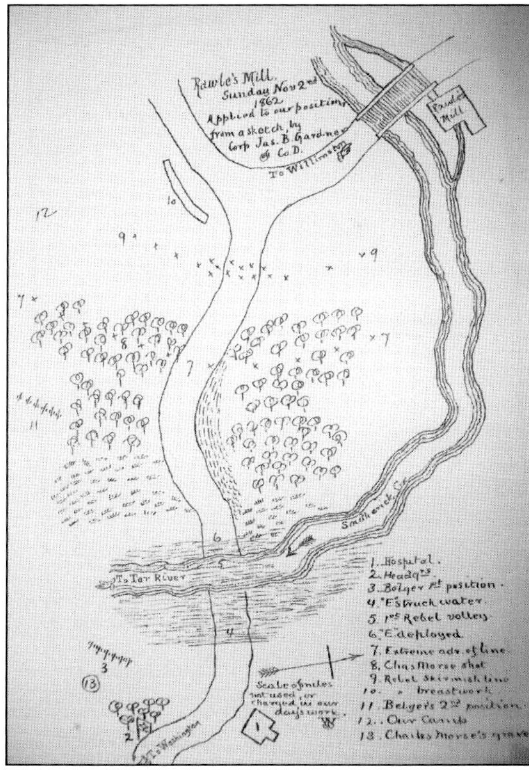

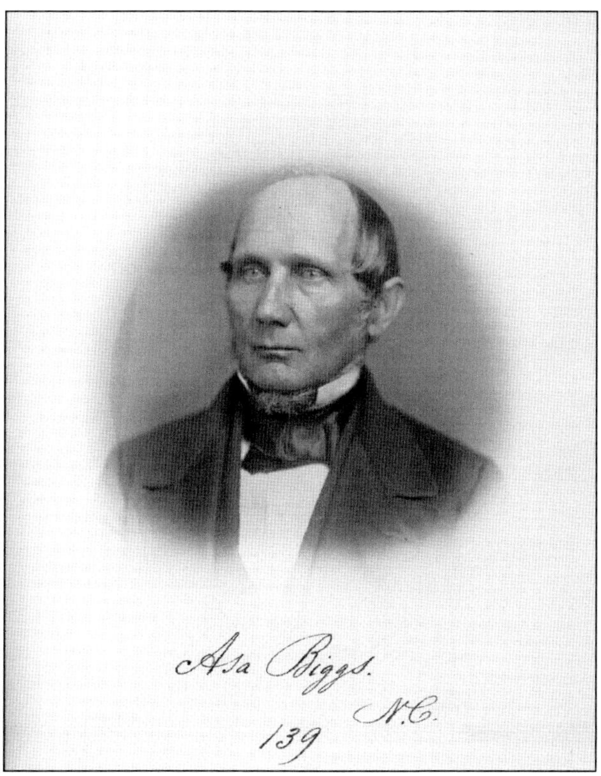

ASA BIGGS, C. 1859. This image of US senator (and later Confederate judge) Asa Biggs of Williamston is taken from *McClees' Gallery of Photographic Portraits of the Senators, Representatives and Delegates of the Thirty-Fifth Congress* (1859). Biggs left Williamston in February 1862 upon the advance of the Union army into inland eastern North Carolina. His home and office were severely pillaged by the invading forces. (Courtesy of the author.)

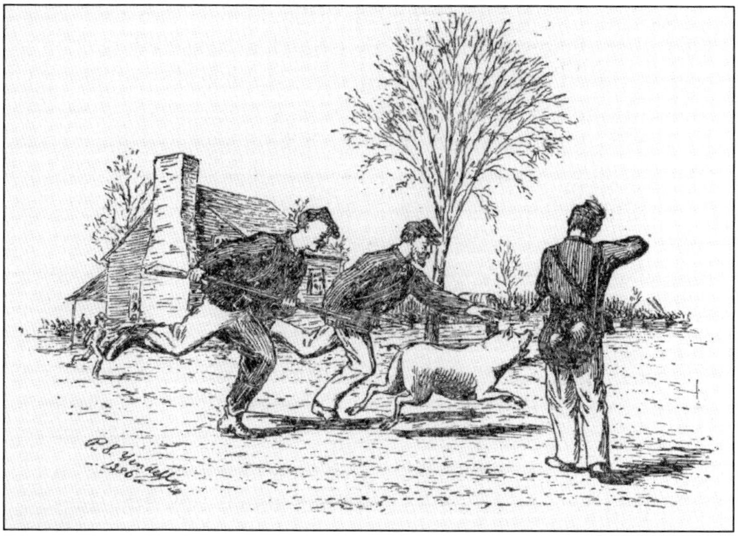

UNION SOLDIERS FORAGING, 1862. Another image from *Record of the Service of the Forty-Fourth Massachusetts Volunteer Militia in North Carolina, August 1862 to May 1863* depicts Union soldiers confiscating pigs during Foster's Raid in November 1862. (Courtesy of the J.Y. Joyner Library, Verona Joyner Langford North Carolina Collection.)

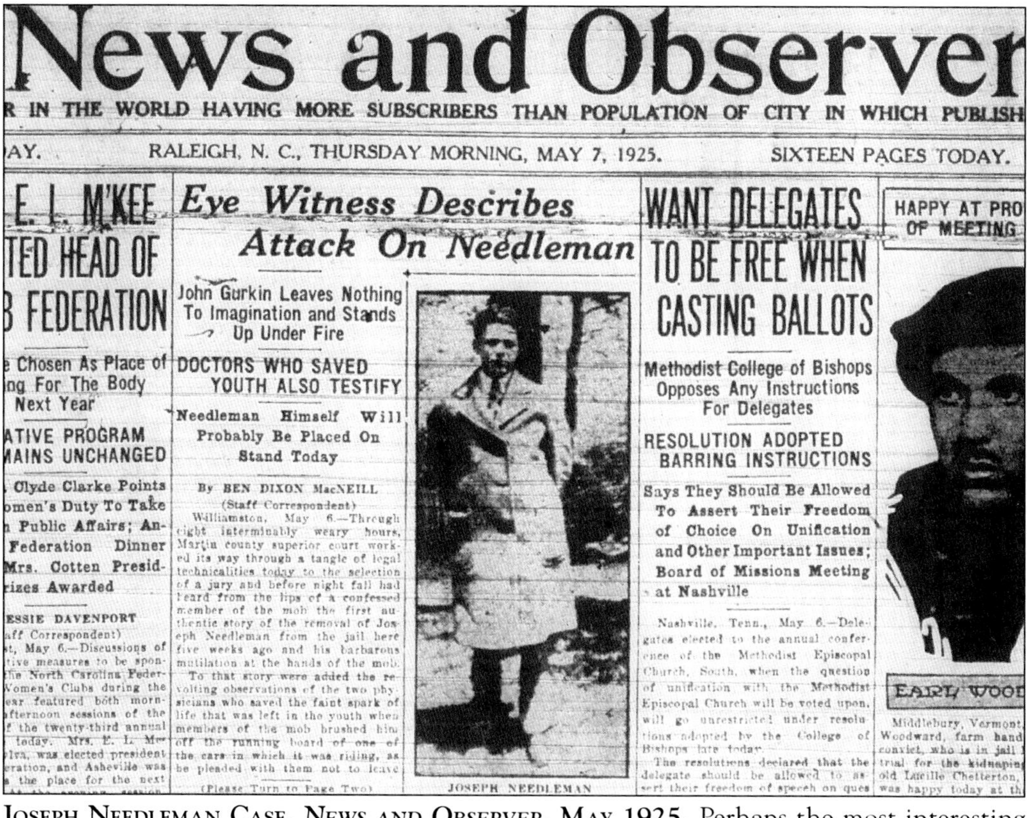

News and Observer

R IN THE WORLD HAVING MORE SUBSCRIBERS THAN POPULATION OF CITY IN WHICH PUBLISH

AY. RALEIGH, N. C., THURSDAY MORNING, MAY 7, 1925. SIXTEEN PAGES TODAY.

E. L. M'KEE
TED HEAD OF
B FEDERATION

e Chosen As Place of
ng For The Body
Next Year

ATIVE PROGRAM
MAINS UNCHANGED

Clyde Clarke Points
omen's Duty To Take
n Public Affairs; An-
Federation Dinner
Mrs. Cotten Presid-
rizes Awarded

ESSIE DAVENPORT
aff Correspondent)

t, May 6.—Discussions of tive measures to be spon- the North Carolina Feder- Women's Clubs during the ear featured both morn- fternoon sessions of the f the twenty-third annual today. Mrs. E. L. Mc- lva, was elected president eration, and Asheville was the place for the next

Eye Witness Describes
Attack On Needleman

John Gurkin Leaves Nothing
To Imagination and Stands
Up Under Fire

DOCTORS WHO SAVED
YOUTH ALSO TESTIFY

Needleman Himself Will
Probably Be Placed On
Stand Today

By BEN DIXON MacNEILL
(Staff Correspondent)

Williamston, May 6.—Through eight interminably weary hours, Martin county superior court worked its way through a tangle of legal technicalities today to the selection of a jury and before night fall had heard from the lips of a confessed member of the mob the first authentic story of the removal of Joseph Needleman from the jail here five weeks ago and his barbarous mutilation at the hands of the mob.

To that story were added the revolting observations of the two physicians who saved the faint spark of life that was left in the youth when members of the mob brushed him off the running board of one of the cars in which it was riding, as he pleaded with them not to leave

(Please Turn to Page Two)

JOSEPH NEEDLEMAN

WANT DELEGATES
TO BE FREE WHEN
CASTING BALLOTS

Methodist College of Bishops
Opposes Any Instructions
For Delegates

RESOLUTION ADOPTED
BARRING INSTRUCTIONS

Says They Should Be Allowed
To Assert Their Freedom
of Choice On Unification
and Other Important Issues;
Board of Missions Meeting
at Nashville

Nashville, Tenn., May 6.—Delegates elected to the annual conference of the Methodist Episcopal Church, South, when the question of unification with the Methodist Episcopal Church will be voted upon, will go unrestricted under resolutions adopted by the College of Bishops late today.

The resolutions declared that the delegate should be allowed to assert their freedom of speech on ques

HAPPY AT PRO
OF MEETING

EARL WOOD

Middlebury, Vermont, Woodward, farm hand convict, who is in jail trial for the kidnaping old Lucille Chetterton, was happy today at th

JOSEPH NEEDLEMAN CASE, *NEWS AND OBSERVER*, MAY 1925. Perhaps the most interesting incident of Martin County's history— still recalled by many living today—is the lynching of Joseph Needleman and the court case that followed. Needleman, a Jewish tobacco salesman, was accused of assaulting a local girl. The case made state and national headlines and also garnered international attention. Fearing a potentially negative effect on the state's business climate, Gov. Angus Maclean took a personal interest in the matter by ordering a special term of court. (Courtesy of the *News and Observer.*)

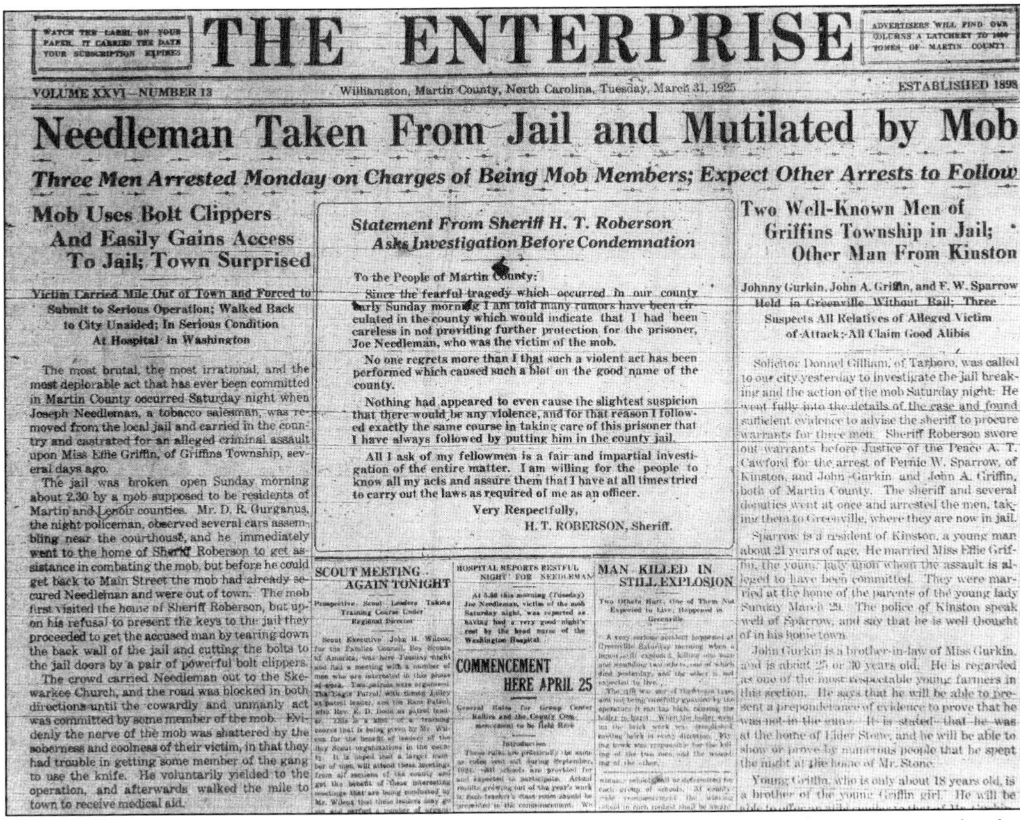

WATCH THE LABEL ON YOUR PAPER. IT CARRIES THE DATE YOUR SUBSCRIPTION EXPIRES

THE ENTERPRISE

ADVERTISERS WILL FIND OUR COLUMNS A LATCHKEY TO 1600 HOMES OF MARTIN COUNTY

VOLUME XXVI—NUMBER 13 Williamston, Martin County, North Carolina, Tuesday, March 31, 1925 ESTABLISHED 1898

Needleman Taken From Jail and Mutilated by Mob

Three Men Arrested Monday on Charges of Being Mob Members; Expect Other Arrests to Follow

Mob Uses Bolt Clippers And Easily Gains Access To Jail; Town Surprised

Victim Carried Mile Out of Town and Forced to Submit to Serious Operation; Walked Back to City Unaided; In Serious Condition At Hospital in Washington

The most brutal, the most irrational, and the most deplorable act that has ever been committed in Martin County occurred Saturday night when Joseph Needleman, a tobacco salesman, was removed from the local jail and carried in the country and castrated for an alleged criminal assault upon Miss Effie Griffin, of Griffins Township, several days ago.

The jail was broken open Sunday morning about 2.30 by a mob supposed to be residents of Martin and Lenoir counties. Mr. D. R. Gurganus, the night policeman, observed several cars assembling near the courthouse, and he immediately went to the home of Sheriff Roberson to get assistance in combating the mob, but before he could get back to Main Street the mob had already secured Needleman and were out of town. The mob first visited the home of Sheriff Roberson, but upon his refusal to present the keys to the jail they proceeded to get the accused man by tearing down the back wall of the jail and cutting the bolts to the jail doors by a pair of powerful bolt clippers.

The crowd carried Needleman out to the Skewarkee Church, and the road was blocked in both directions until the cowardly and unmanly act was committed by some member of the mob. Evidenly the nerve of the mob was shattered by the soberness and coolness of their victim, in that they had trouble in getting some member of the gang to use the knife. He voluntarily yielded to the operation, and afterwards walked the mile to town to receive medical aid.

Statement From Sheriff H. T. Roberson Asks Investigation Before Condemnation

To the People of Martin County:

Since the fearful tragedy which occurred in our county early Sunday morning I am told many rumors have been circulated in the county which would indicate that I had been careless in not providing further protection for the prisoner, Joe Needleman, who was the victim of the mob.

No one regrets more than I that such a violent act has been performed which caused such a blot on the good name of the county.

Nothing had appeared to even cause the slightest suspicion that there would be any violence, and for that reason I followed exactly the same course in taking care of this prisoner that I have always followed by putting him in the county jail.

All I ask of my fellowmen is a fair and impartial investigation of the entire matter. I am willing for the people to know all my acts and assure them that I have at all times tried to carry out the laws as required of me as an officer.

Very Respectfully,
H. T. ROBERSON, Sheriff.

SCOUT MEETING AGAIN TONIGHT

Prospective Scout Leaders Taking Training Course Under Regional Director

HOSPITAL REPORTS RESTFUL NIGHT FOR NEEDLEMAN

At 5.30 this morning (Tuesday) Joe Needleman, victim of the mob Saturday night, was reported as having had a very good night's rest by the head nurse of the Washington Hospital.

COMMENCEMENT HERE APRIL 25

General Rules for Group Center Rallies and the County Commencement to be Held Here

Introduction

MAN KILLED IN STILL EXPLOSION

Two Others Hurt, One of Them Not Expected to Live; Happened in Greenville

Two Well-Known Men of Griffins Township in Jail; Other Man From Kinston

Johnny Gurkin, John A. Griffin, and F. W. Sparrow Held in Greenville Without Bail; Three Suspects All Relatives of Alleged Victim of Attack; All Claim Good Alibis

Solicitor Donnel Gilliam, of Tarboro, was called to our city yesterday to investigate the jail breaking and the action of the mob Saturday night. He went fully into the details of the case and found sufficient evidence to advise the sheriff to procure warrants for three men. Sheriff Roberson swore out warrants before Justice of the Peace A. T. Cawford for the arrest of Fernie W. Sparrow, of Kinston, and John Gurkin and John A. Griffin, both of Martin County. The sheriff and several deputies went at once and arrested the men, taking them to Greenville, where they are now in jail.

Sparrow is a resident of Kinston, a young man about 21 years of age. He married Miss Effie Griffin, the young lady upon whom the assault is alleged to have been committed. They were married at the home of the parents of the young lady Sunday March 29. The police of Kinston speak well of Sparrow, and say that he is well thought of in his home town.

John Gurkin is a brother-in-law of Miss Gurkin, and is about 25 or 30 years old. He is regarded as one of the most respectable young farmers in this section. He says that he will be able to present a preponderance of evidence to prove that he was not in the gang. It is stated that he was at the home of Elder Stone, and he will be able to show or prove by numerous people that he spent the night at the home of Mr. Stone.

Young Griffin, who is only about 18 years old, is a brother of the young Griffin girl. He will be

NEEDLEMAN CASE, THE *ENTERPRISE*, MARCH 1925. Numerous local personalities were involved in some shape or form with the events surrounding the Needleman affair. Days when sentences were handed down to those judged guilty of various criminal actions were times of great moaning and weeping in the old Martin County Courthouse. A mob of men broke into the local jail using bolt clippers, took Needleman a mile outside of town, and castrated him behind Skewarkey Primitive Baptist Church. (Courtesy of Martin County Historical Society.)

SKEWARKEY PRIMITIVE BAPTIST CHURCH. Shown here as it appeared in 1936, the structure, built in 1857, is the second building for the congregation, whose roots go back to the 1780s. The area behind the church was the scene of an assault on Joseph Needleman in the spring of 1925. (Courtesy of Martin County Historical Society.)

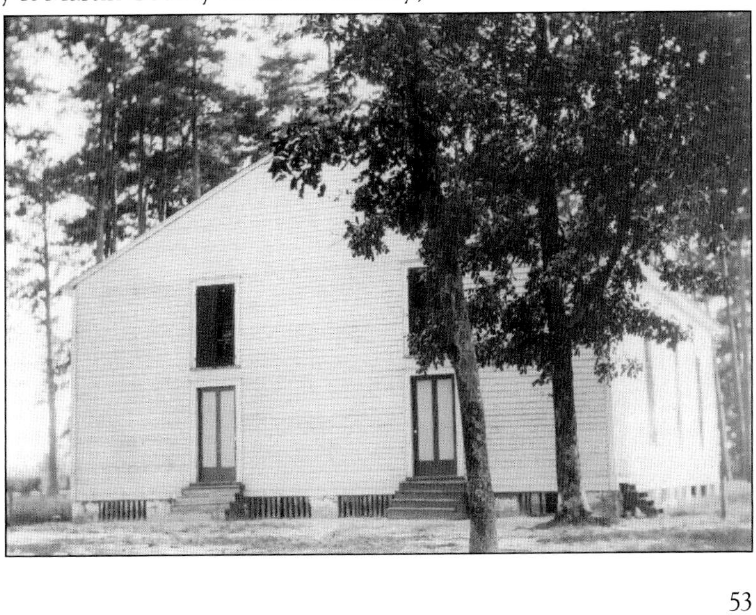

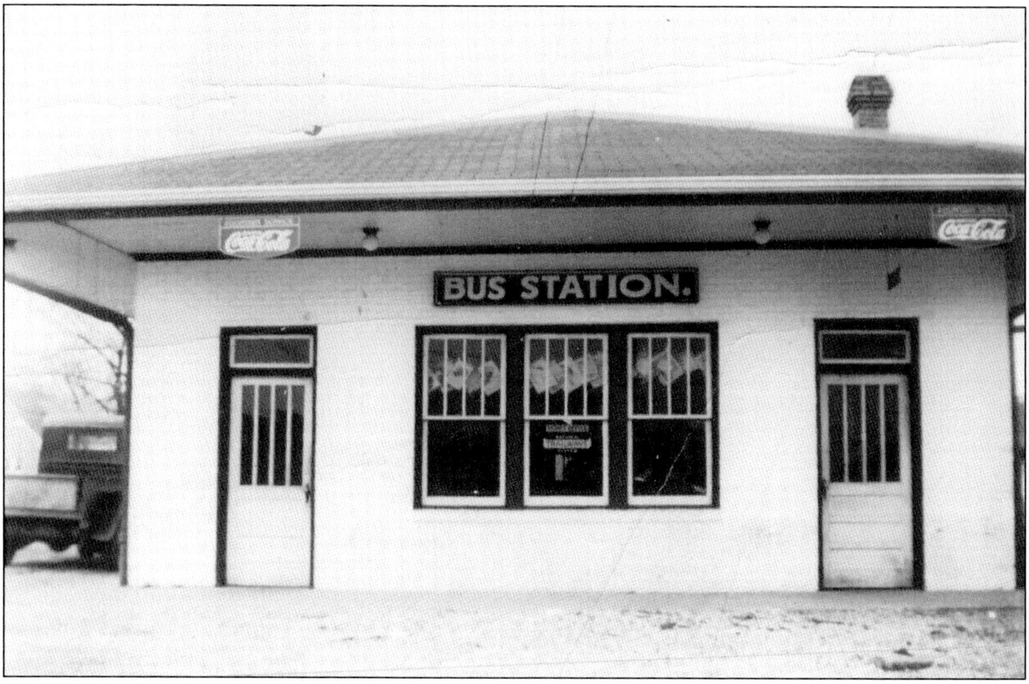

OLD WILLIAMSTON BUS STATION. Williamston's first bus station was located in the area now referred to as 200 West Main Street, the current site of Schewels Furniture and the previous location of the Belk-Tyler department store. Many County men drafted for service during World War II passed through here. (Courtesy of Martin County Historical Society.)

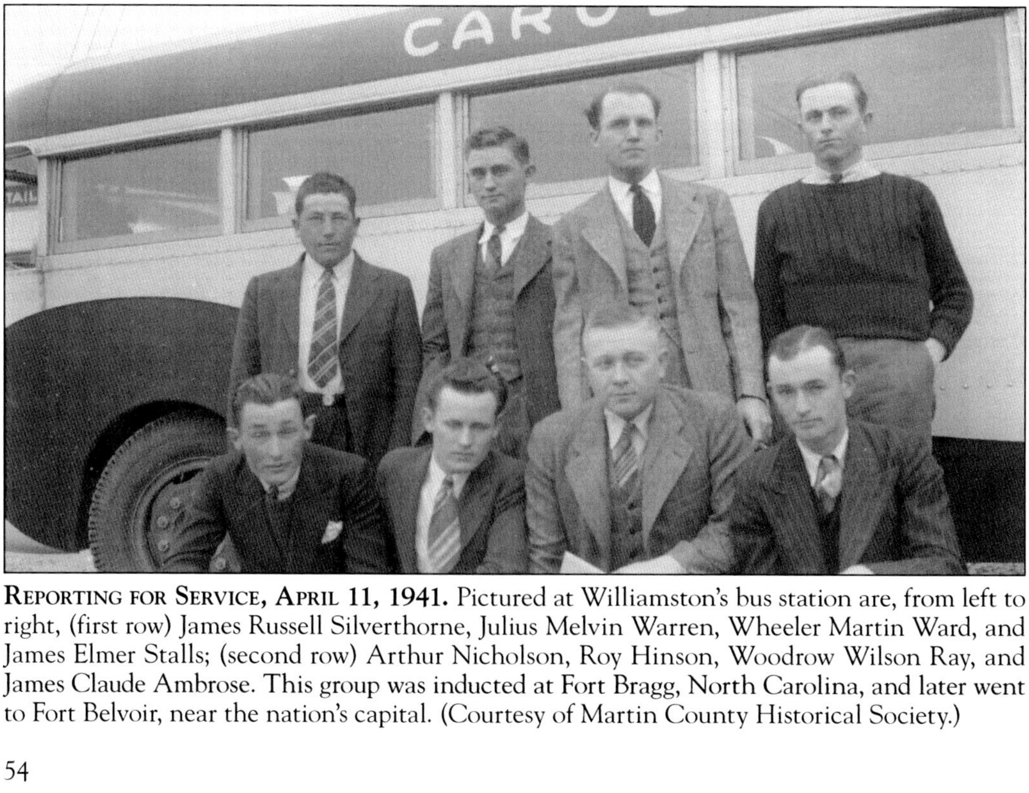

REPORTING FOR SERVICE, APRIL 11, 1941. Pictured at Williamston's bus station are, from left to right, (first row) James Russell Silverthorne, Julius Melvin Warren, Wheeler Martin Ward, and James Elmer Stalls; (second row) Arthur Nicholson, Roy Hinson, Woodrow Wilson Ray, and James Claude Ambrose. This group was inducted at Fort Bragg, North Carolina, and later went to Fort Belvoir, near the nation's capital. (Courtesy of Martin County Historical Society.)

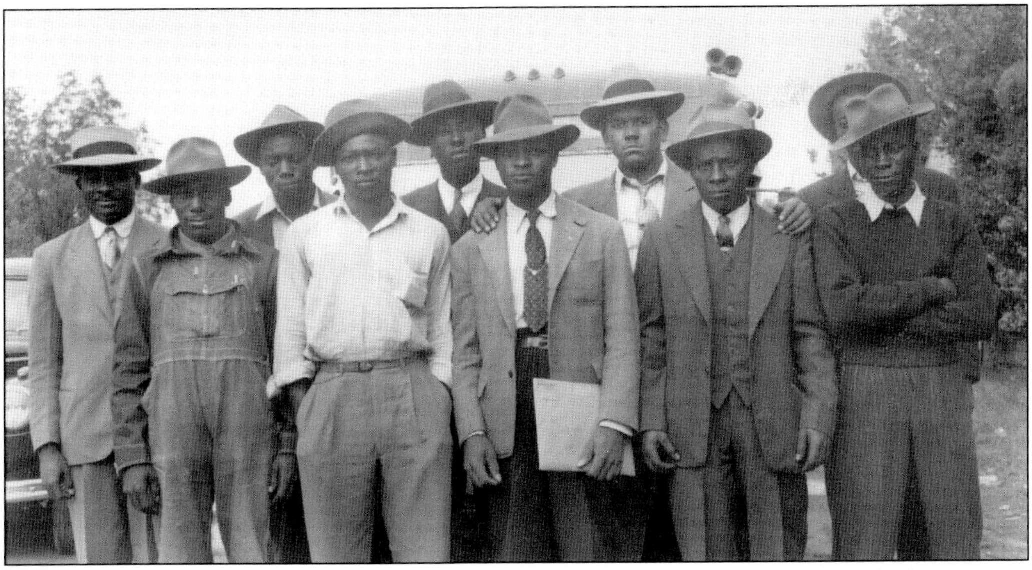

Reporting for Service, November 21, 1941. These men, also photographed at the bus station, are, from left to right, (first row) Richard Hyman, Milton Rollins, James Morris Cherry, Willie Grover Mason, and Shelbert Ore; (second row) Woodrow Narrow, Milton Roberson, Eddie Lee Smith, Edmond Pierce, and Jeremiah Brown. (Courtesy of Martin County Historical Society.)

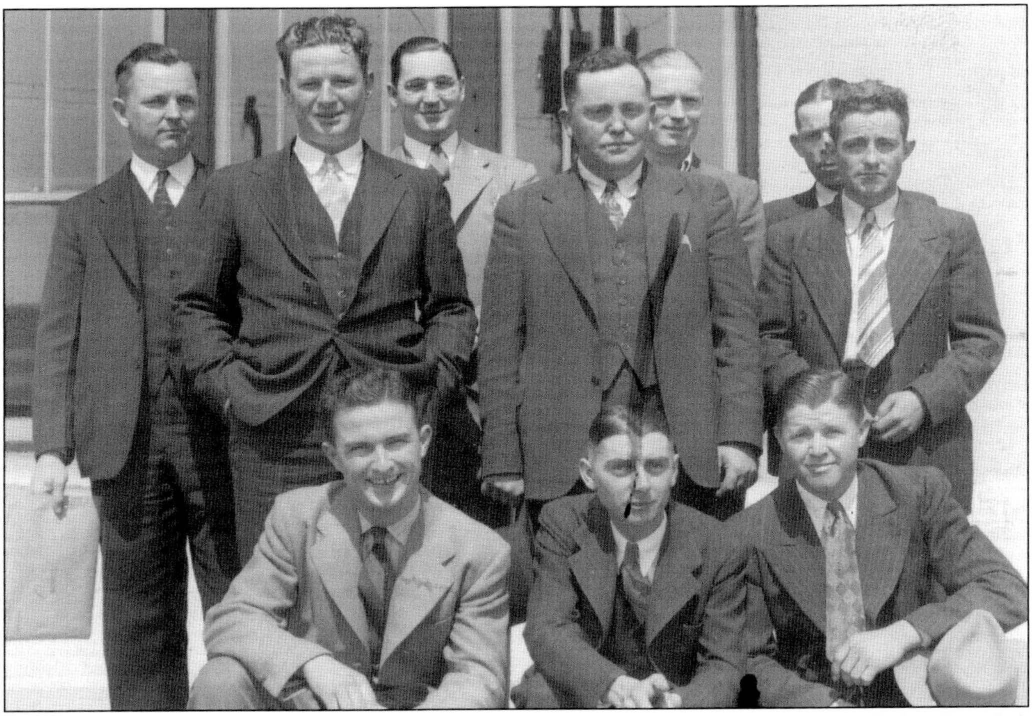

Reporting for Service, April 18, 1941. This group of men at the bus station includes, from left to right, (first row) William Daniel Peel, Ben Ollie Coburn, and Thomas Leroy Taylor; (second row) Eddie Gurley Leggett, Robert Bailey, and Willis Robert Crandall; (third row) Jimmy Lindsey Dickens, Dallas Gaylord Waters, Steve Elias Stevenson, and Johnny Thomas Mobley. (Courtesy of Martin County Historical Society.)

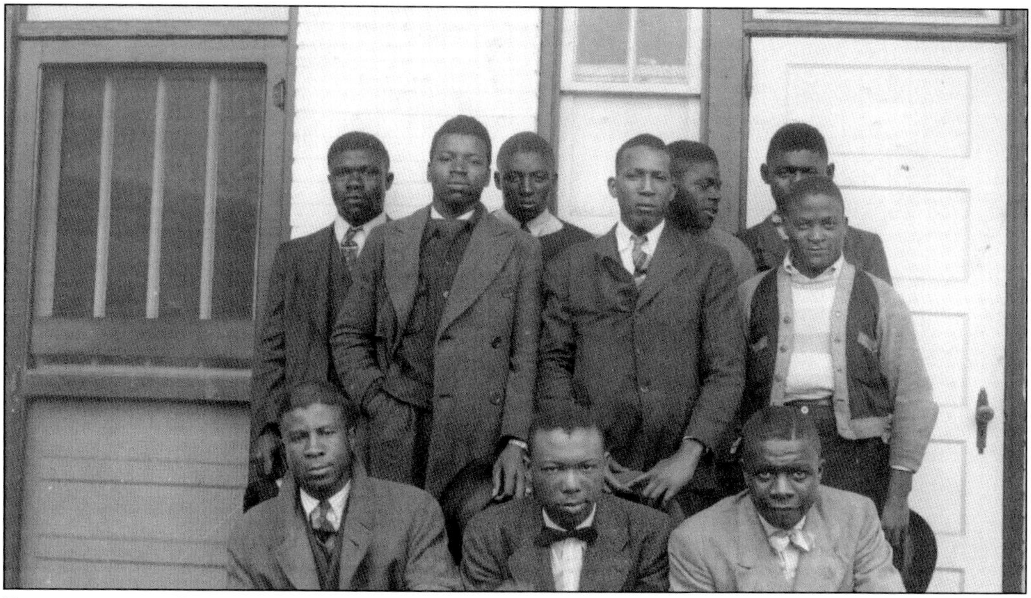

Reporting for Service, April 11, 1941. Pictured here at the bus station are, from left to right, (first row) Wesley Moore, Herbert Louis Peel, and Samuel Davis Slade; (second row) Ordele Little, Thomas Lee Hawkins, Penberton Benson Swarner, John D. Gainer, Jesse Walston, Louis Reddick, and unidentified. (Courtesy of Martin County Historical Society.)

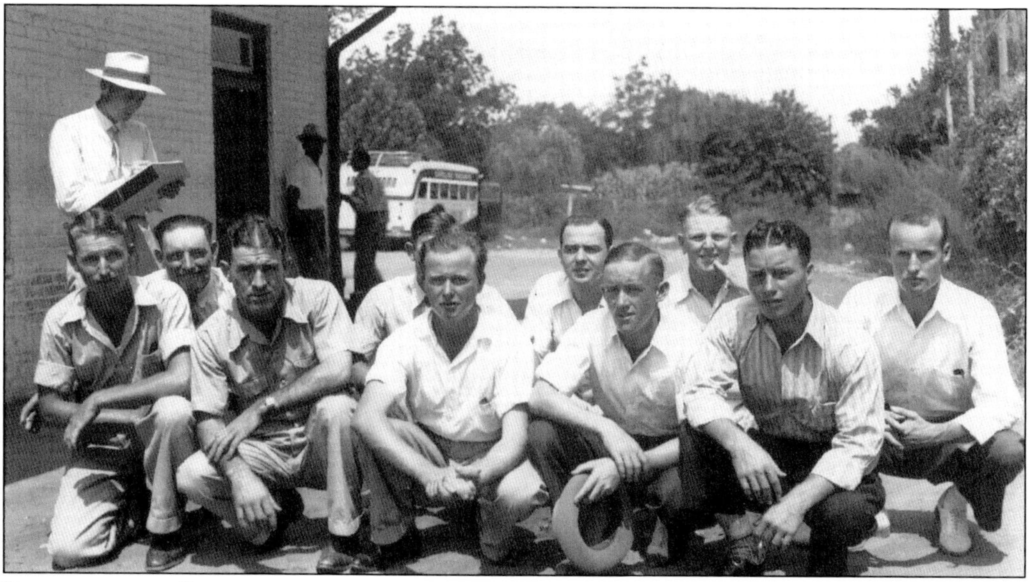

Reporting for Service, August 6, 1941. Kneeling at the bus station are, from left to right, (first row) Ed Moore, Dallie Merry, Morris Lynch, Jessie Griffin, and Julius Revels; (second row) Dallas Harden, Jessie Wynne, Elbert Whichard, Bill Haislip, and Paul Swinson. (Courtesy of Martin County Historical Society.)

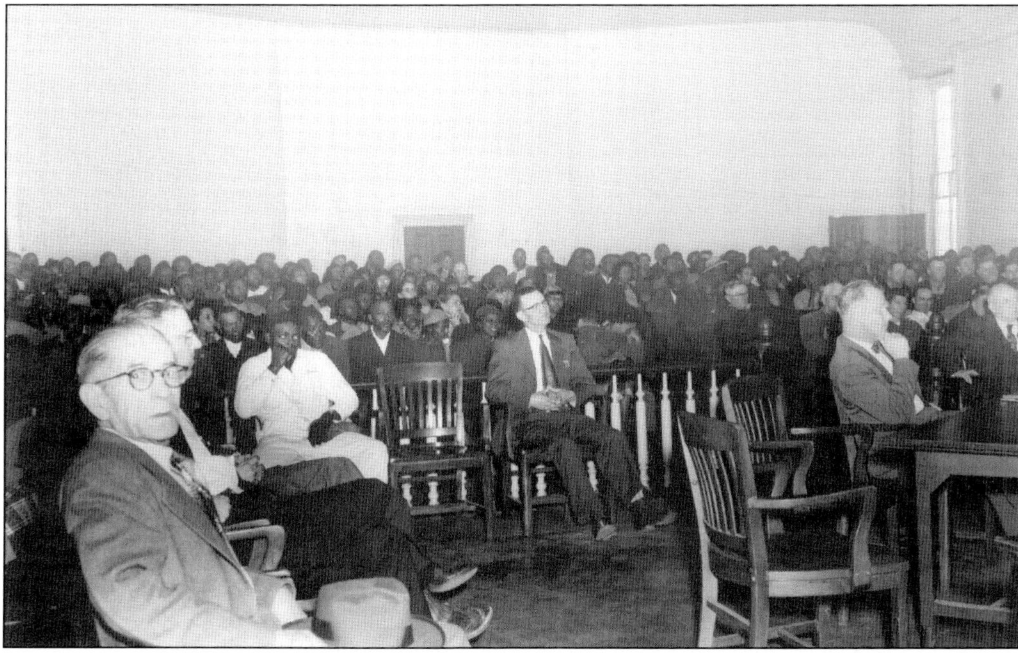

Bootlegger Trials, February 1953. A photograph from the Royal Photographic Studio of Williamston records proceedings taking place in the old Martin County Courthouse. (Courtesy of Martin County Historical Society.)

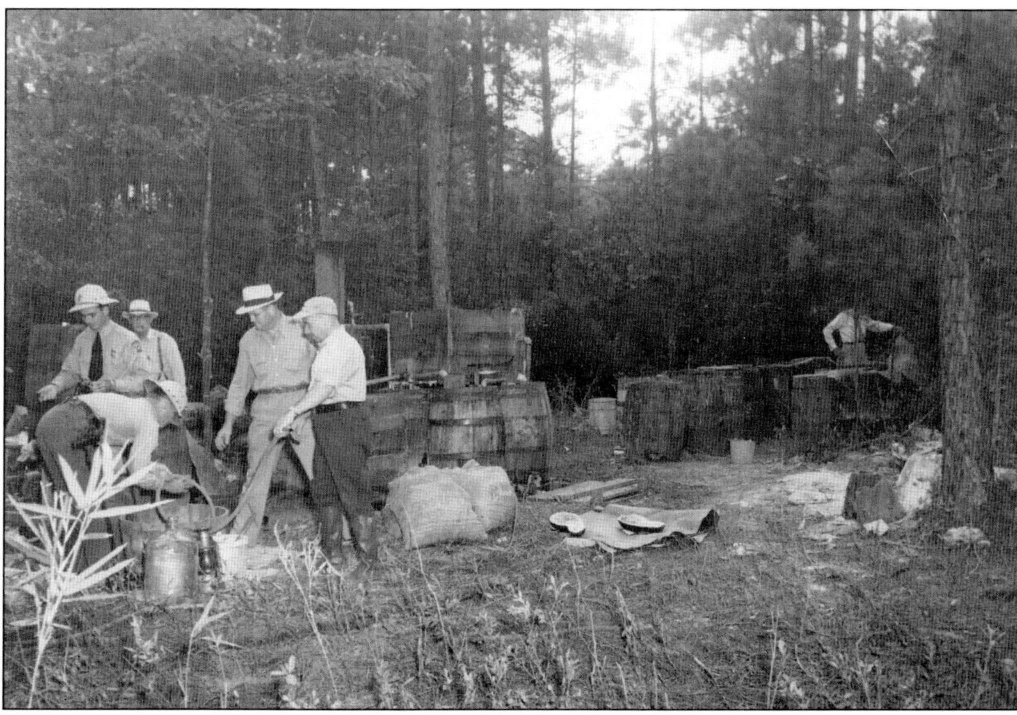

Officials Breaking Up Moonshine Operation, c. 1950. This image is attributed to the Royal Photographic Studio of Williamston, North Carolina, Identified second from right is Buck Holloman. (Courtesy of Jesse Silverthorne.)

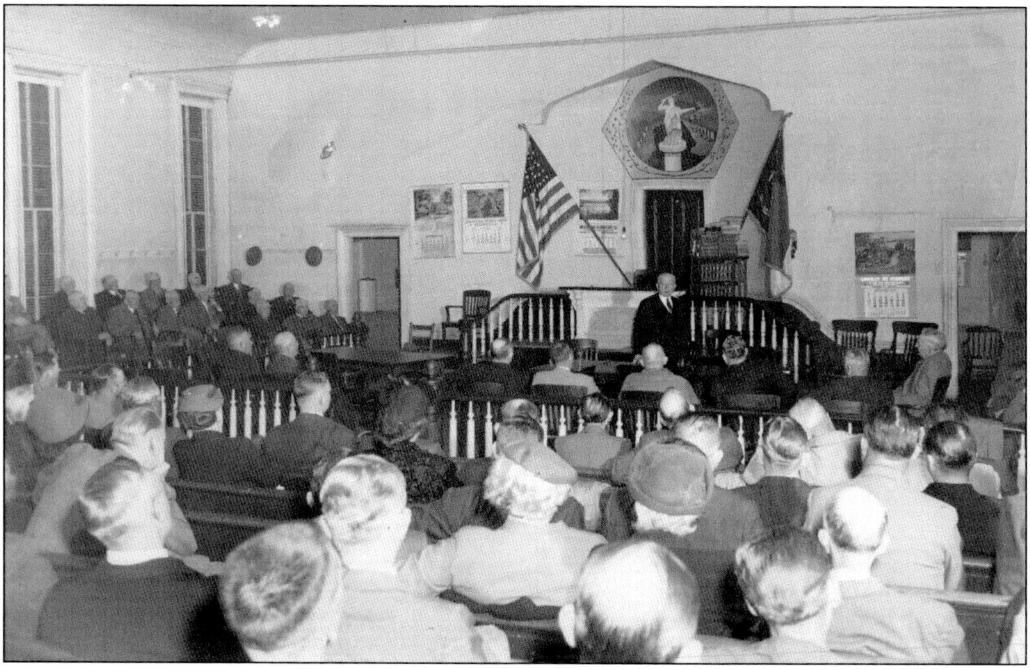

TRIAL SCENE IN OLD MARTIN COUNTY COURTHOUSE, OCTOBER 1948. This interesting view by the Royal Photographic Studio shows the courtroom as it appeared before the introduction of knotty pine paneling in the 1950s. (Courtesy of Jesse Silverthorne.)

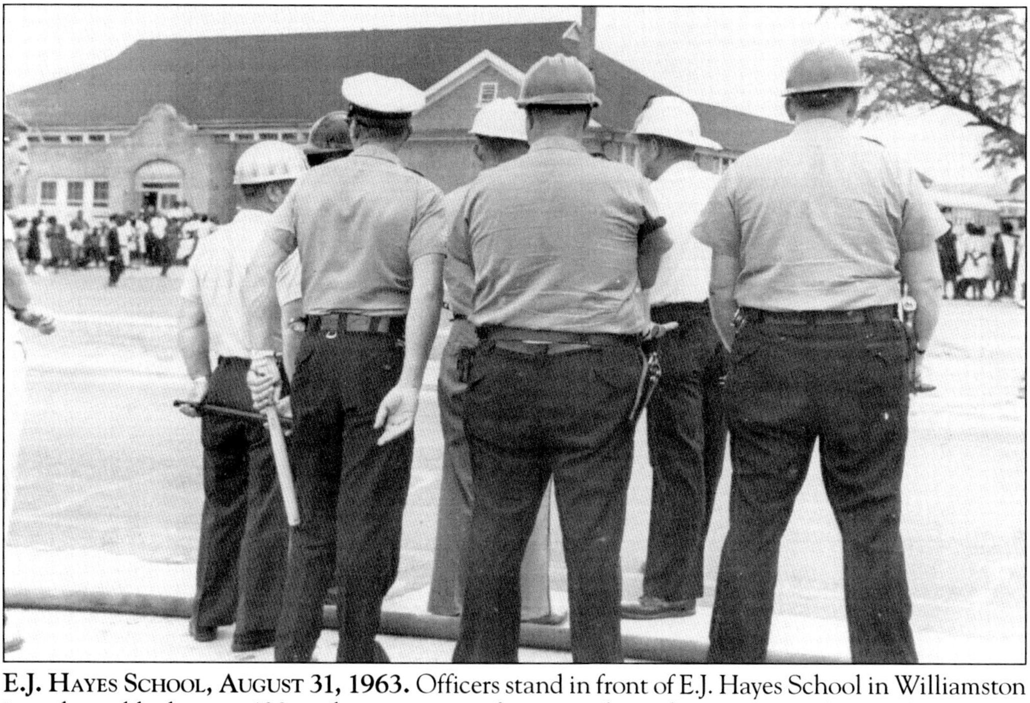

E.J. HAYES SCHOOL, AUGUST 31, 1963. Officers stand in front of E.J. Hayes School in Williamston in order to block some 400 student protestors from marching downtown on August 31, 1963, in one of the more heated civil rights protests during the so-called Williamston Freedom Movement. Much national media attention was focused on the town. (Courtesy of the author.)

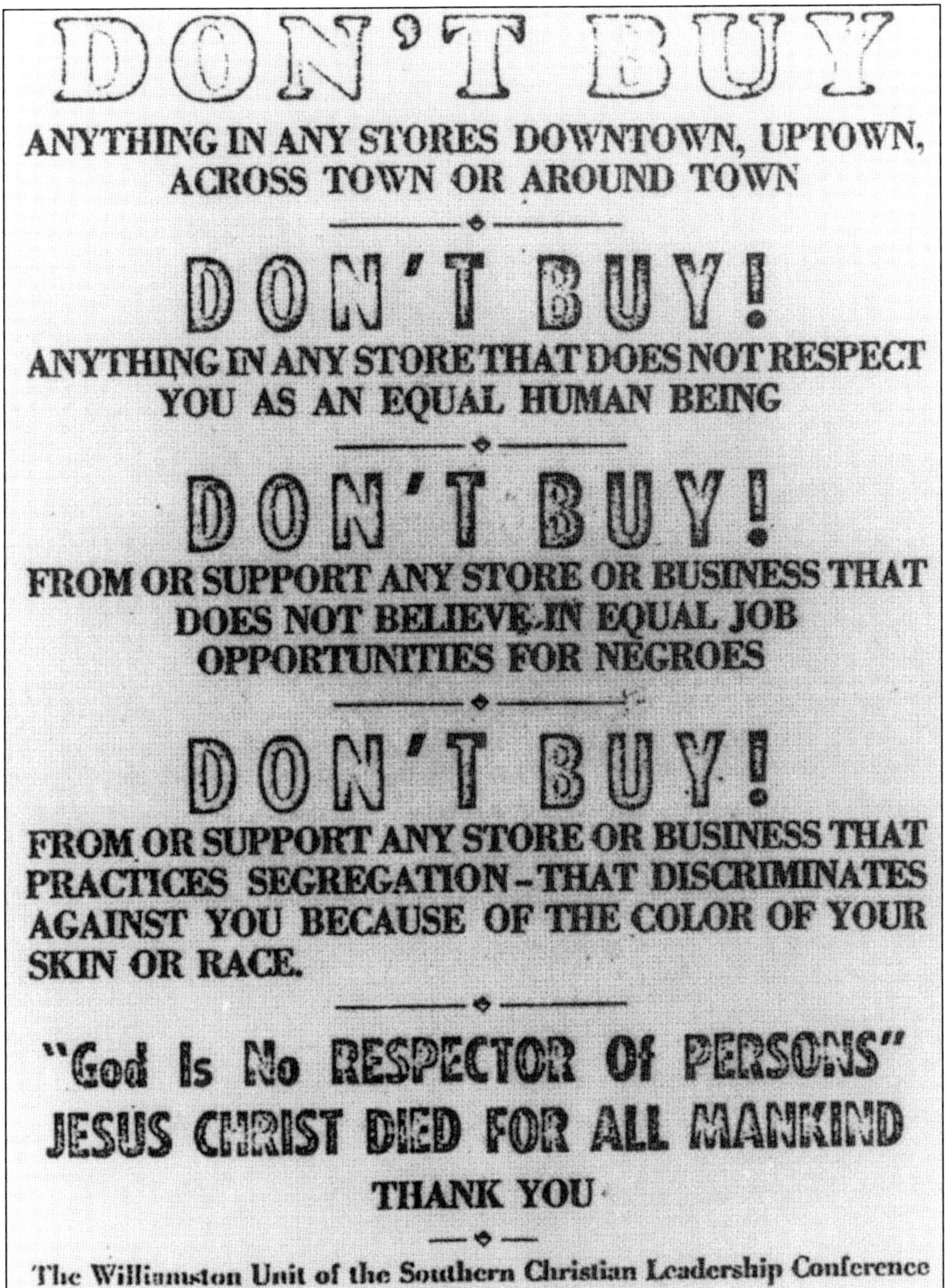

DON'T BUY

ANYTHING IN ANY STORES DOWNTOWN, UPTOWN, ACROSS TOWN OR AROUND TOWN

DON'T BUY!

ANYTHING IN ANY STORE THAT DOES NOT RESPECT YOU AS AN EQUAL HUMAN BEING

DON'T BUY!

FROM OR SUPPORT ANY STORE OR BUSINESS THAT DOES NOT BELIEVE IN EQUAL JOB OPPORTUNITIES FOR NEGROES

DON'T BUY!

FROM OR SUPPORT ANY STORE OR BUSINESS THAT PRACTICES SEGREGATION – THAT DISCRIMINATES AGAINST YOU BECAUSE OF THE COLOR OF YOUR SKIN OR RACE.

"God Is No RESPECTOR OF PERSONS"
JESUS CHRIST DIED FOR ALL MANKIND

THANK YOU

The Williamston Unit of the Southern Christian Leadership Conference

WILLIAMSTON BOYCOTT, 1963. This broadside dating from the fall of 1963 urges black citizens to refrain from buying goods in Williamston's business district. The boycott had a definite effect as retail sales in Williamston plummeted. It was called off two days before Christmas when organizers achieved their objective in having segregation signage removed from publicly owned buildings and a nondiscrimination policy approved for county and municipal employment. (Courtesy of Martin County Historical Society.)

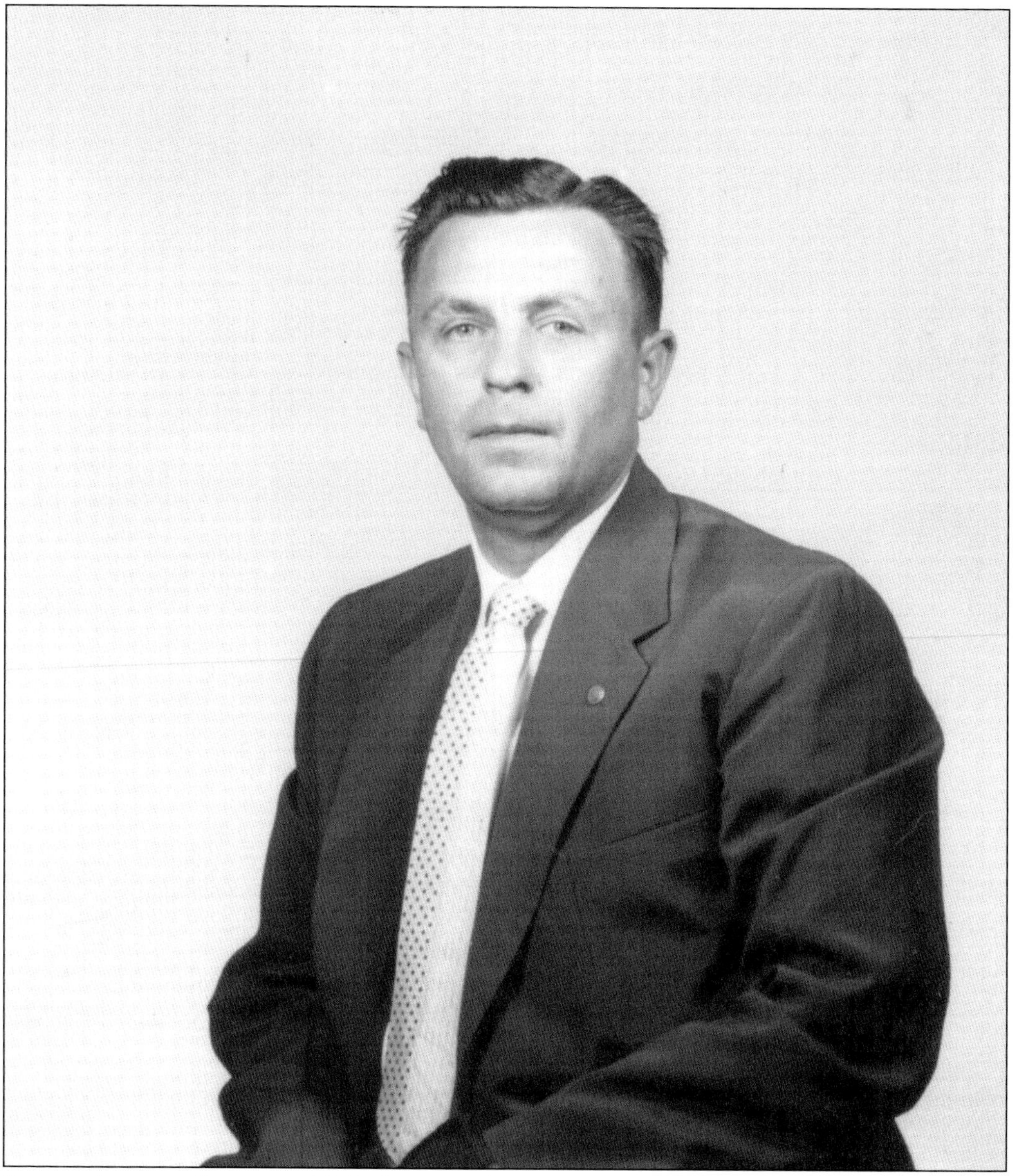

SHERIFF RAYMOND RAWLS, C. 1960. Serving as Martin County sheriff during the 1950s and 1960s, Raymond Rawls played an active role in the drama surrounding the local struggle for civil rights. He directed a freight train passing through town to stop in the area of Hayes School to block protestors from reaching their destination in the protest march of August 31, 1963. (Courtesy of Jesse Silverthorne.)

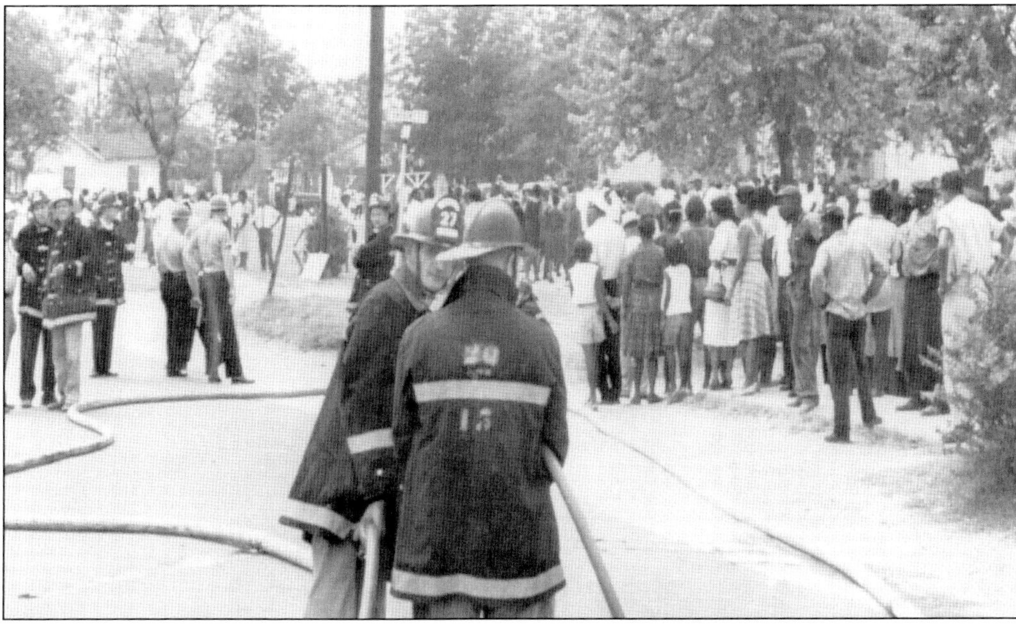

Firemen Attempt to Block Civil Rights March in Williamston, August 30, 1963. Crowds, law enforcement, and firemen gather along Andrews Street toward Washington Street as 400 students from E.J. Hayes High School prepare for a protest march to the uptown area. The protest, in response to the August 29 arrest of 11 demonstrators, ended with bottles and rocks being thrown and several demonstrators and policemen receiving minor wounds; remarkably, no serious injuries occurred. (Courtesy of the author.)

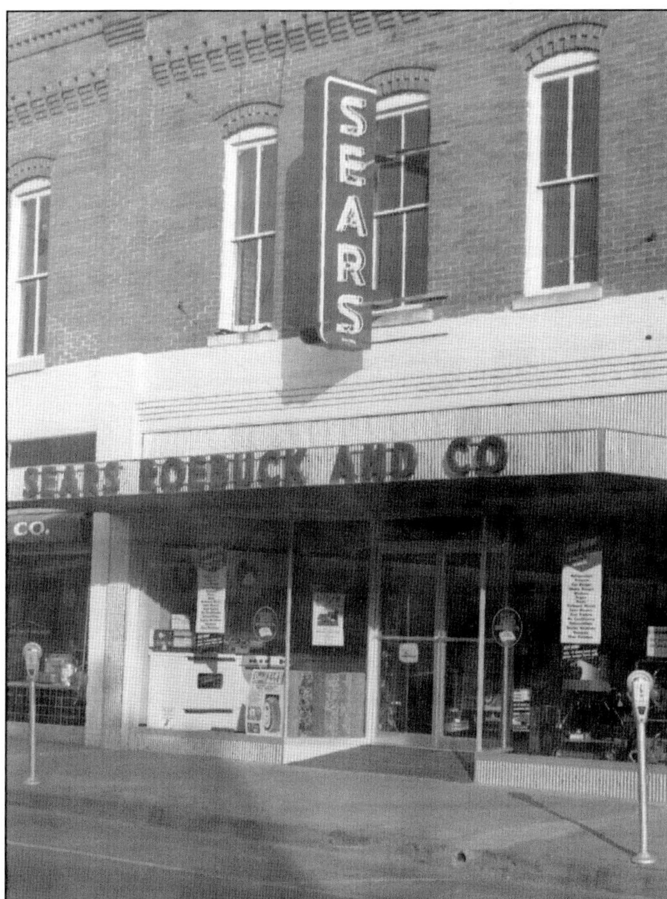

Williamston Sears Store, 1960. The Sears on Williamston's Main Street was the scene of a sensational segregation protest in which a group of Massachusetts women was arrested in the spring of 1964. (Courtesy Martin County Historical Society.)

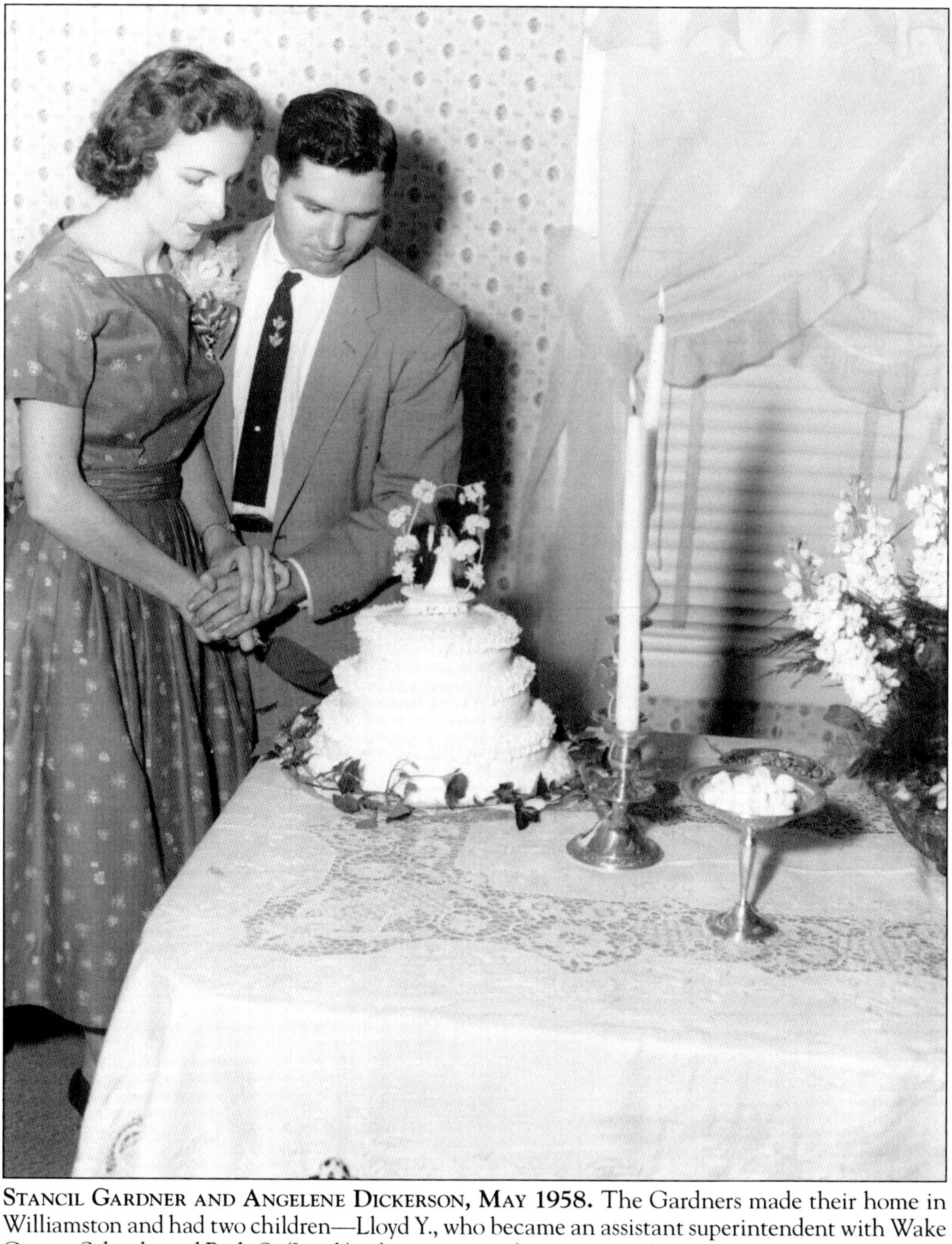

STANCIL GARDNER AND ANGELENE DICKERSON, MAY 1958. The Gardners made their home in Williamston and had two children—Lloyd Y., who became an assistant superintendent with Wake County Schools, and Beth G. (Lamb), who went on to become a teacher in the Williamston schools. L. Stancil Gardner was employed for over 40 years with East Carolina Supply in Plymouth, North Carolina; Angelene "Angie" worked for the Martin County Board of Education. (Photograph by B.W. Parker, courtesy of the author.)

Five

CELEBRATIONS AND SOCIAL GATHERINGS

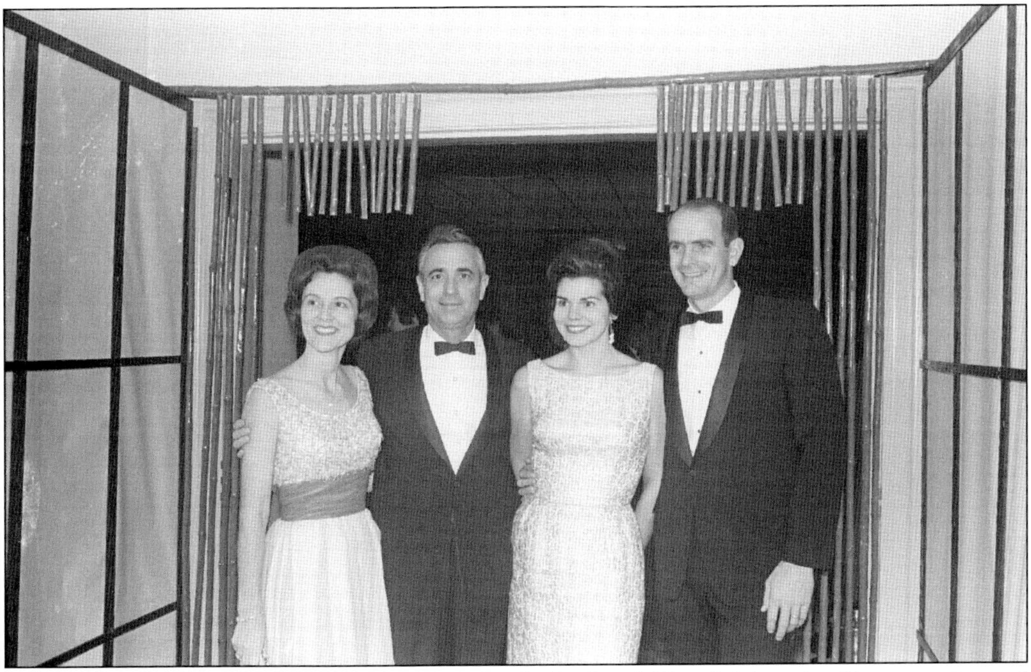

THE PERRYS AND THE SCALES, FEBRUARY 1967. Gaylord and Blanch Manning Perry are pictured at right with W.M. "Booger" Scales Jr. and his wife, Virginia, at the Service League Charity Ball in Greenville in February 1967. Perry gained a great deal of notoriety and attention during his baseball career, and in 1974 he authored *Me and the Spitter: An Autobiographical Confession*. (Courtesy of the J.Y. Joyner Library, East Carolina Manuscript Collection.)

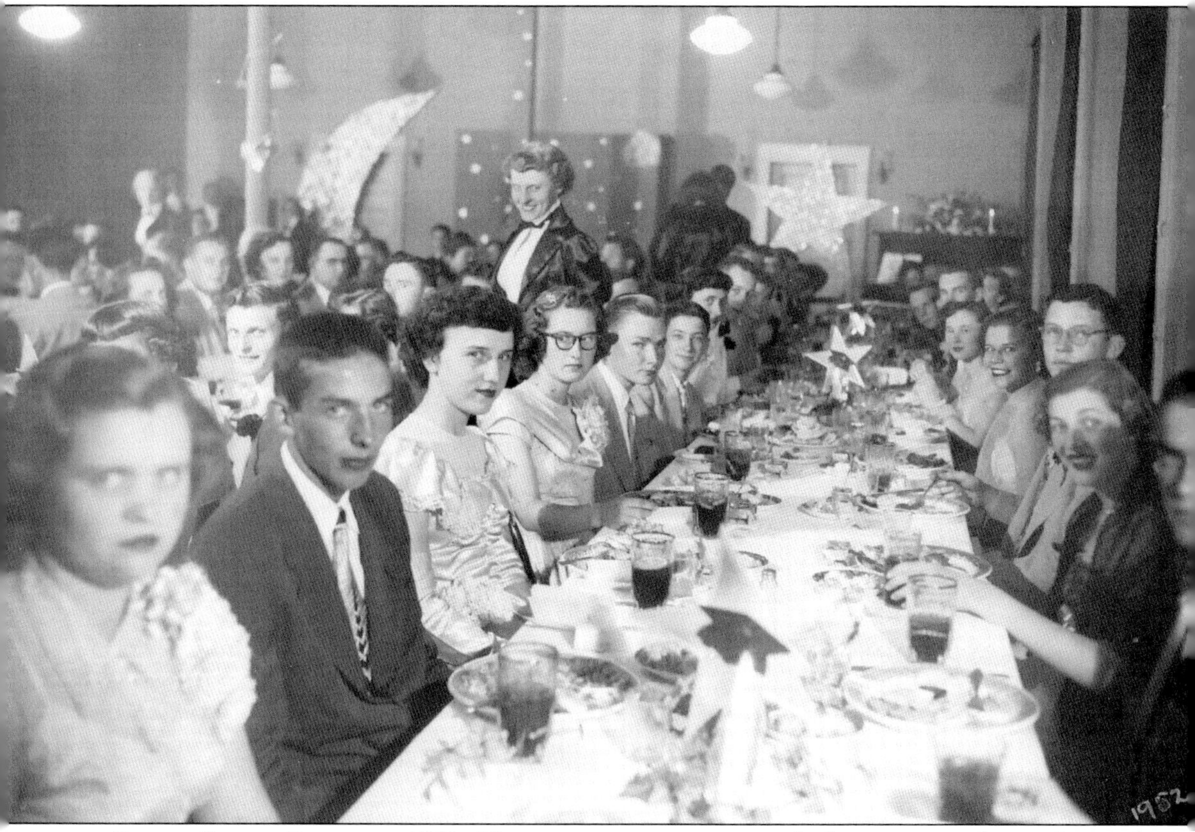

JUNIOR-SENIOR BANQUET, 1952. The postwar years saw a marked increase in the quality and sophistication of events like the Williamston High School celebration pictured. (Courtesy of Martin County Historical Society.)

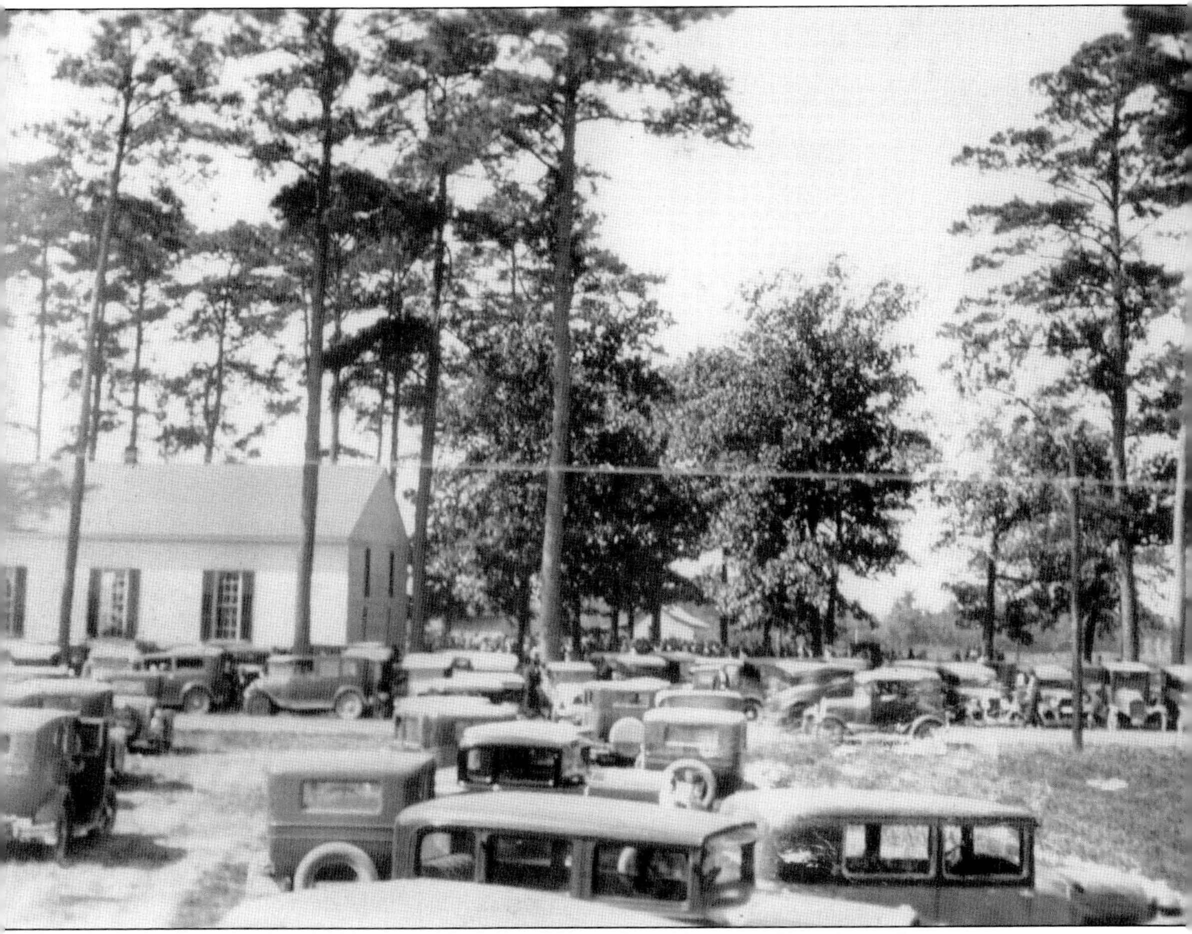

SKEWARKEY PRIMITIVE BAPTIST CHURCH, 1936. With the exception of its surrounding environment, this church building, pictured during a Kehukee Association meeting, has seen little physical change since its construction in 1857. (Courtesy of Martin County Historical Society.)

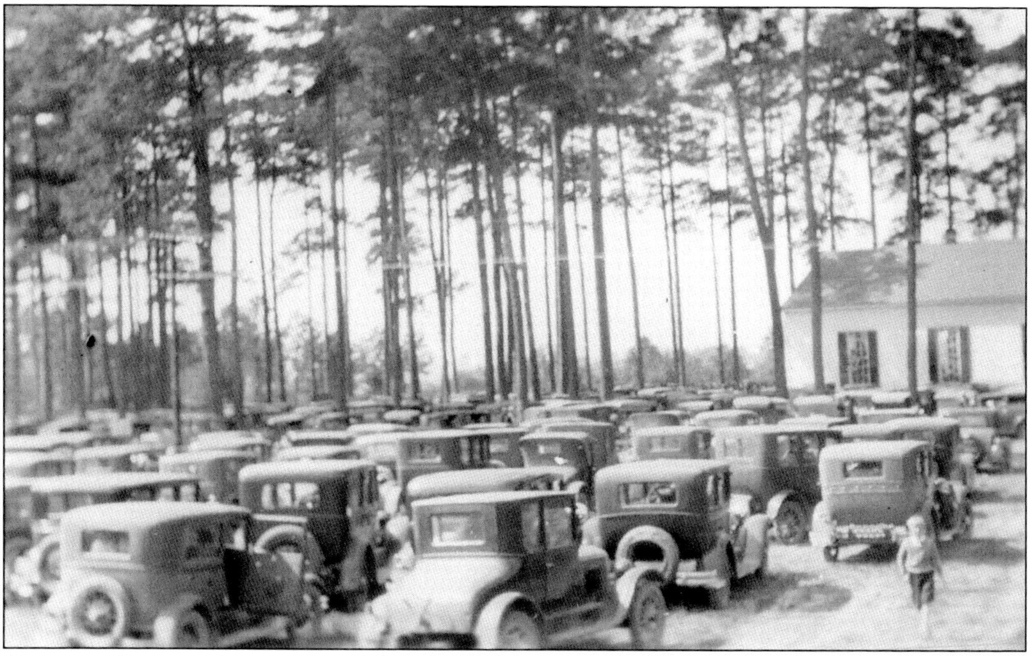

Kehukee Baptist Association Meeting at Skewarkey Church, 1936. During the period before the Civil War, members' servants and slaves sat in an upstairs balcony at the rear of the church. This architectural feature remains intact today. The last black member of the church died in 1954. The Kehukee Baptist Association, formed in 1769, consisted of members with strong Calvinistic beliefs. Skewarkey Church joined the group in 1787. (Courtesy of Martin County Historical Society.)

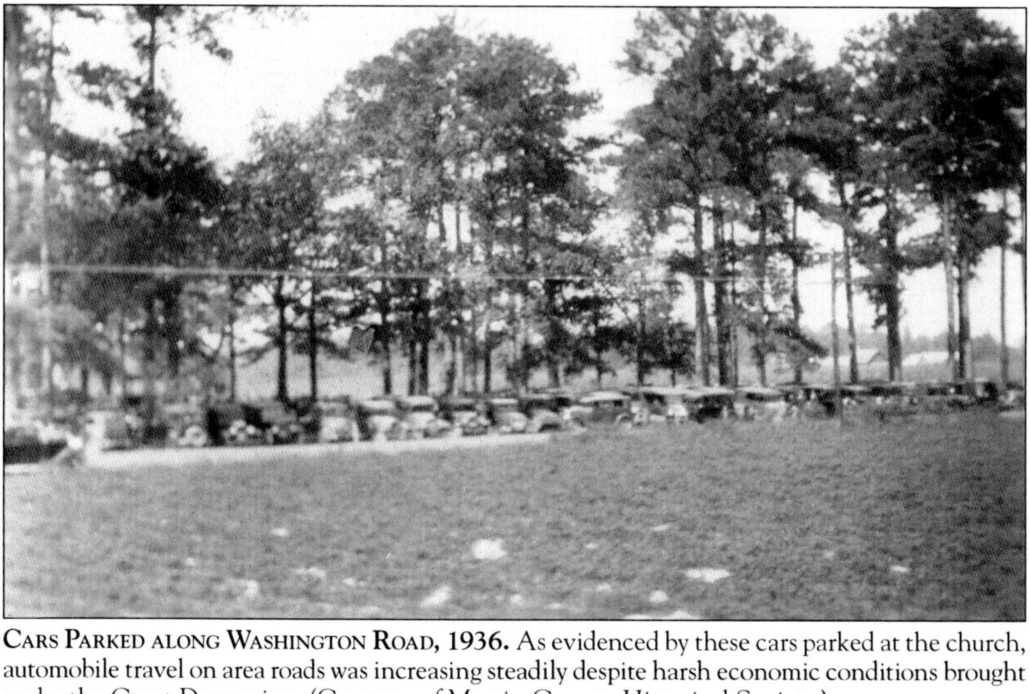

Cars Parked along Washington Road, 1936. As evidenced by these cars parked at the church, automobile travel on area roads was increasing steadily despite harsh economic conditions brought on by the Great Depression. (Courtesy of Martin County Historical Society.)

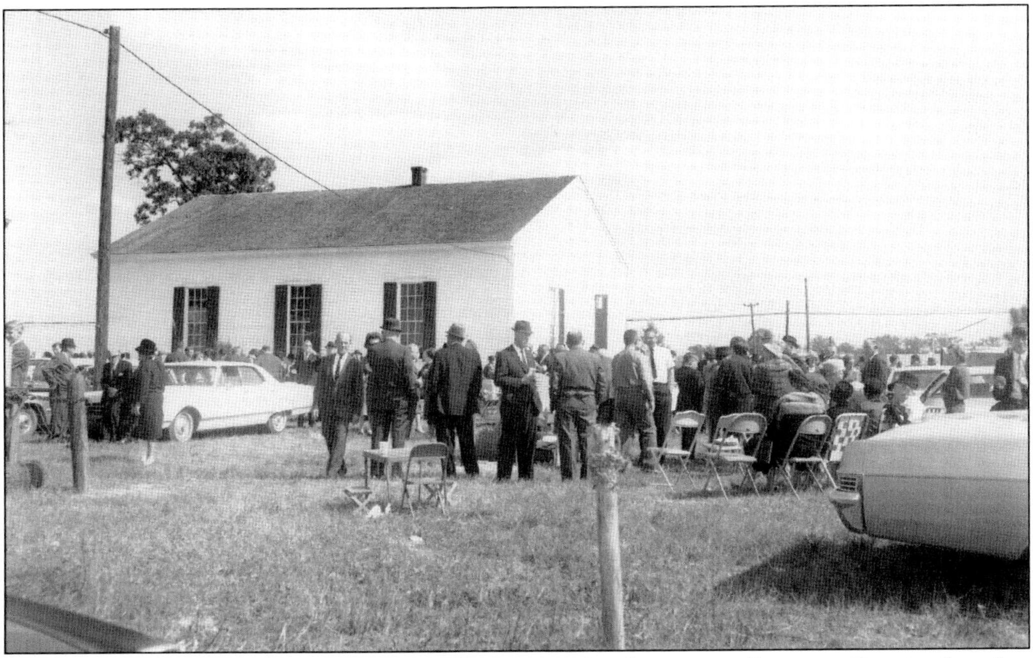

KEHUKEE ASSOCIATION MEETING, 1967. Though membership in area Primitive Baptist churches fell off to a large degree by the mid-20th century, family connections and support for gatherings like this continued to remain strong through the 1960s. (Photograph by B.W. Parker, courtesy of the author.)

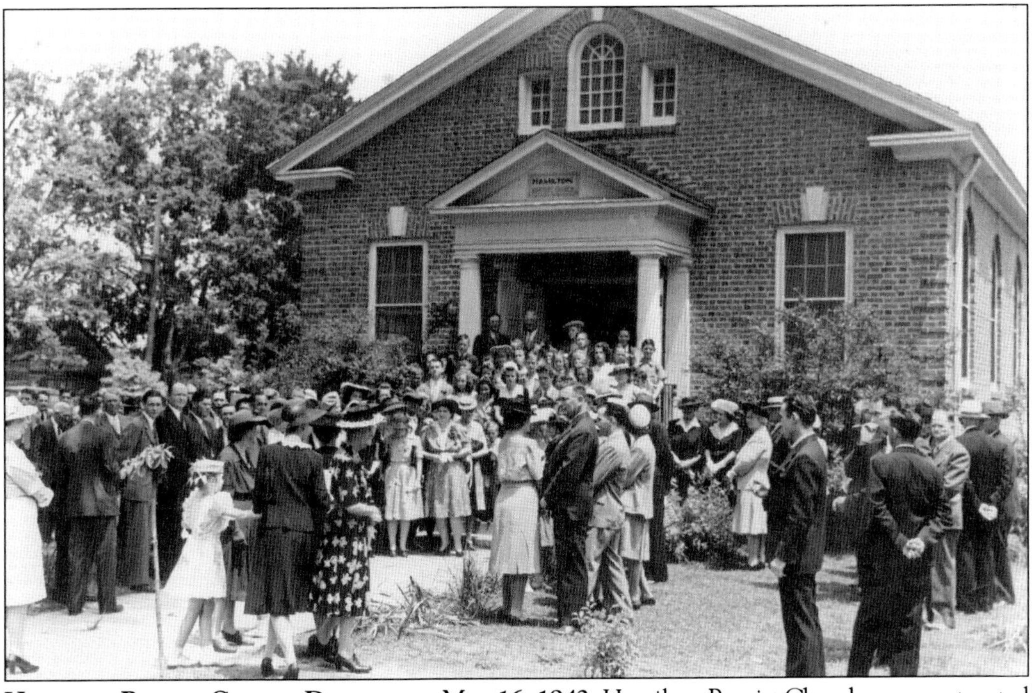

HAMILTON BAPTIST CHURCH DEDICATION, MAY 16, 1943. Hamilton Baptist Church was constructed in 1929—though it was not dedicated at that time—at a cost of $10,000. (Courtesy of Martin County Historical Society.)

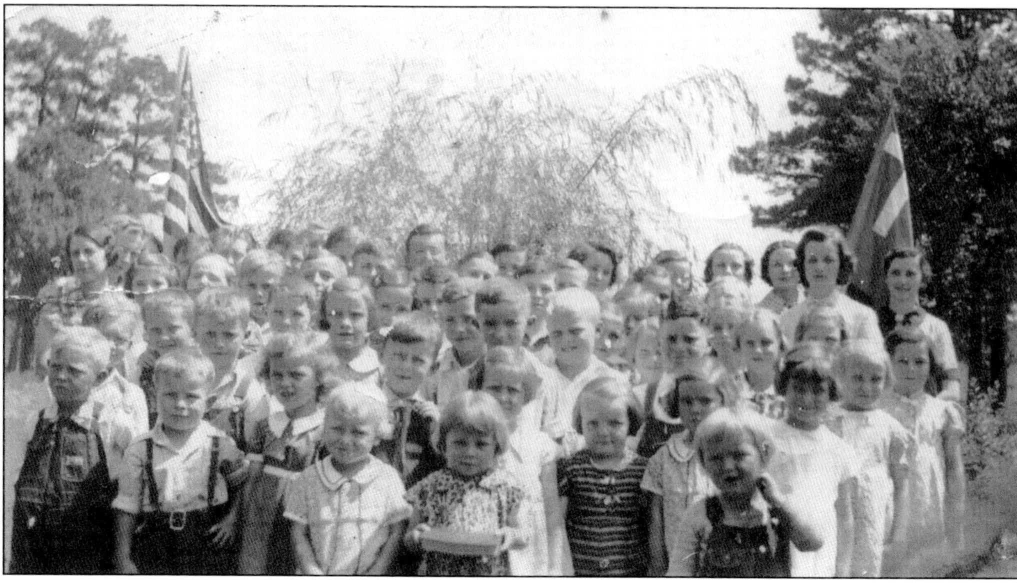

Bible School, c. 1935–1940. Some of those identified in this image of the Bear Grass Presbyterian Church Bible school are Dillon Cherry, Gene Rogers, Louise Wynn Cherry, Martha Mendenhall Peele, Tommy Wynne, Julia Harrison Biggs, Louis Taylor Wynn, Jack Williamson, Russell Mobley, Randolph Rogerson, A.D. Bailey, and teacher Mildred Ward. (Courtesy of R. Eugene Rogers.)

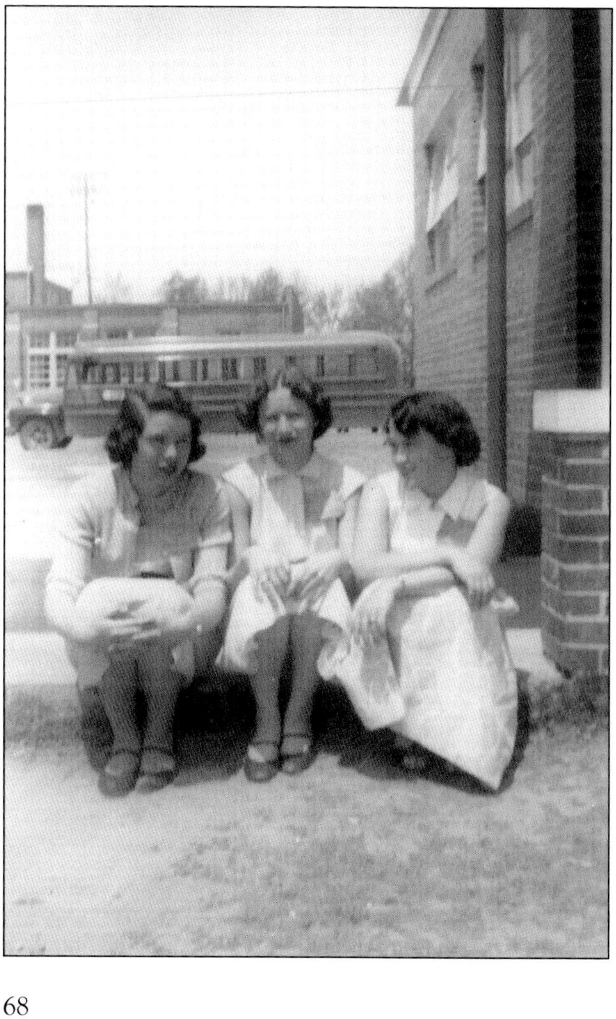

Girls on Williamston High School Campus, c. 1955. Pictured, from left to right, are Ann Holliday, Peggy Wynne, and Loretta Simpson. (Courtesy of Ann H. Harrison.)

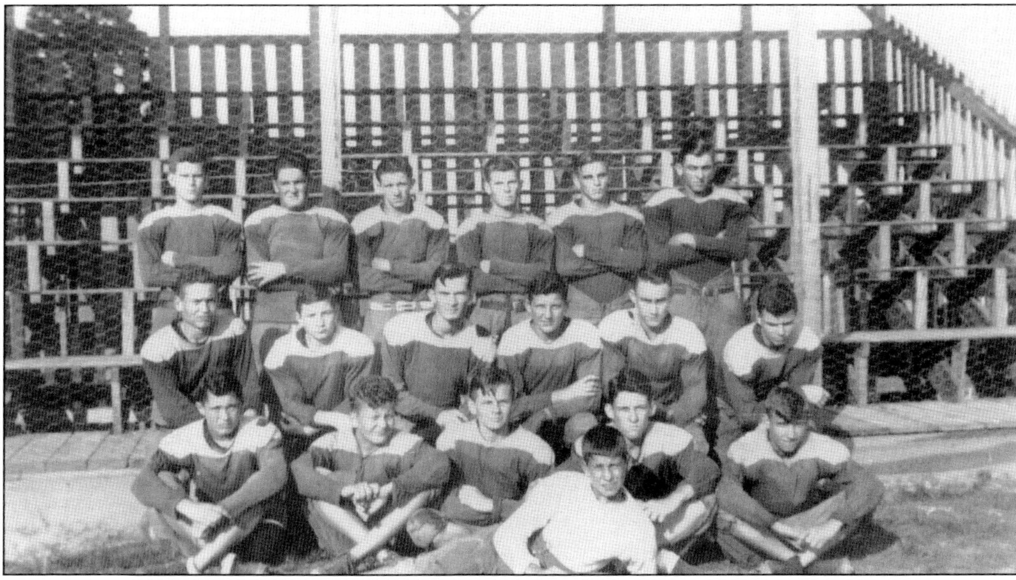

WILLIAMSTON HIGH SCHOOL FOOTBALL TEAM, C. 1935. During the 1930s, the high school football field was located behind the 1929 high school building off School Drive. (Courtesy of Martin County Historical Society.)

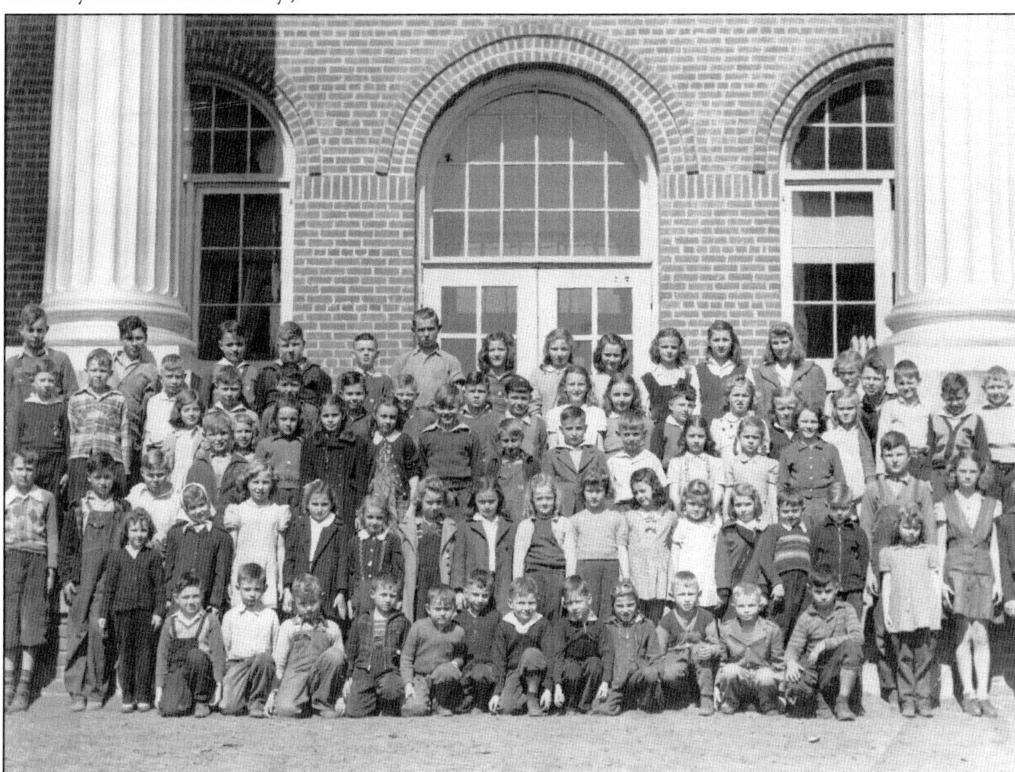

CHURCH STREET GRAMMAR SCHOOL, C. 1939–1940. This photograph appears to include children of various grade levels attending the school during the period. (Photograph by Eugene Rice, courtesy of Martin County Historical Society.)

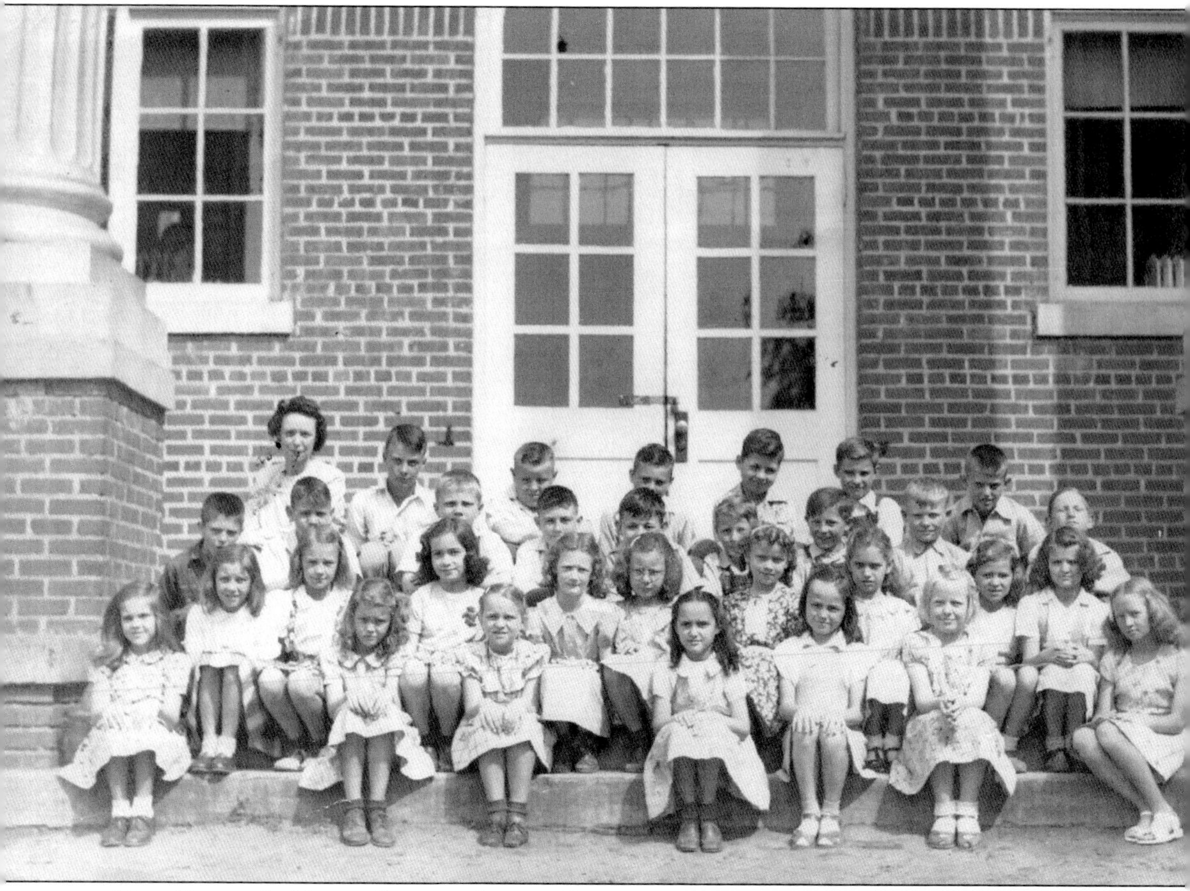

Mrs. Elliott's Class, Church Street Grammar School, 1945. Those identified are Mrs. Elliott, Odis Whitaker, Randolph Coker, Jimmy Hardison, Freddie Harrison (fourth row, third from right), David Davis Jr., Wayne Lilley, George Harris Jr., Tommy Hardison, Bill Glover, Calvin Chesson, W.B. Bullock, Johnny Hardison, Grover Barber, Lois Beach, Theresa Modlin, Martha D. Kimbell, Janet Ross, Betty Lou Gardner, Judy Ayers, Betty Sue Clark, Doris Bowen, Judy Rogers, Dan Peele, Christian Wells, Patty Williams, Rose Taylor, Janice Taylor, and Betty Jean Mizell. (Photograph by Eugene Rice, courtesy of Judith A. Critcher.)

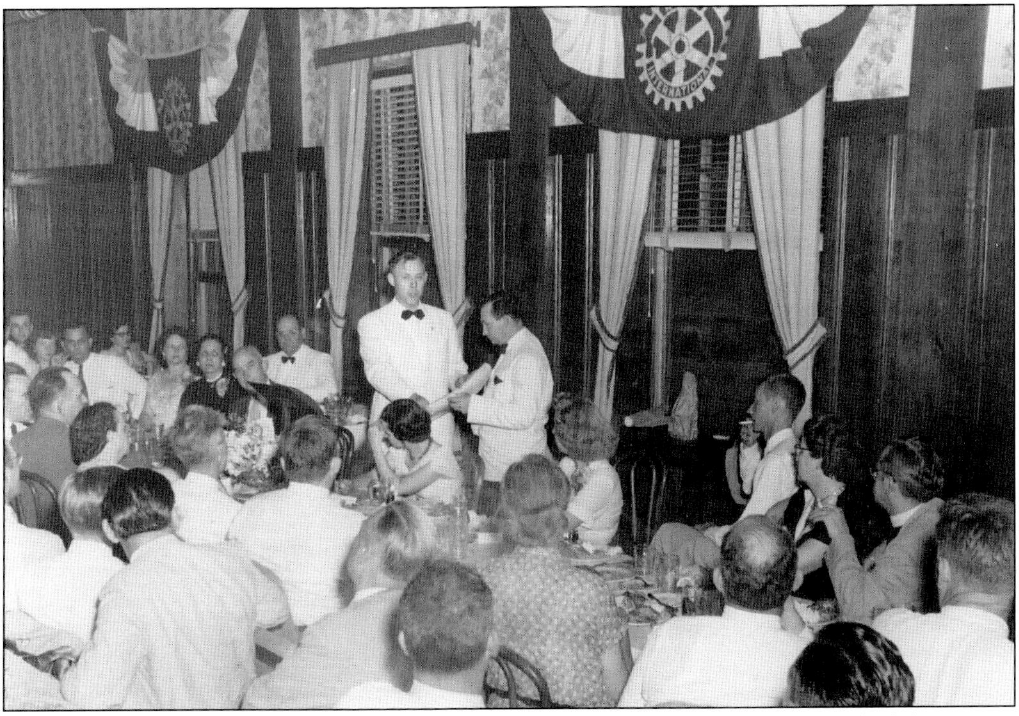

Williamston Rotary Club Banquet, 1951. Dr. Charles Harris is seen at center stage (right) receiving honors during an event at the George Reynolds Hotel. (Courtesy of Jesse Silverthorne.)

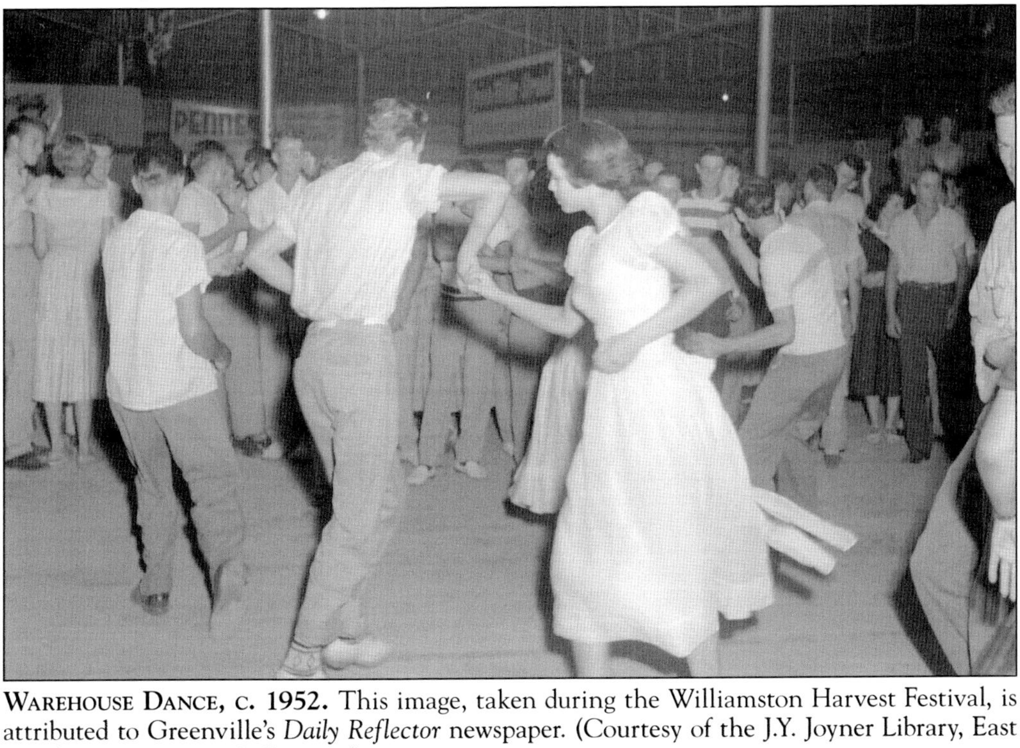

Warehouse Dance, c. 1952. This image, taken during the Williamston Harvest Festival, is attributed to Greenville's *Daily Reflector* newspaper. (Courtesy of the J.Y. Joyner Library, East Carolina Manuscript Collection.)

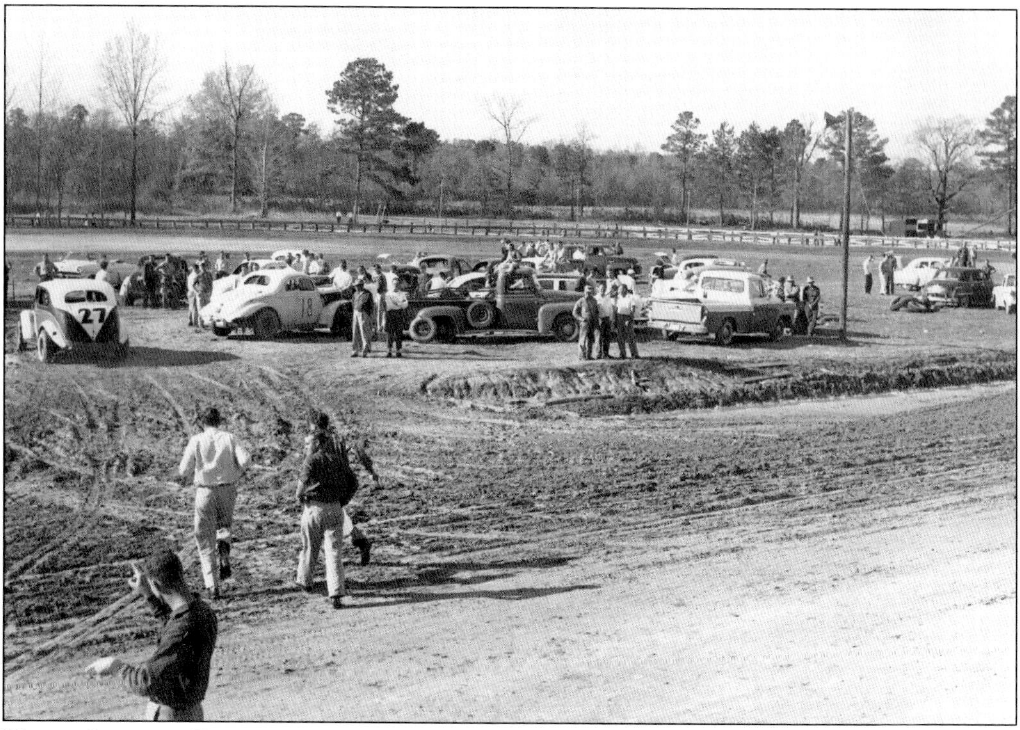

Henry Johnson Racetrack, November 17, 1957. This once popular venue was succeeded in the early 1990s with the opening of the East Carolina Motor Speedway near Robersonville. (Courtesy of Martin County Historical Society.)

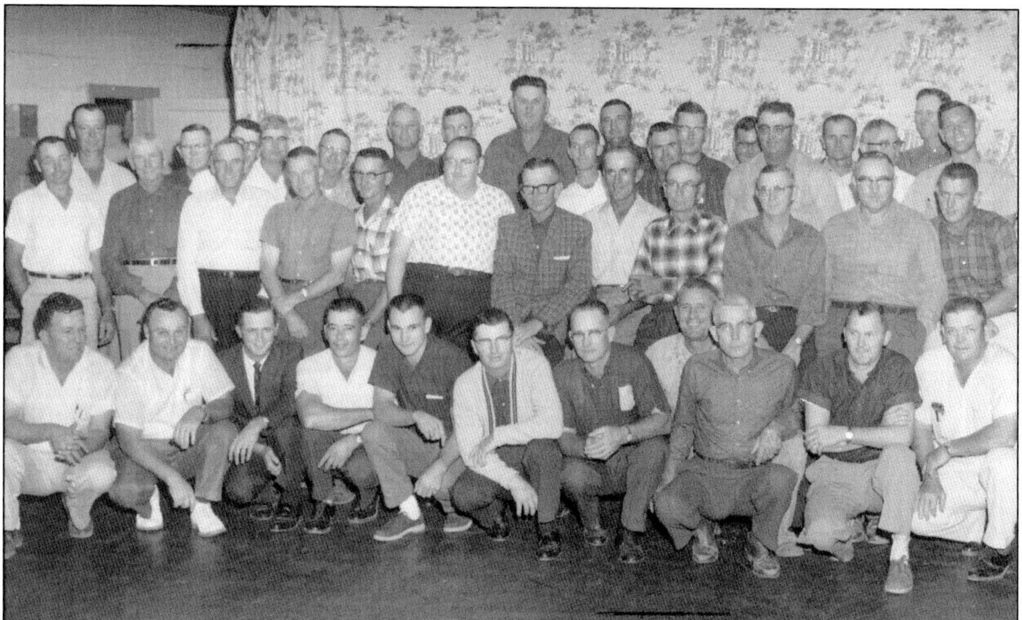

Farm Life Ruritan Club, 1962. Ruritan Clubs were and continue to be an integral part of nearly every community in Martin County. This group was based in Griffins Township. (Courtesy of Martin County Historical Society.)

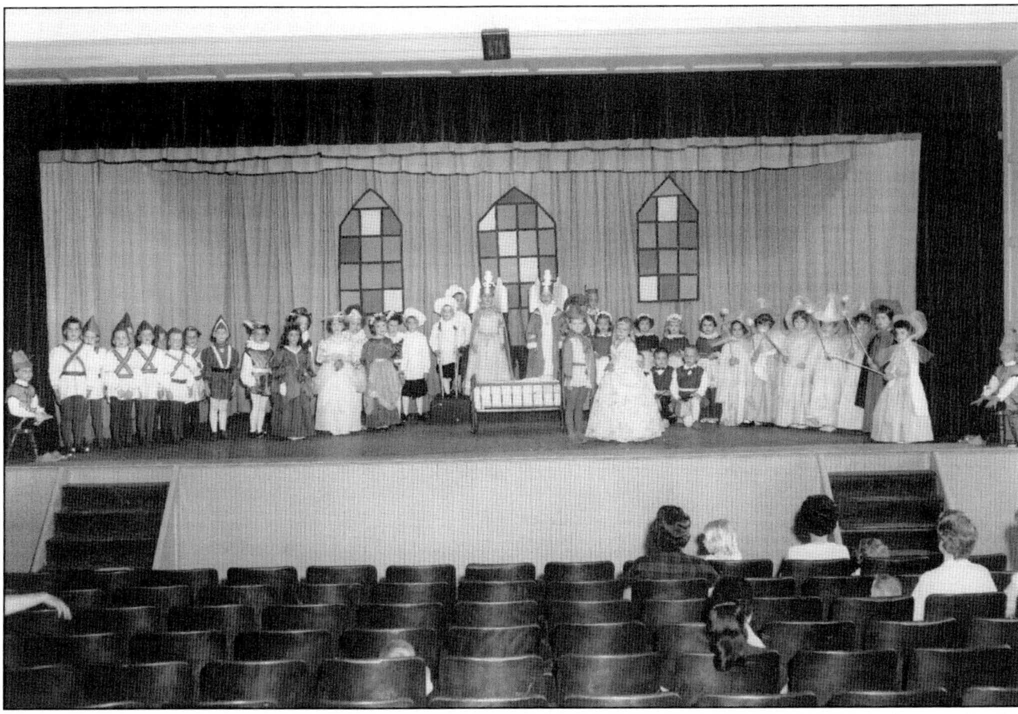

Church Street School Play, 1962. During this period, pageants were popular with the Community Kindergarten, which, though not affiliated with the school, was permitted to use the auditorium. (Courtesy of Judith A. Critcher.)

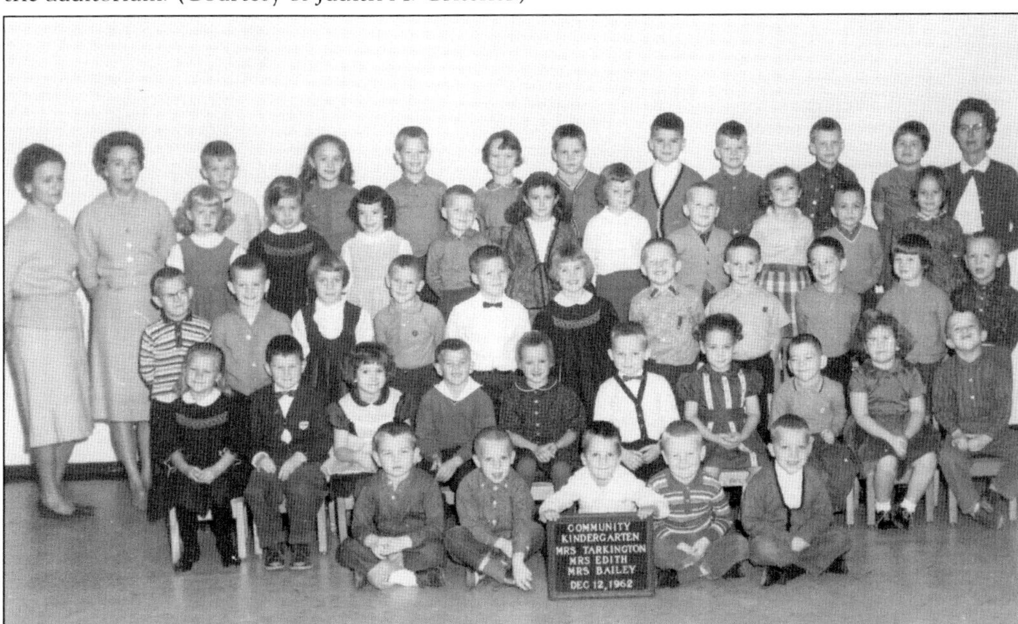

Community Kindergarten, December 12, 1962. Begun in the 1950s, the Community Kindergarten was supported by the Williamston Ministerial Association and was discontinued in the 1970s. (Courtesy of Judith A. Critcher.)

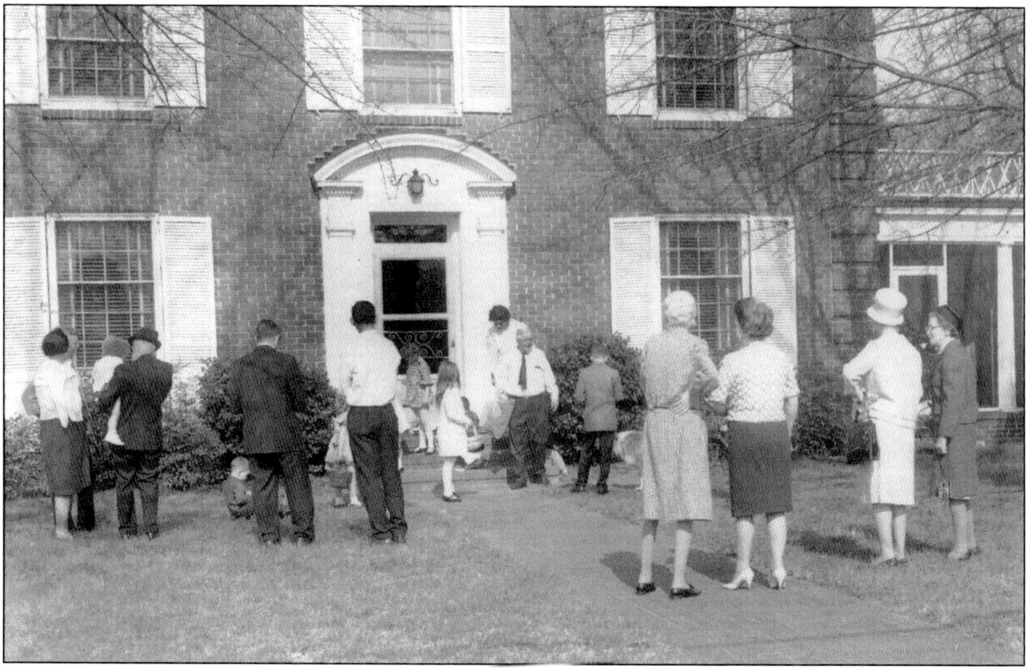

Easter Egg Hunt, c. 1965. Francis Manning, who hosted this Easter egg hunt at his home, is seen at center of the image. (Courtesy of Martin County Historical Society.)

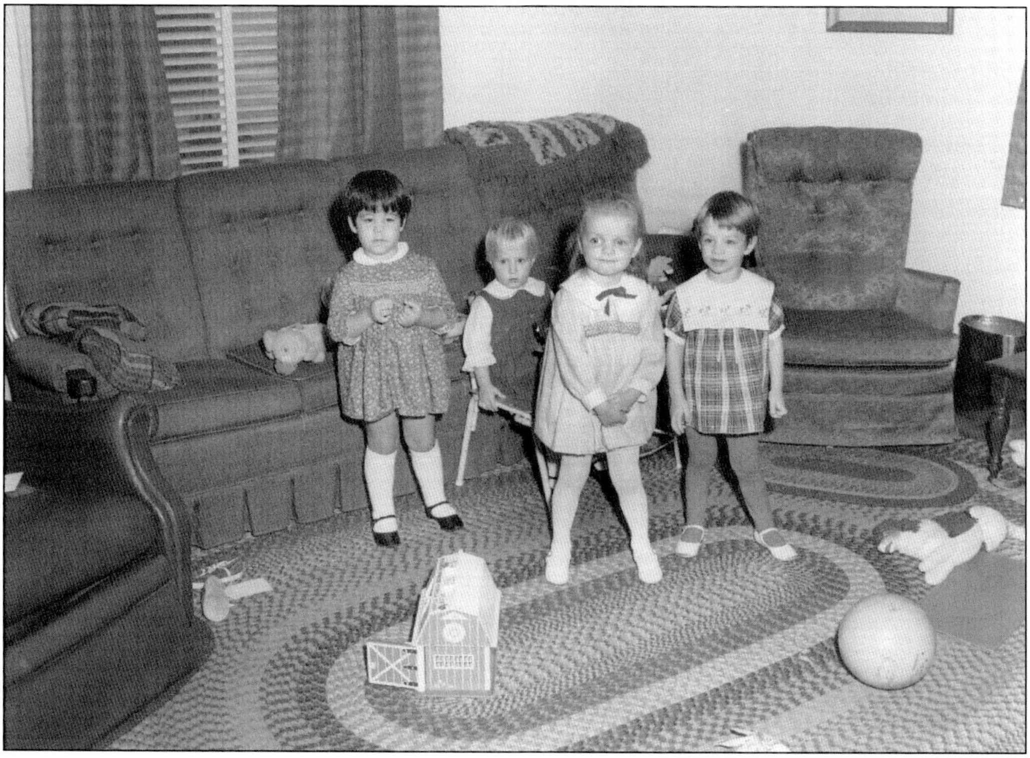

Birthday Party, Fall 1969. Amy Roberson, the birthday girl, stands second from the right. Also identified is Leigh Ann Harrison, at far left. (Courtesy of Elizabeth W. Roberson.)

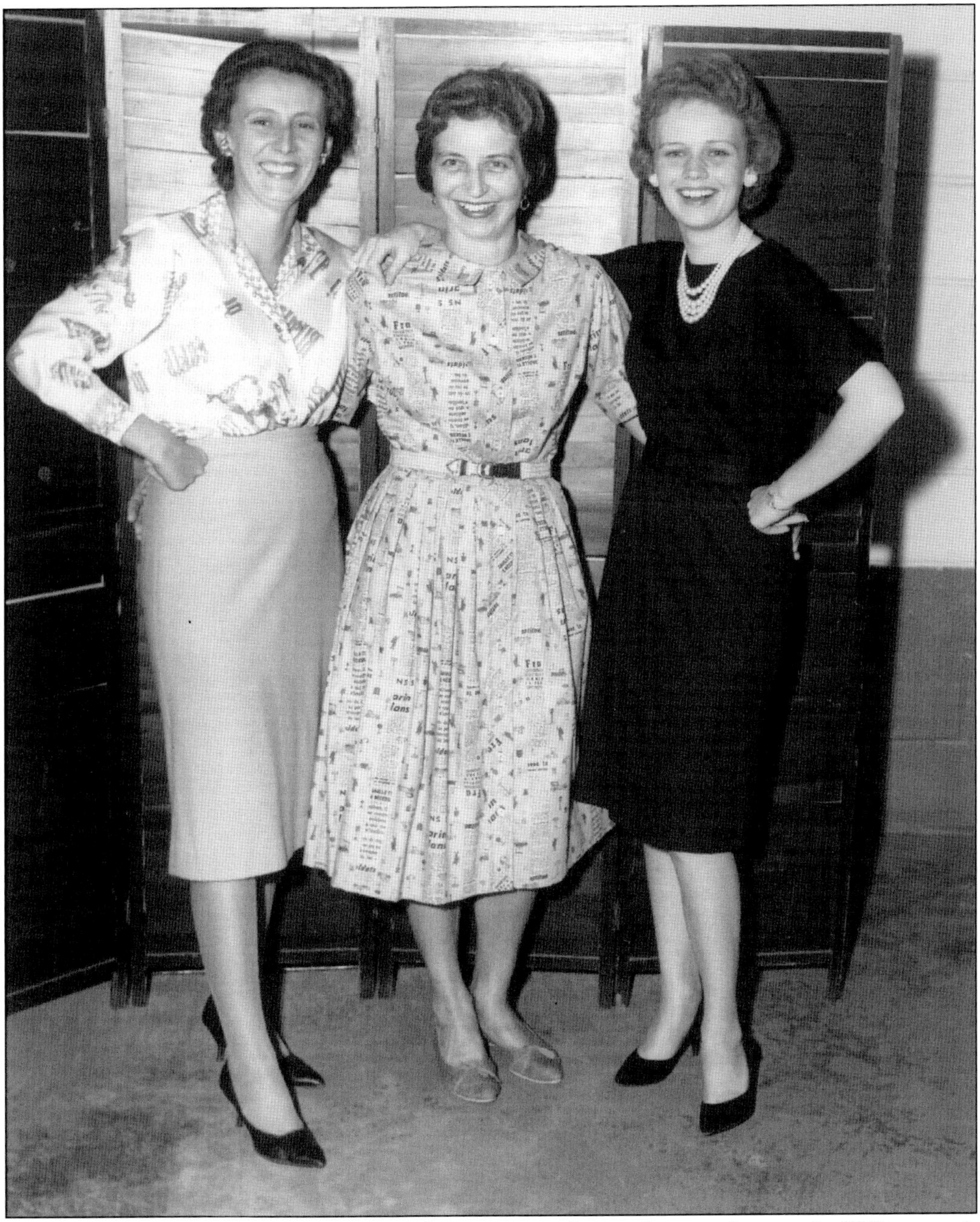

FASHION SHOW CHARITY, c. 1965. One of many events during the period put on by Williamston's Episcopal congregation, Church of the Advent, this scene recalls Williamston's vibrant mix of social, civic, and religious life during the 1960s. Seen here are Sylvia Newell (left), Mary Charles Coppage (center), and Judy Critcher. (Courtesy of Martin County Historical Society.)

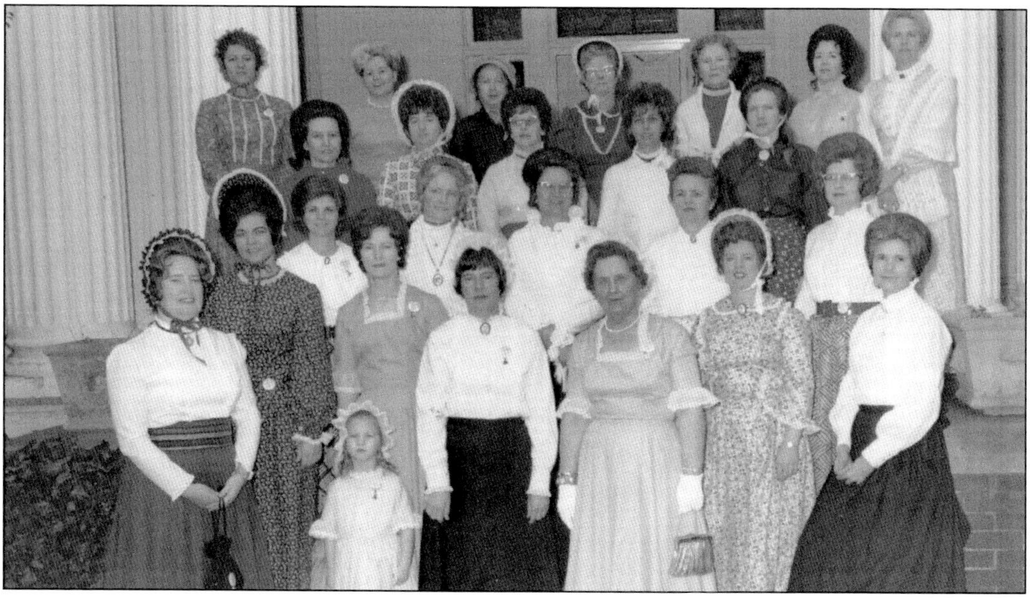

Celebrating Robersonville's Centennial, 1972. Ladies in period costume stand at the entrance to the Vance Roberson home. The honored guest for this occasion was US first lady Pat Nixon. (Courtesy of Patsy R. Miller.)

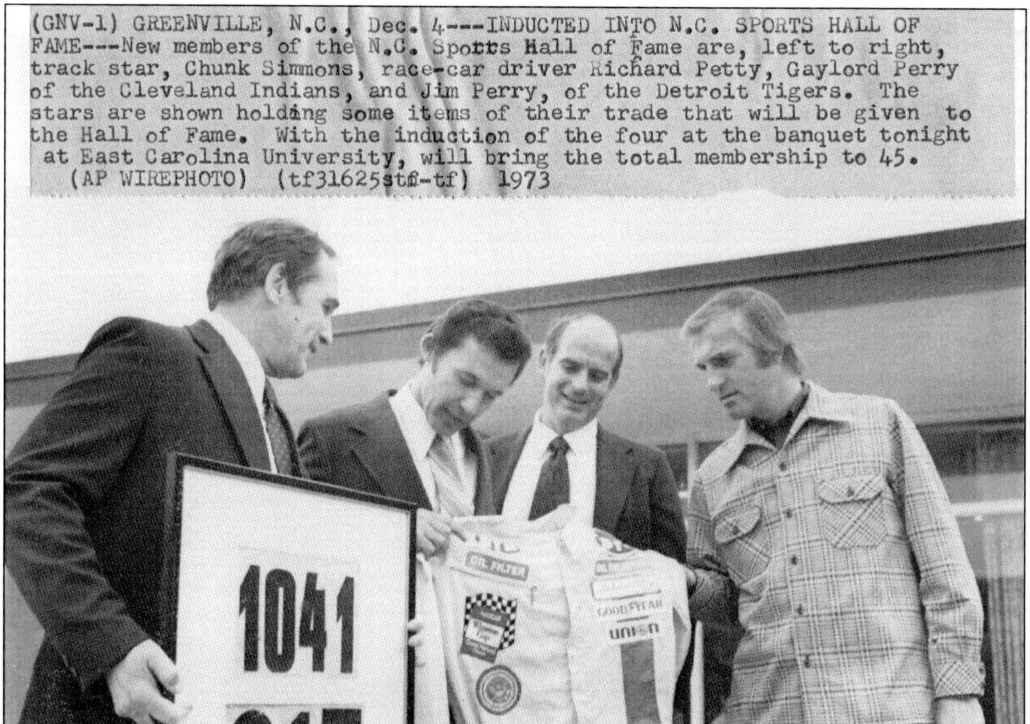

North Carolina Sports Hall of Fame Induction, 1973. Brothers and major-league baseball greats Jim (far right) and Gaylord (second from right) Perry grew up in the Farm Life community of Griffins Township in Martin County. (Courtesy of the J.Y. Joyner Library, East Carolina Manuscript Collection.)

George and Mary Ida Roberson Crofton, 1944. The couple poses for the camera outside their home on South Haughton Street in Williamston in celebration of their 50th wedding anniversary in December. (Courtesy of Judith A. Critcher.)

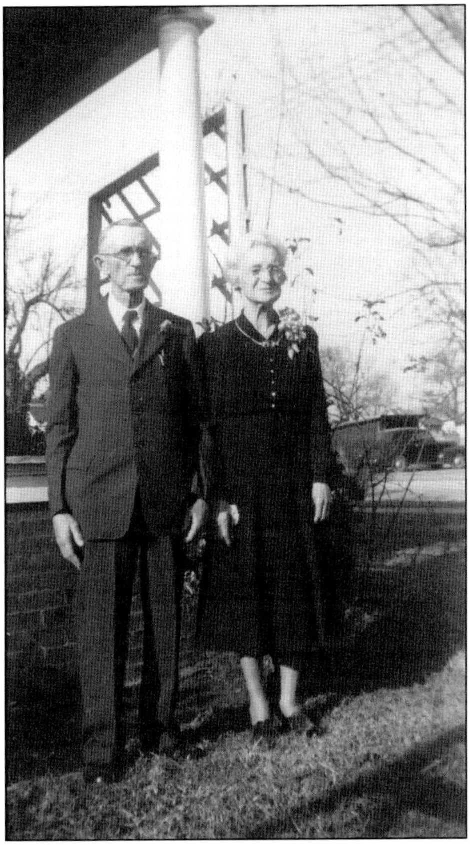

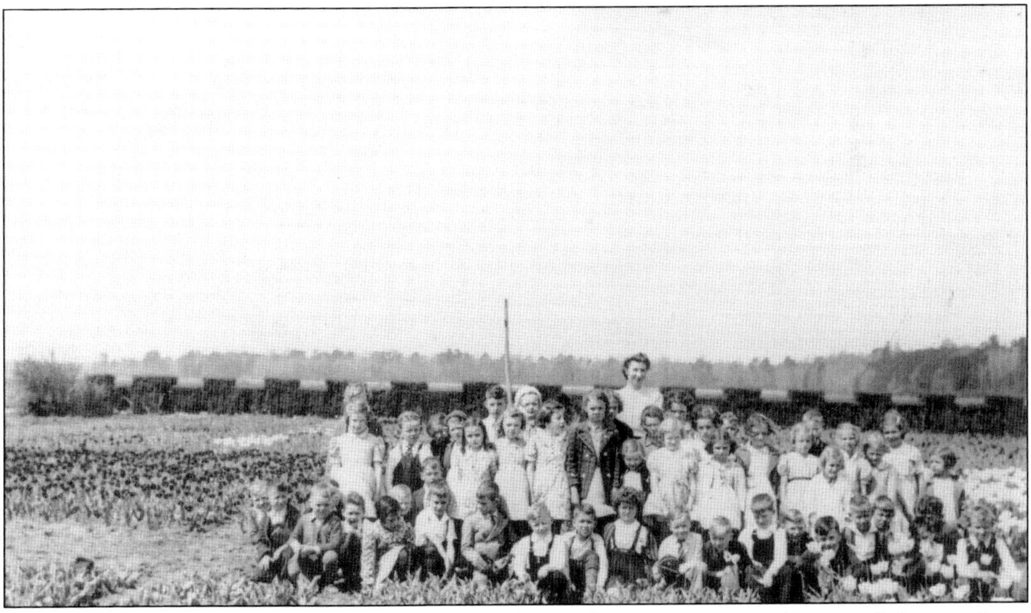

Betty Courtney's First-Grade Class, 1939. Betty Courtney, pictured here with her students at Farm Life School, was a longtime educator in Martin County. In later years, she assisted with the Williamston Community Kindergarten. (Courtesy of Jean G. Rogers.)

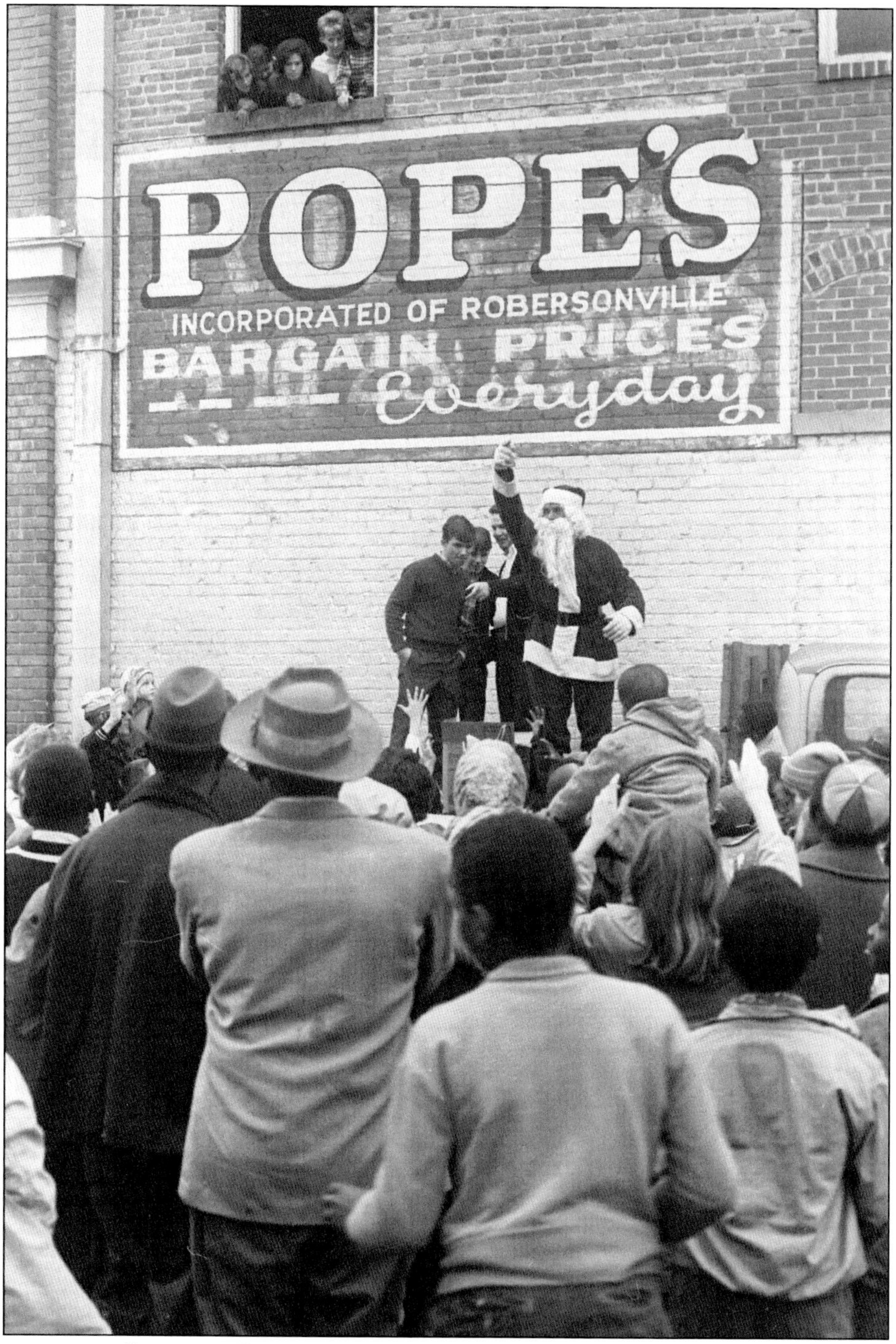

ROBERSONVILLE CHRISTMAS PARADE, DECEMBER 1965. Established in 1872, Robersonville gained importance as a railroad stop along the Atlantic Coast Line route between Raleigh and Williamston in the 1880s and later as the county's first tobacco marketing center. By the 1920s, this town's importance rivaled in many ways that of Williamston, the county seat. (Courtesy of the J.Y. Joyner Library, East Carolina Manuscript Collection.)

Six

PROGRESSIVE ROBERSONVILLE

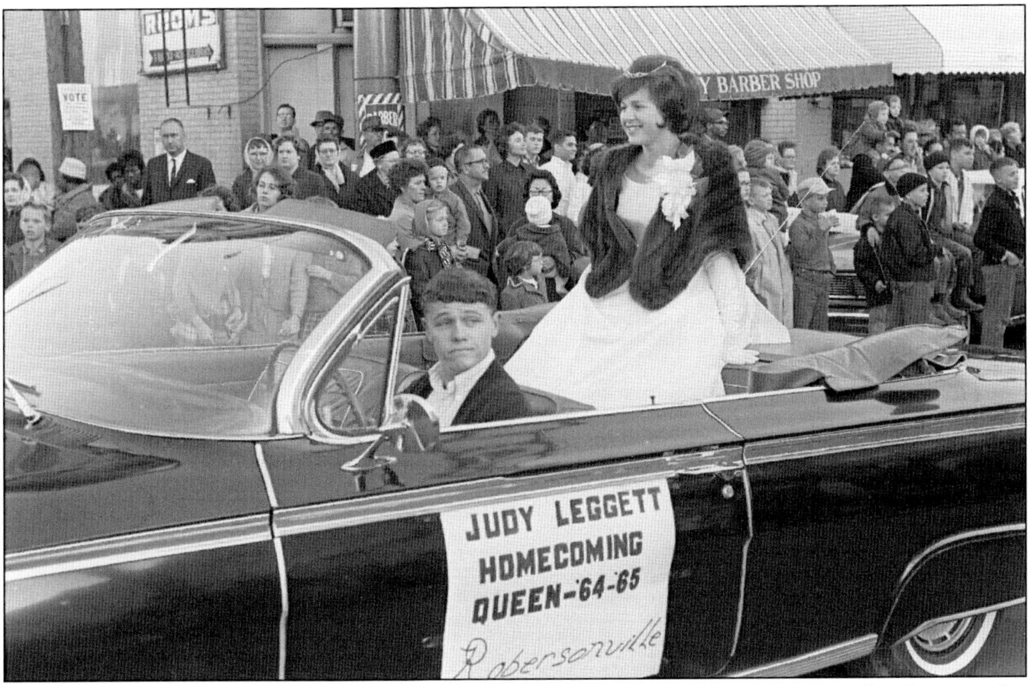

ROBERSONVILLE HIGH HOMECOMING QUEEN, 1964. Judy Leggett is pictured riding in the Robersonville Christmas parade. This image is attributed to Greenville's *Daily Reflector* newspaper. (Courtesy of the J.Y. Joyner Library, East Carolina Manuscript Collection.)

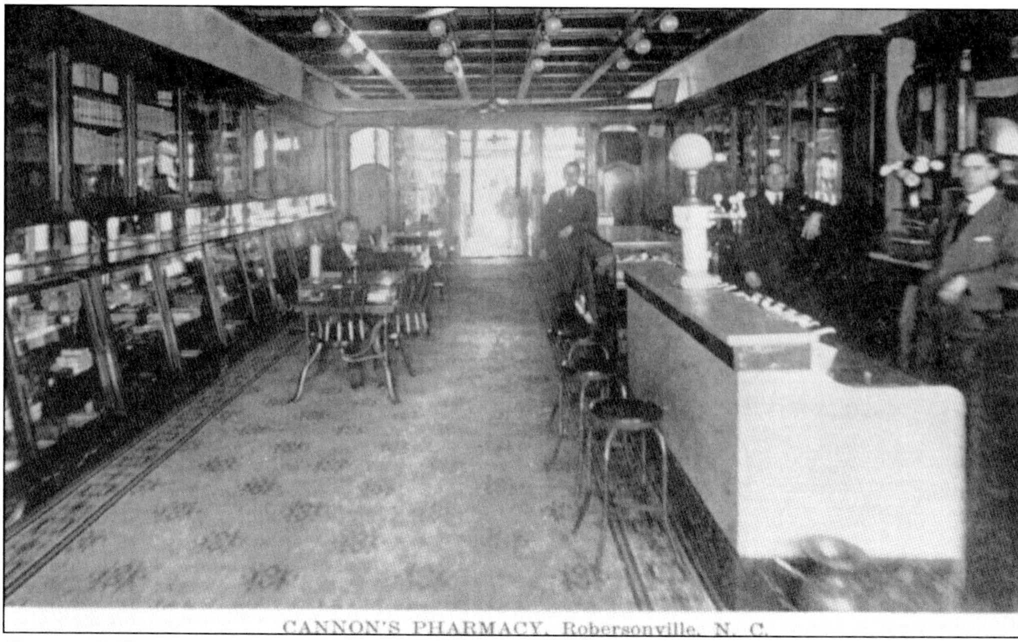

Cannon's Pharmacy, 1916. David Grimes, a popular Robersonville druggist, began his career with the Cannon Pharmacy before starting his own business in 1922. The David Grimes Drug Store celebrated its 50th anniversary in 1972. (Courtesy of the J.Y. Joyner Library, East Carolina Manuscript Collection.)

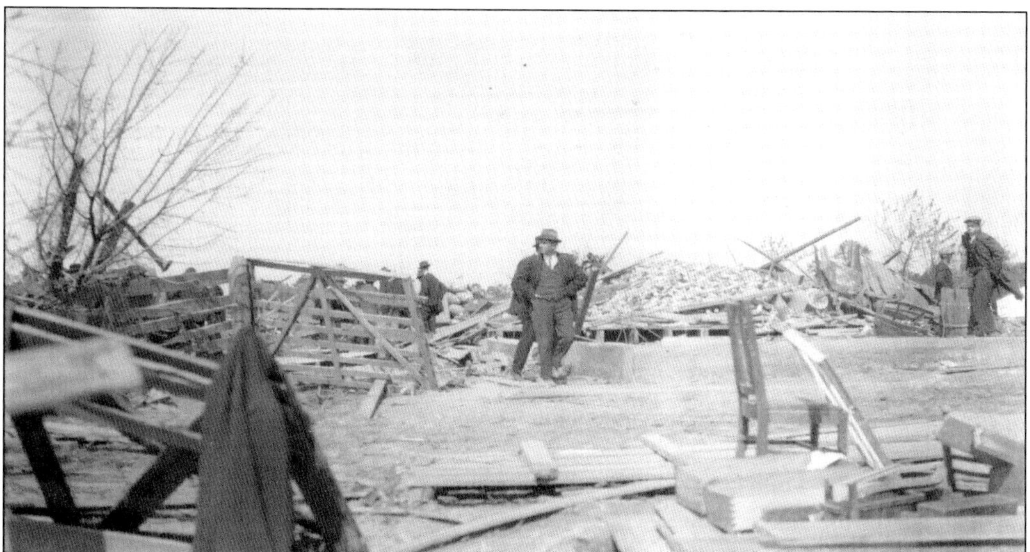

Tornado Destruction, April 1924. These men are pictured surveying the wreckage of the Lee House homestead in the Robersonville area. This particular F3-level storm was one of 26 tornadoes occurring between April 29 and 30, 1924, over Martin County and cut a significant path of destruction, leveling some large homes and buildings between Robersonville and the Roanoke River. (Courtesy of Martin County Historical Society.)

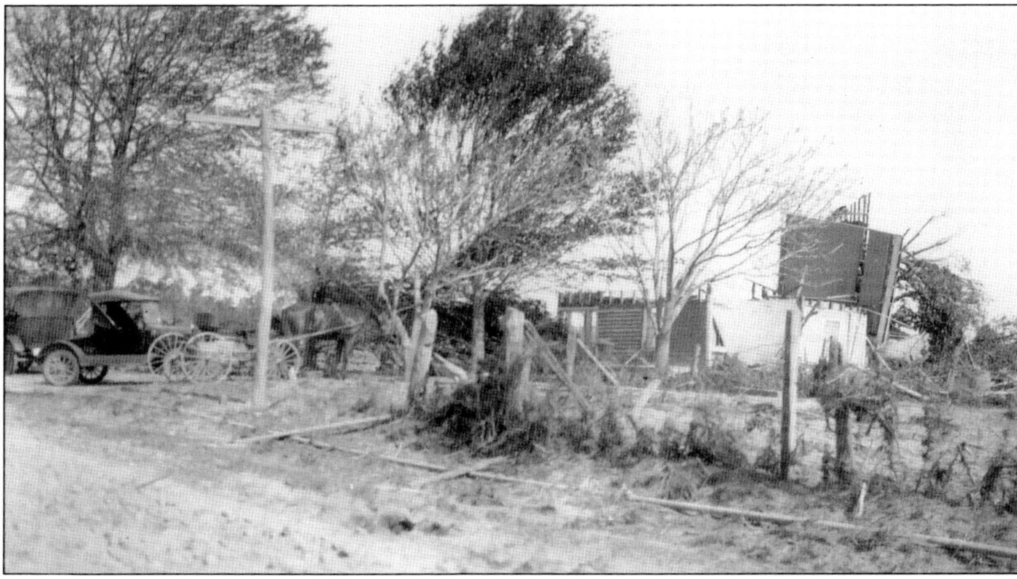

TORNADO DAMAGE. Though somewhat forgotten today, the tornado of 1924 did a considerable amount of damage in Martin County. This view shows the destruction at George Keel's residence. (Courtesy of Martin County Historical Society.)

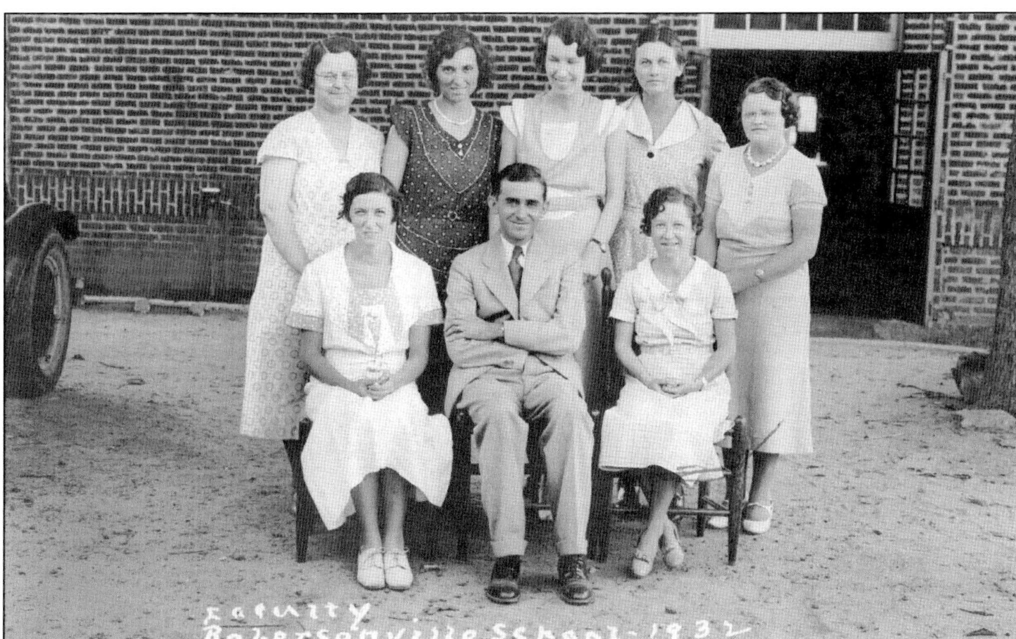

ROBERSONVILLE GRAMMAR SCHOOL FACULTY, 1932. Among the faculty members pictured here are Marvin Everett (first row, center) and Minnie Lee Cochran (second row, far left). (Courtesy of the J.Y. Joyner Library, East Carolina Manuscript Collection.)

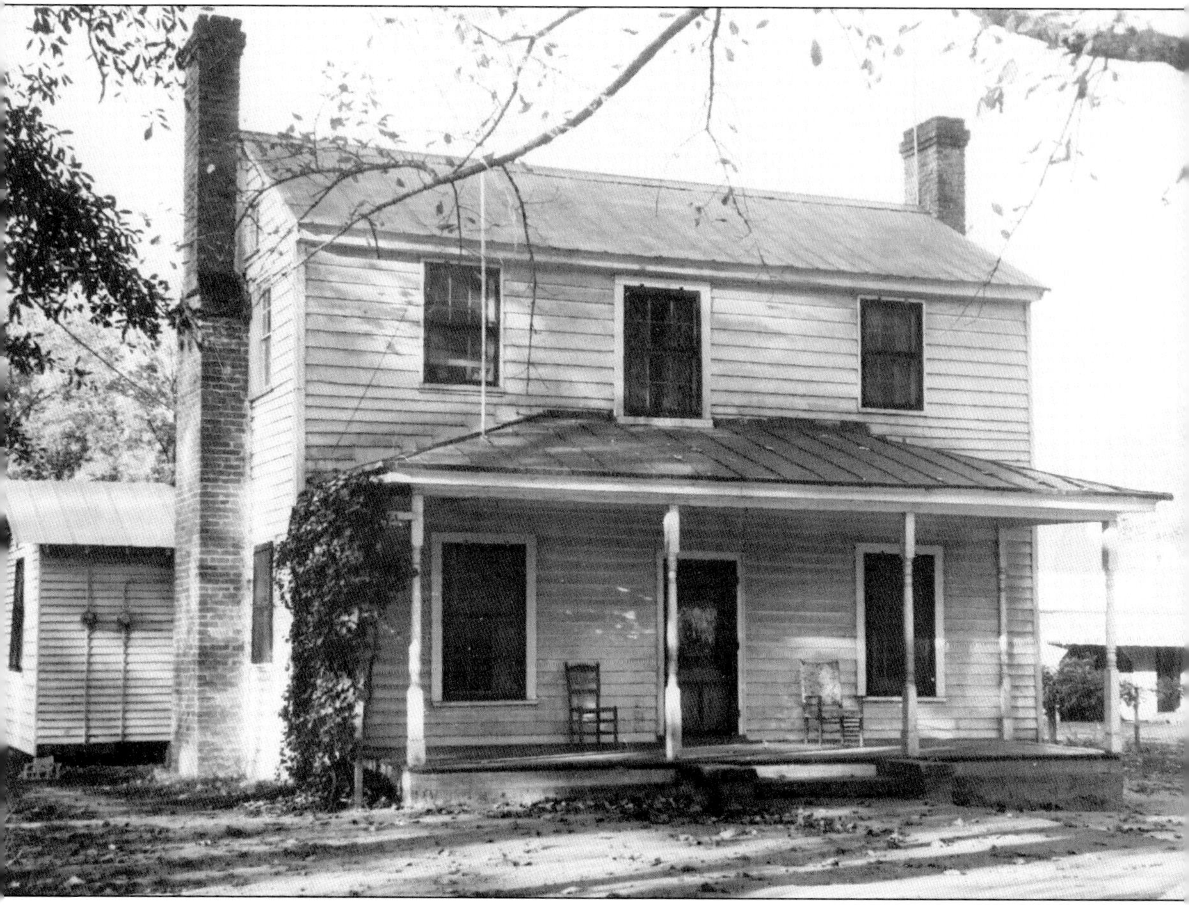

Old Dave Roberson Home, c. 1960. David Franklin Roberson, who lived on Railroad Street, was the last surviving Civil War veteran in Martin County when he died in 1935. The home was demolished sometime in the late 1980s or early 1990s, and the property was converted into a parking lot for the local Baptist church. (Courtesy of Martin County Historical Society.)

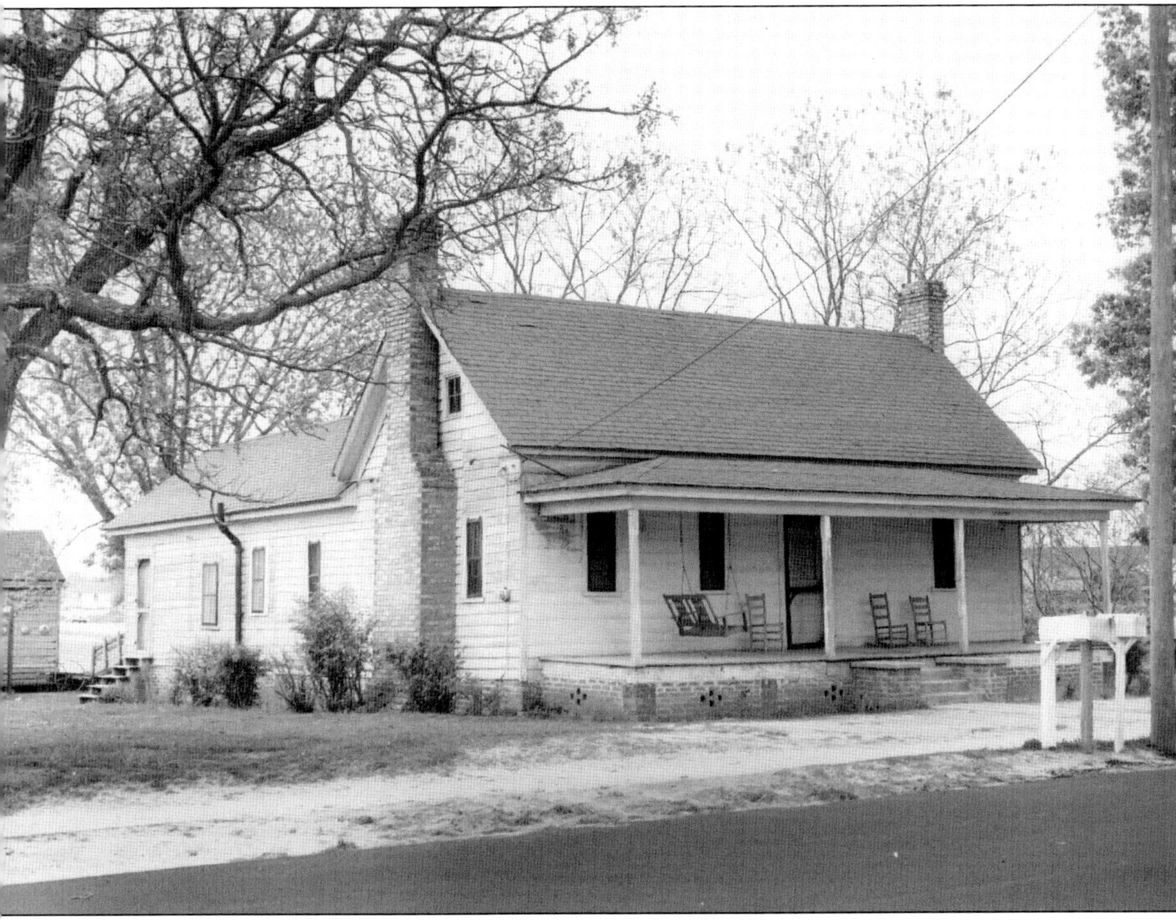

Former Billy Roberson Home, c. 1960. Thought to be the oldest structure still standing in Robersonville as of 2013, this house on West Academy Street was originally home to one of Robersonville's founders. As of 2013, it continues to serve as a private residence. (Courtesy of Martin County Historical Society.)

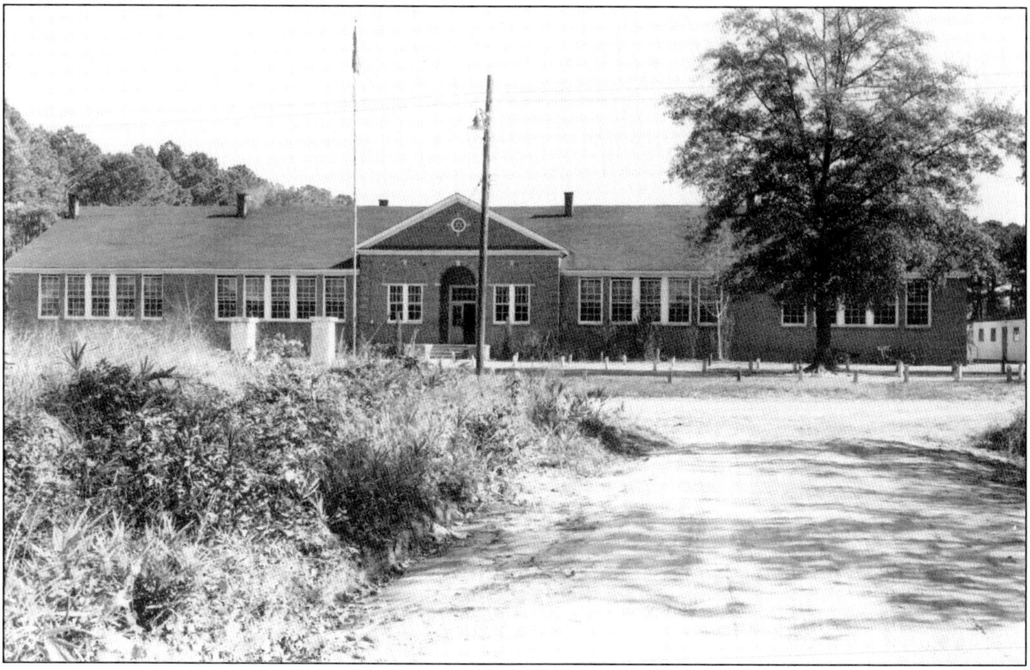

East End School, 1936. This facility originally served Robersonville's black student population. (Courtesy of Martin County Historical Society.)

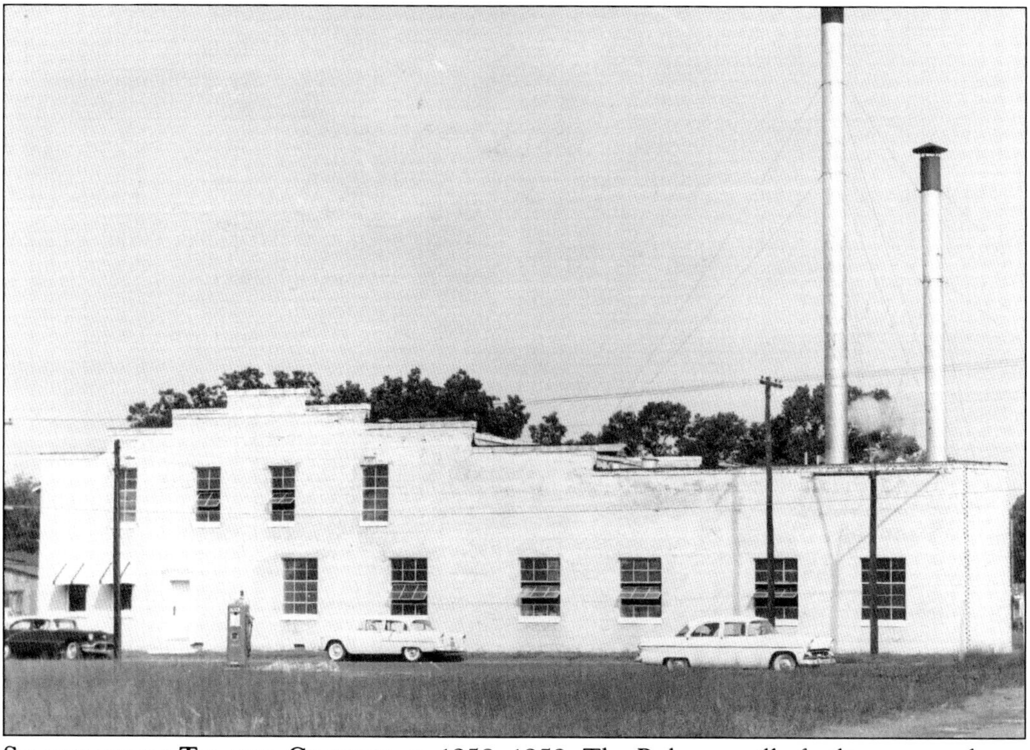

Southeastern Tobacco Company, c. 1958–1959. The Robersonville facility operated as a tobacco-redrying plant from 1952 to 1971. (Courtesy of Martin County Historical Society.)

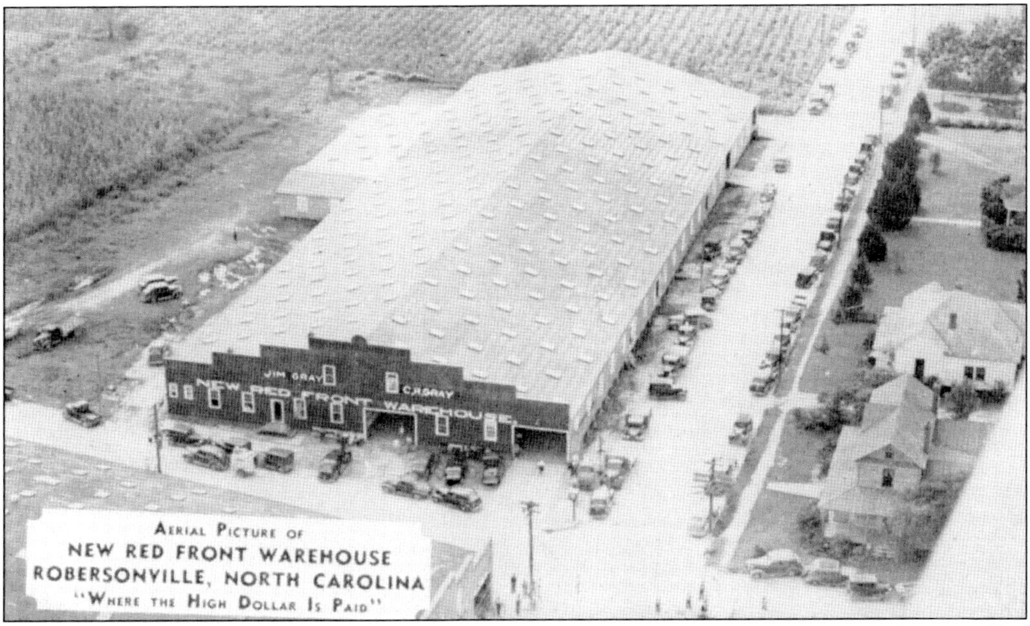

NEW RED FRONT WAREHOUSE, C. 1940. This aerial view records a portion of Robersonville's once bustling tobacco-market district. (Courtesy of the author.)

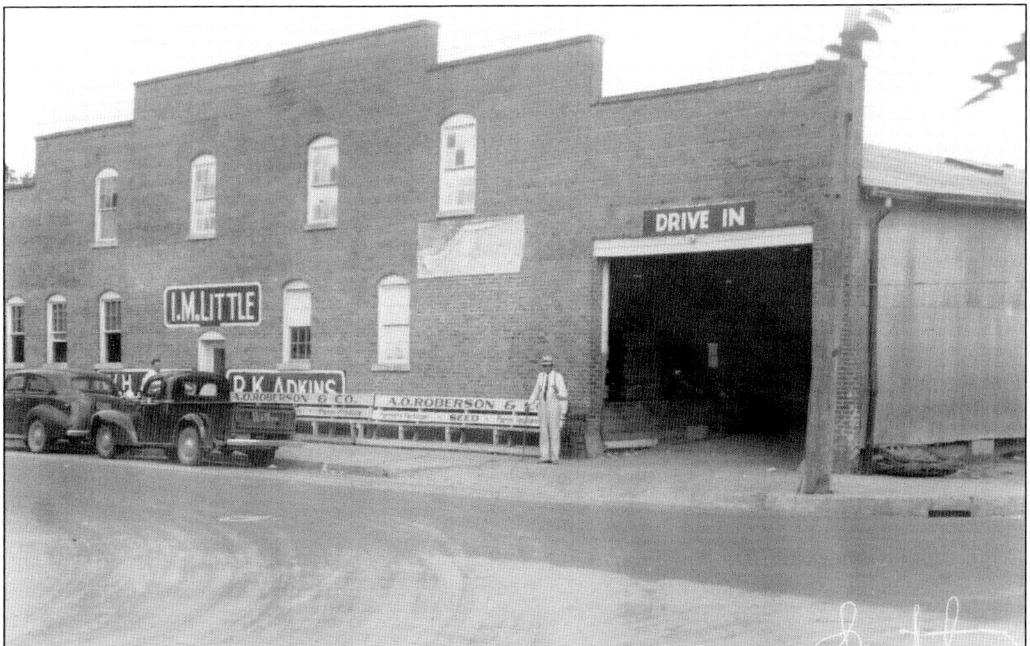

ADKINS-BAILEY-LITTLE TOBACCO WAREHOUSE, C. 1940. This photograph was taken by Irving L. Smith Sr., a Robersonville merchant who was also, for many years, the town's event and portrait photographer. The warehouse burned in 1968. (Courtesy of Irving L. Smith Jr.)

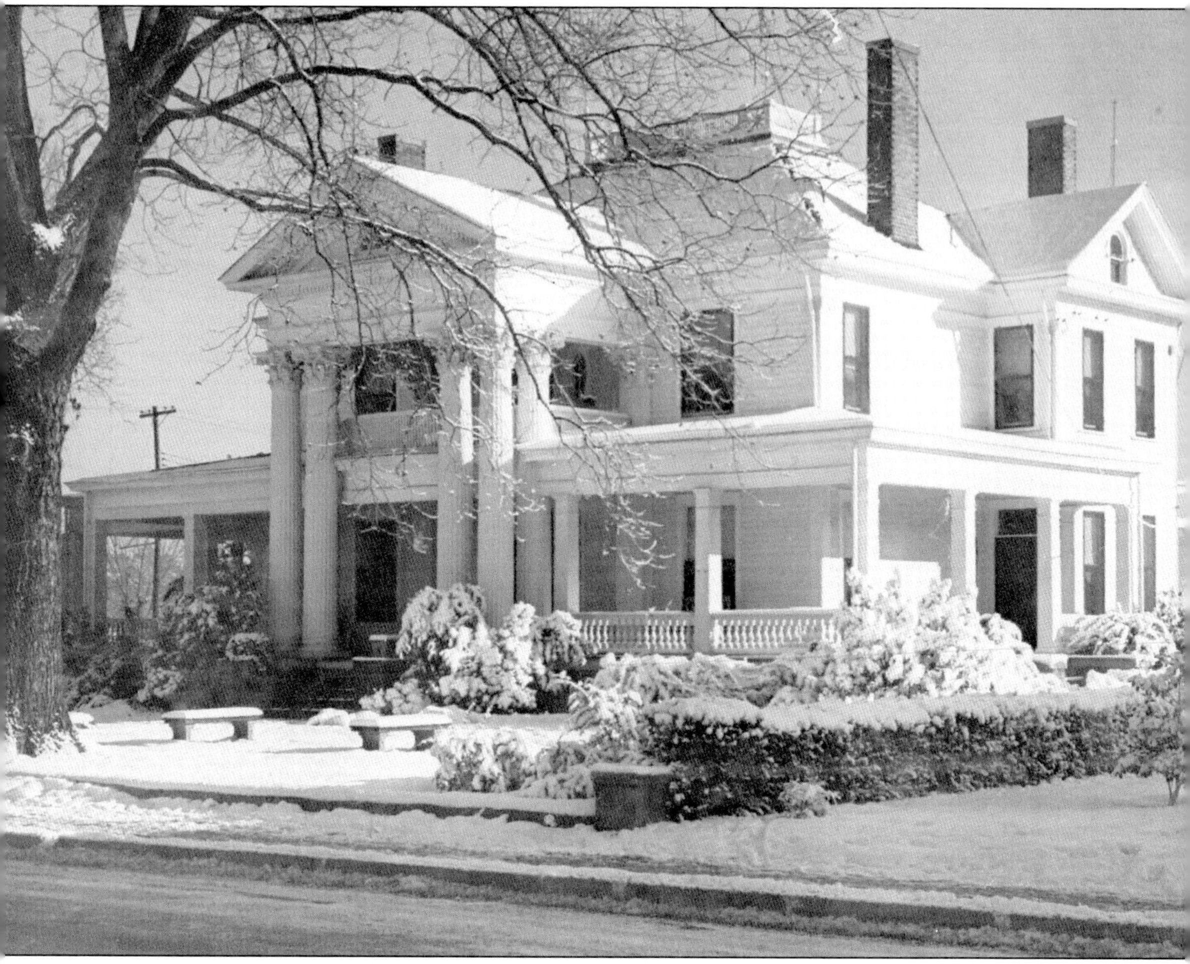

J.H./Vance Roberson Home, c. 1940. Built in 1913 on the corner of Main and Academy Streets, the house originally neighbored the home of J.H. Roberson's father to the south. The earlier home was moved to West Academy Street sometime after the completion of the younger Roberson's residence. Vance Roberson later occupied the structure. (Courtesy of Patsy R. Miller.)

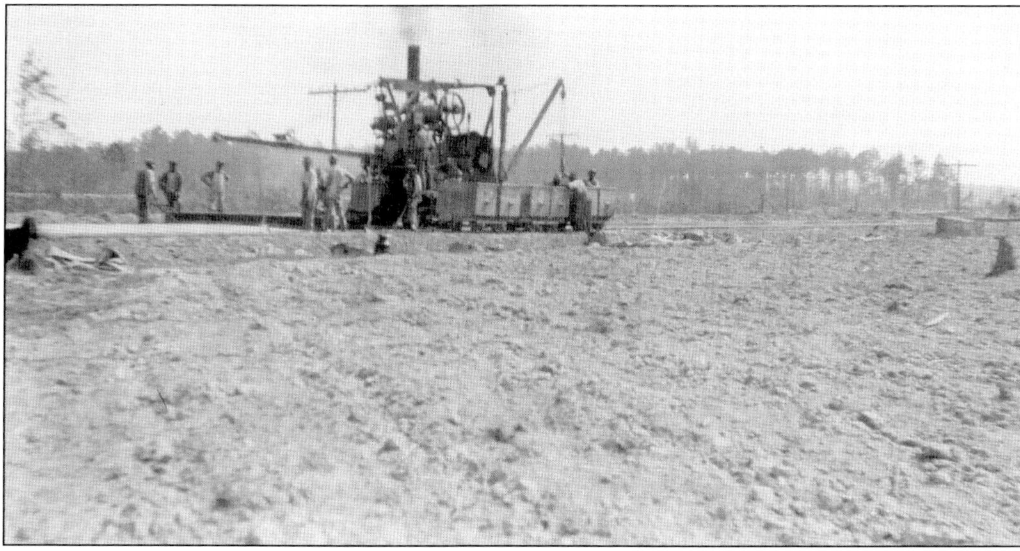

Paving of US Highway 64, 1924. North Carolina Highway 90, later redesignated US Highway 64 in the 1930s, was one of the very first paved roads in Martin County. Interesting in this view is the steam-powered equipment used in the paving process. (Courtesy of Martin County Historical Society.)

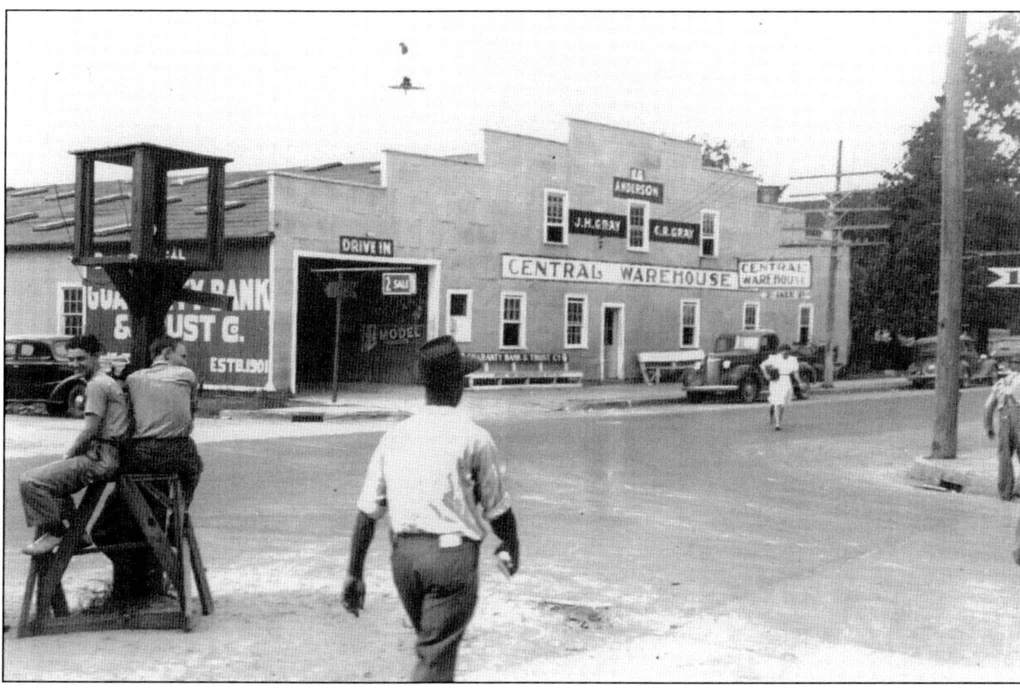

Central Warehouse, c. 1940. This scene depicts a lull in activity along Main and Third Streets during tobacco-market season. (Courtesy of Irving L. Smith Jr.)

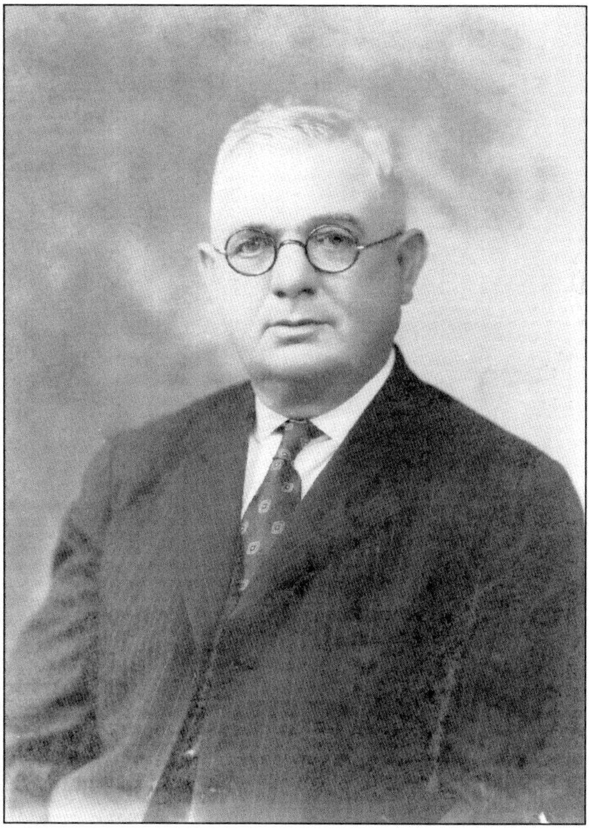

James Harvey Roberson, c. 1925. A native of the Gold Point community, J.H. Roberson (1873–1936) went on to establish a successful mercantile business in Robersonville. (Courtesy of Patsy R. Miller.)

R.L. Smith and Co. Store, 1918. Among those pictured in this interior view of the Main Street store are Bob Smith, Jim Gray, and Lon Roberson. (Courtesy of Patsy R. Miller.)

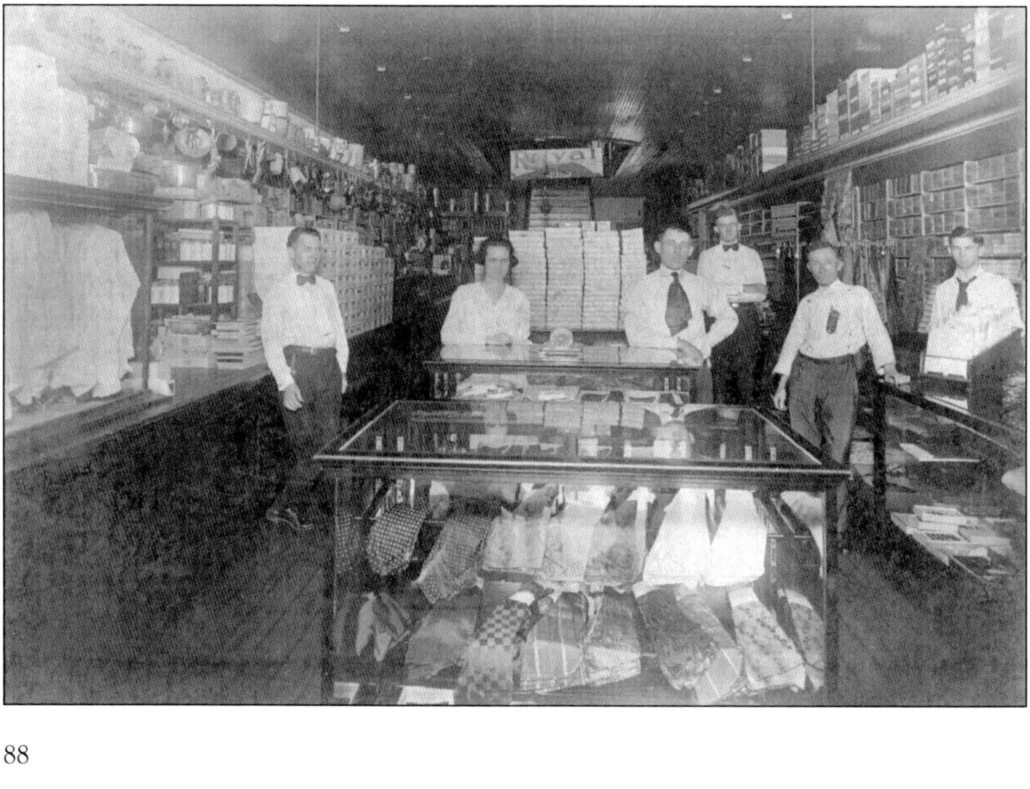

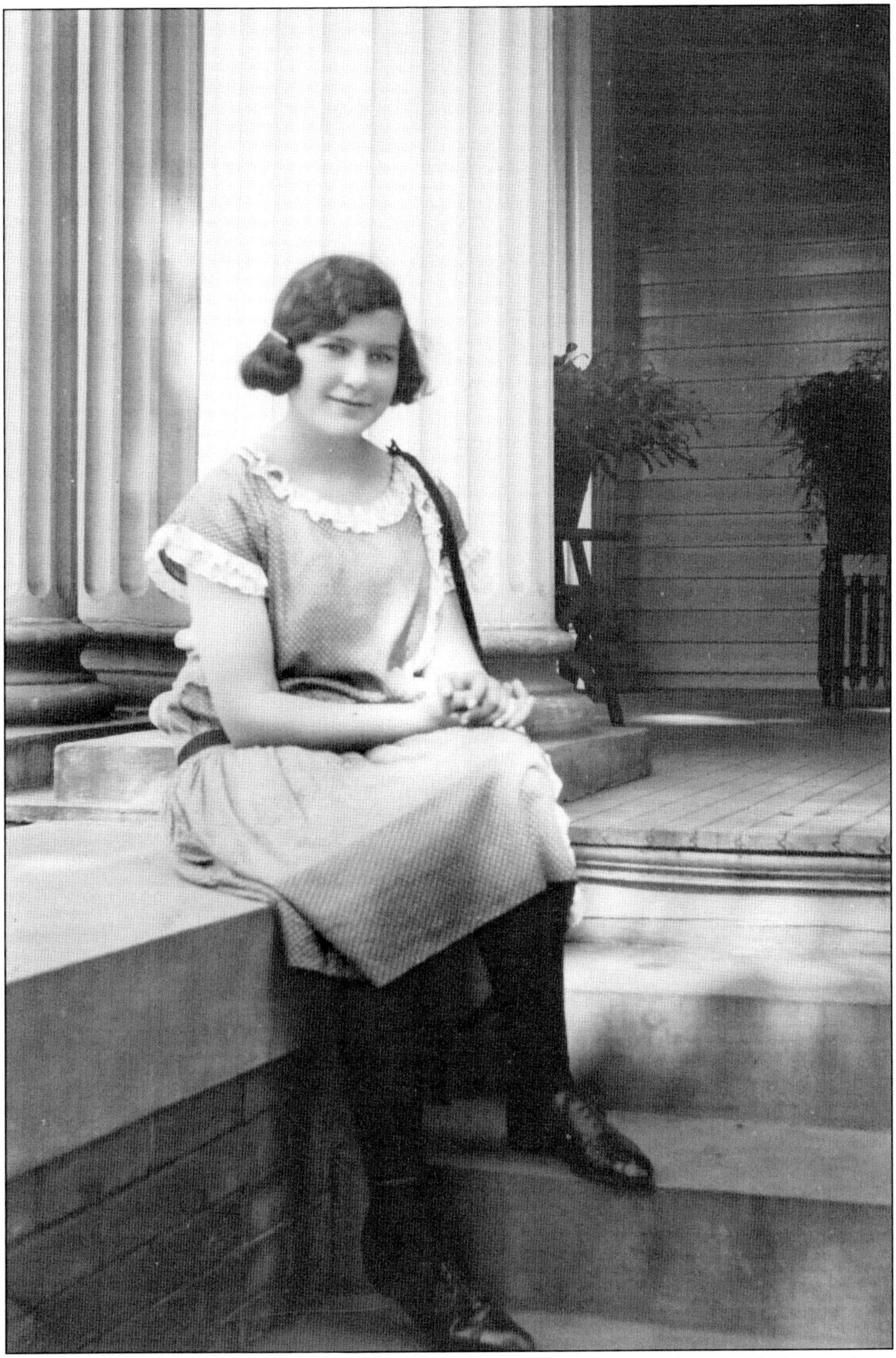

DELLA ROBERSON GILLIAM, C. 1925. Daughter of J.H. and Hattie Little Roberson, Della was described as a great storyteller. She married John B. Gilliam in 1939 and became a resident of Windsor, North Carolina. She had inherited her parents' home upon the death of her father in 1936 but sold it to her brother Vance Roberson upon moving to Windsor. (Courtesy of Patsy R. Miller.)

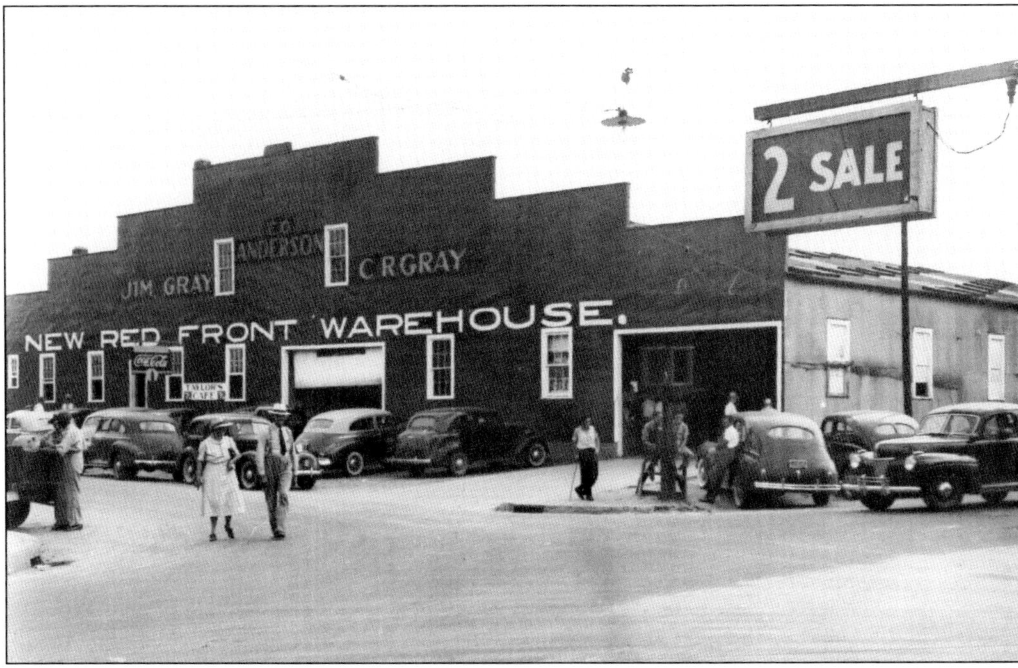

GRAY'S NEW RED FRONT WAREHOUSE, C. 1940. Built in 1930, this warehouse proved successful enough in its first few years of operation to warrant a sizable expansion in 1935. (Photograph by Irving Smith, courtesy of Irving L. Smith Jr.)

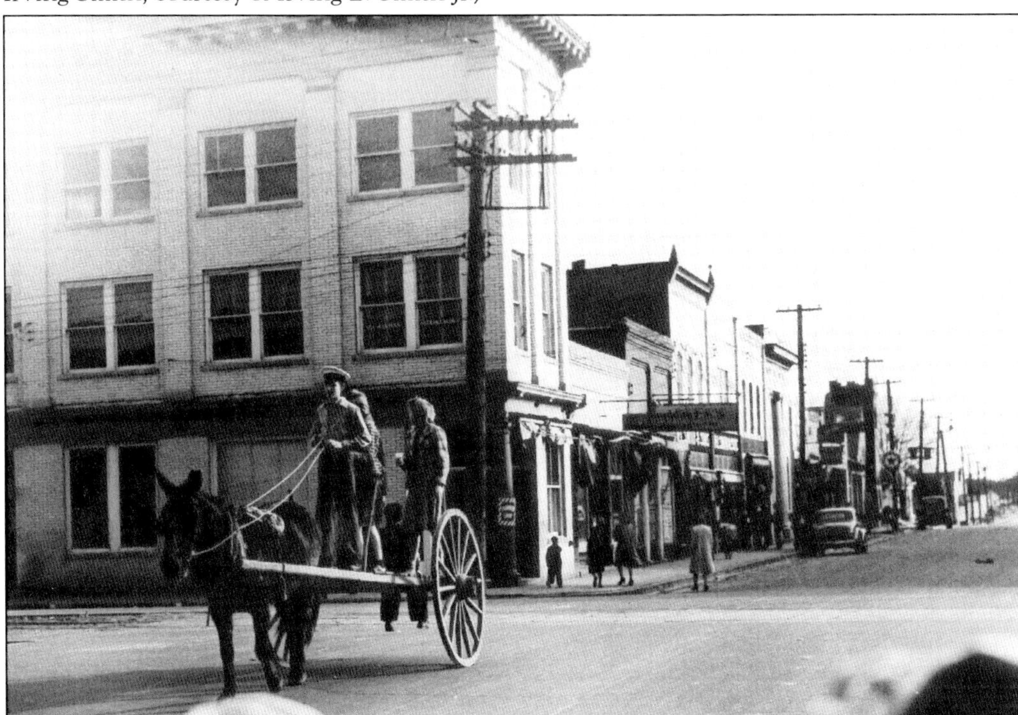

ROBERSONVILLE STREET SCENE, C. 1940. Unidentified youngsters on a mule-drawn cart pose for the camera in the intersection of Main and Railroad Streets. (Courtesy of Irving L. Smith Jr.)

Measles Quarantine, c. 1939. Irving L. Smith Jr. is pictured here, confined to his Grimes Street home in what was one of the last measles quarantines in Martin County. (Courtesy of Irving L. Smith Jr.)

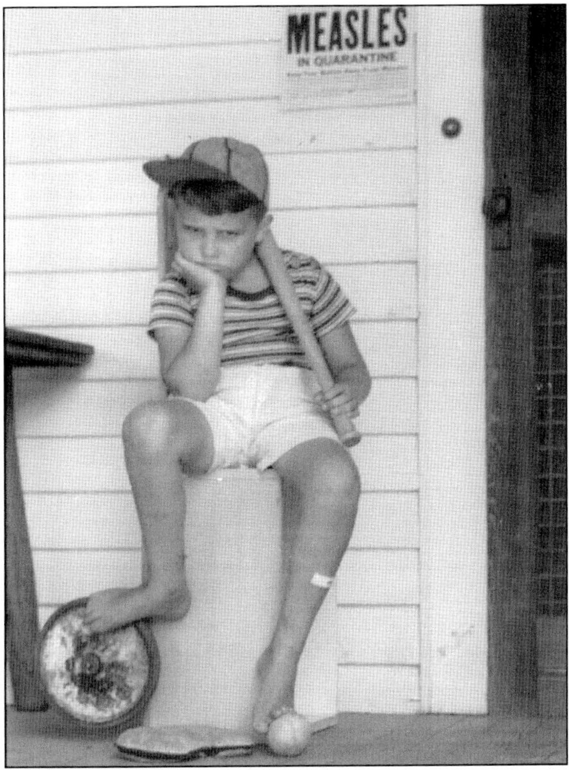

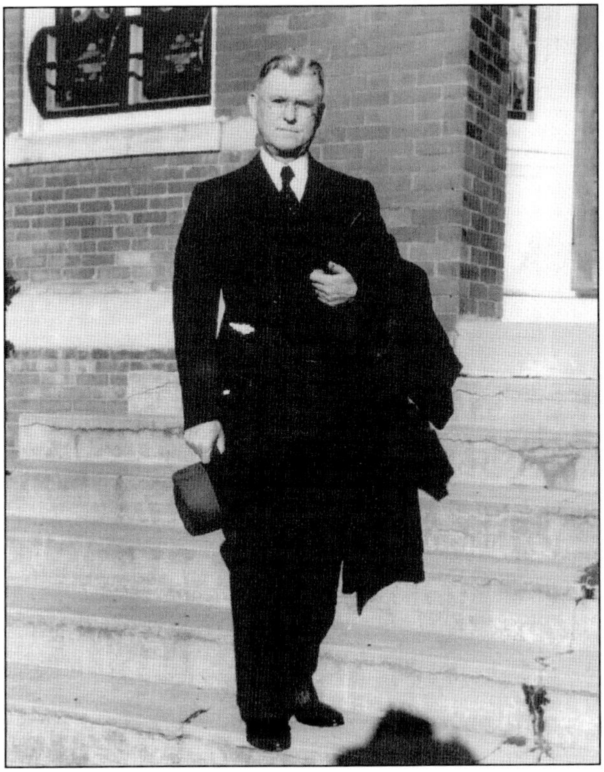

Rev. J.M. Perry, c. 1940. Reverend Perry is pictured on the steps of Robersonville First Christian Church, dedicated on October 19, 1919. (Courtesy of Irving L. Smith Jr.)

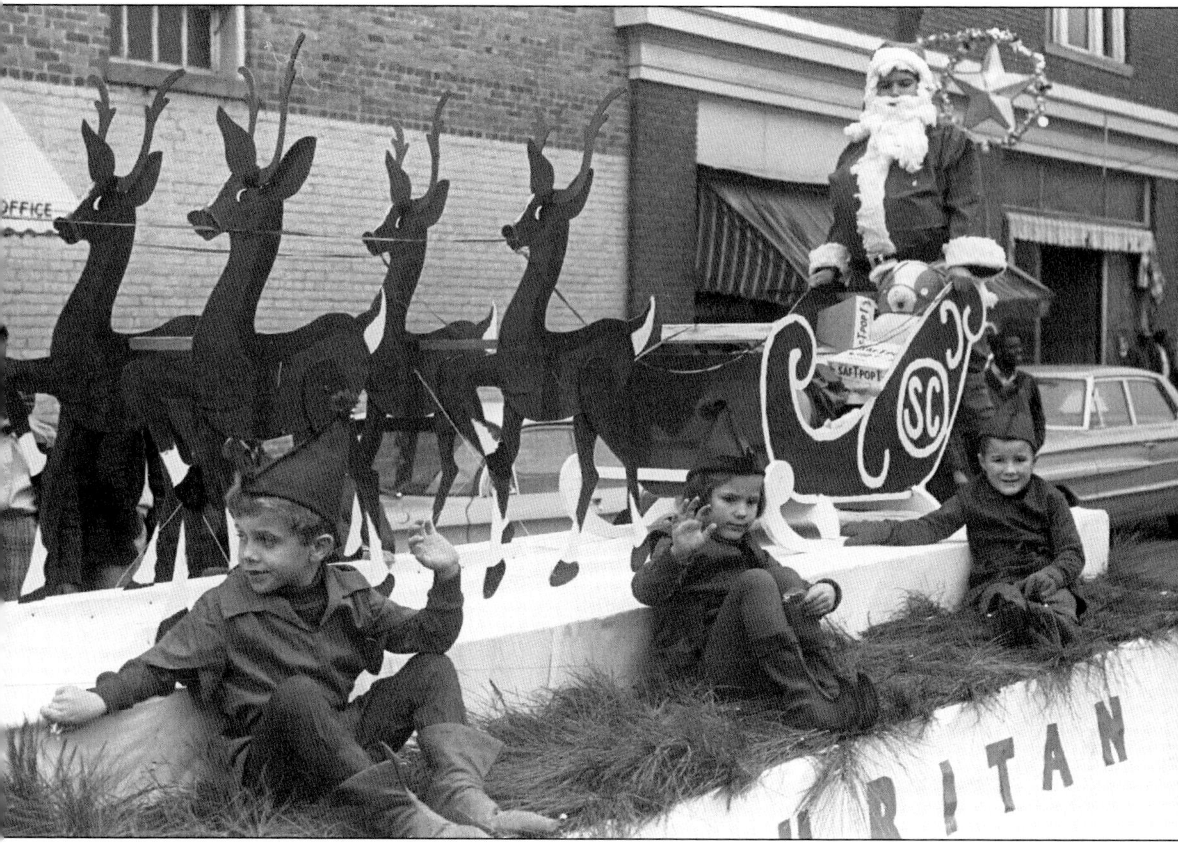

Robersonville Christmas Parade, December 1965. This image of Santa with his little helpers is attributed to Greenville, North Carolina's *Daily Reflector* newspaper. (Courtesy of the J.Y. Joyner Library, East Carolina Manuscript Collection.)

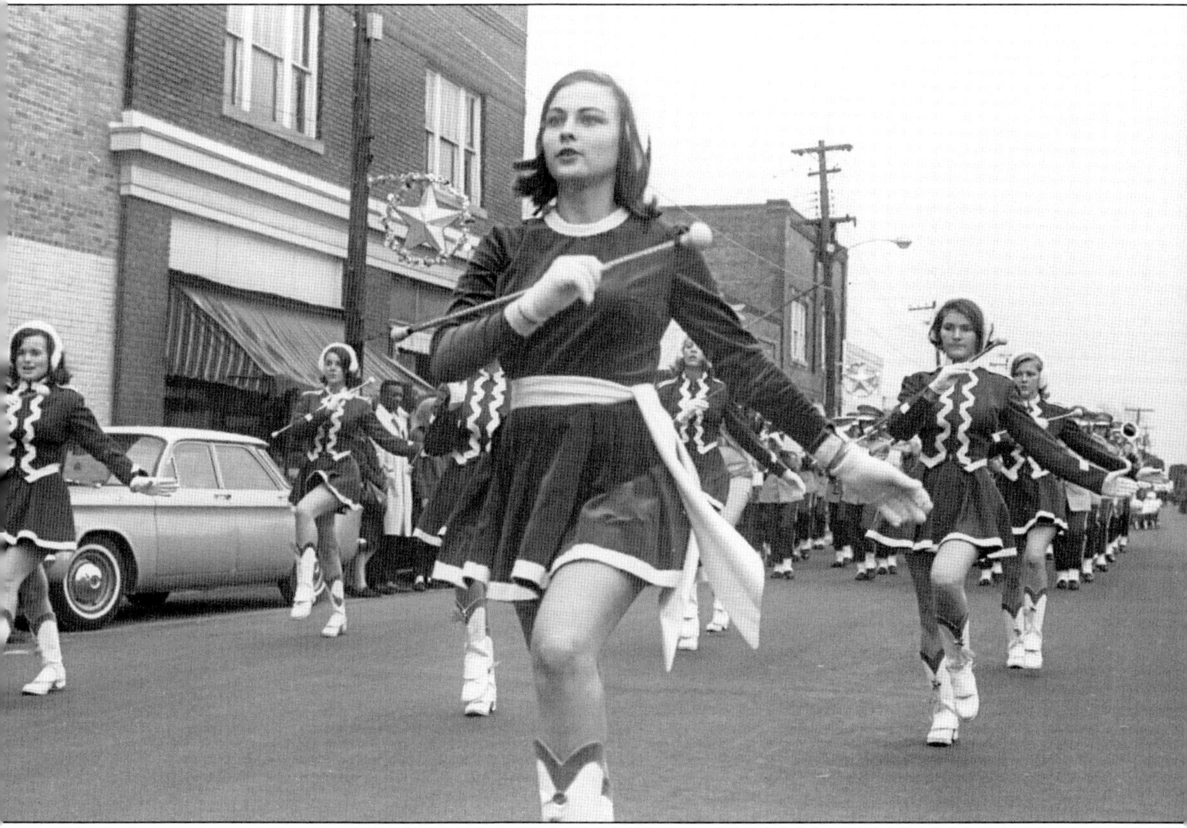

Christmas Parade Drum Majorettes, 1965. The Robersonville High School Band, seen here along Railroad Street, boasts a long and successful history going back to the 1930s. (Courtesy of the J.Y. Joyner Library, East Carolina Manuscript Collection.)

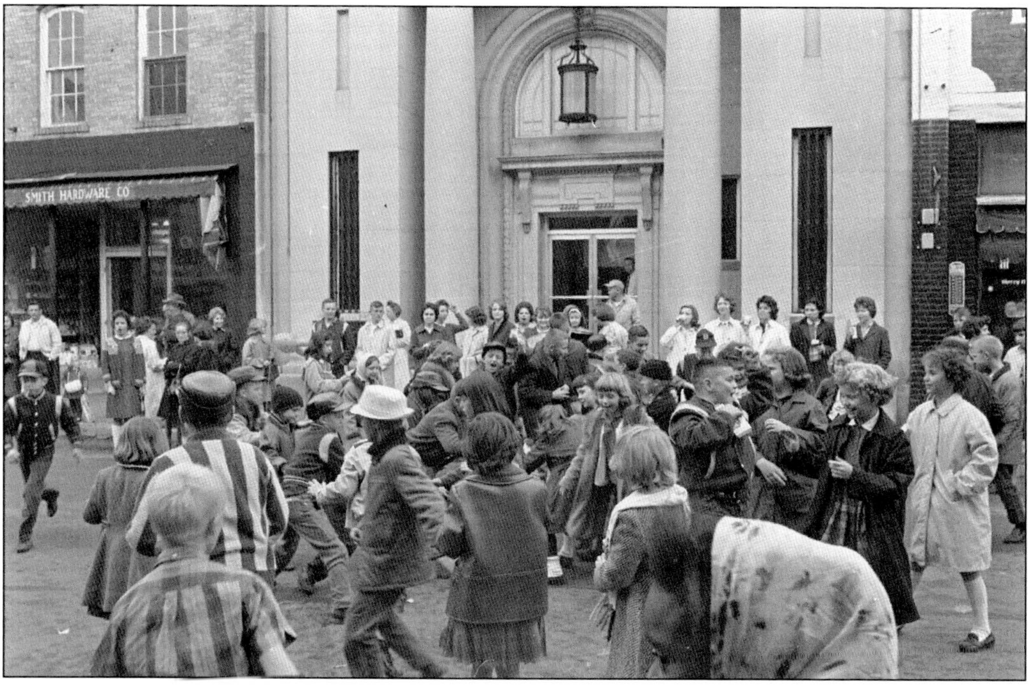

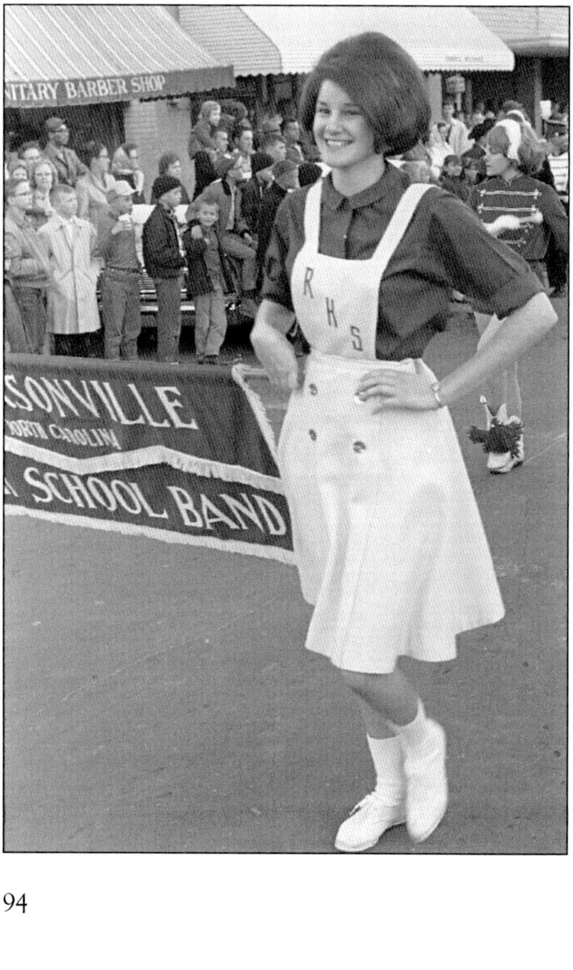

ROBERSONVILLE CHRISTMAS PARADE, 1963. This image, attributed to Greenville's *Daily Reflector* newspaper, shows the scene prior to the Robersonville Christmas parade of 1963. (Courtesy of the J.Y. Joyner Library, East Carolina Manuscript Collection.)

ROBERSONVILLE CHRISTMAS PARADE, 1964. This image of the 1964 parade is also credited to the *Daily Reflector.* (Courtesy of the J.Y. Joyner Library, East Carolina Manuscript Collection.)

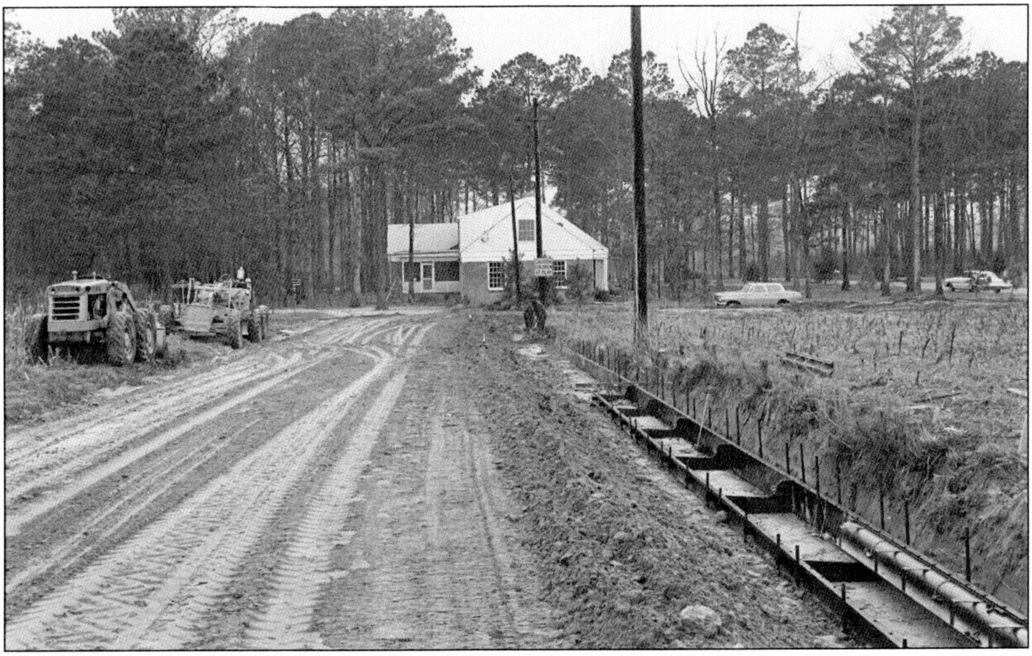

Residential Street Construction, February 1964. The area shown appears to be the intersection of Robersonville's Dogwood and South Broad Streets. (Courtesy of the J.Y. Joyner Library, East Carolina Manuscript Collection.)

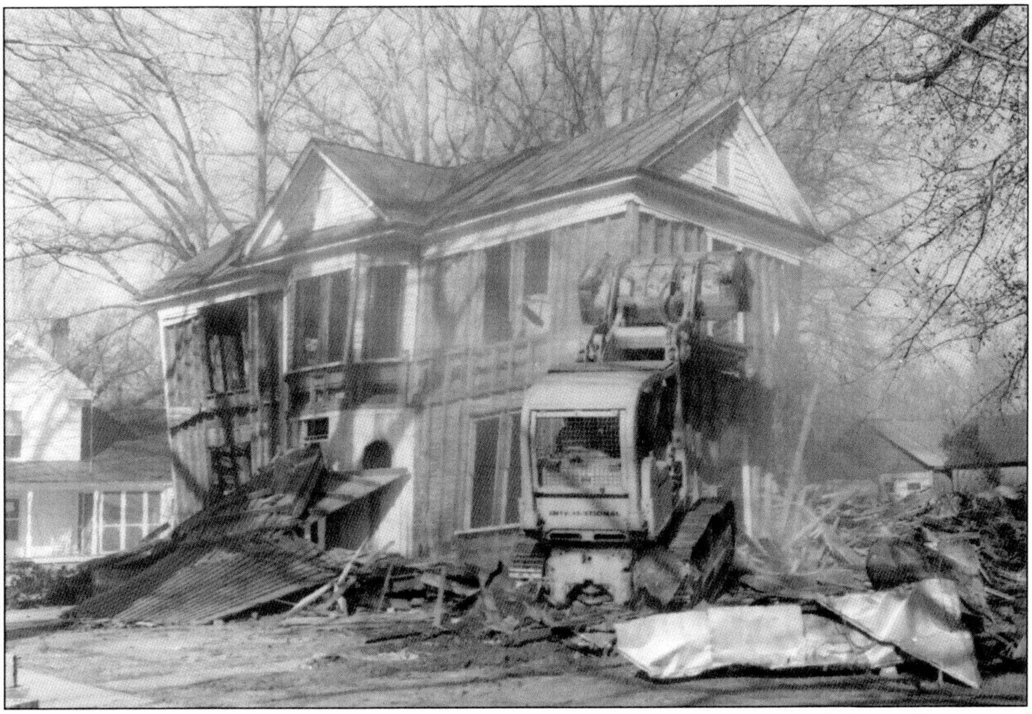

A.S. Roberson Home Demolition, 1976. This house on Railroad Street belonged to one of Robersonville's early merchants and was replaced by a banking institution, Cooperative Savings and Loan. (Courtesy of Martin County Historical Society.)

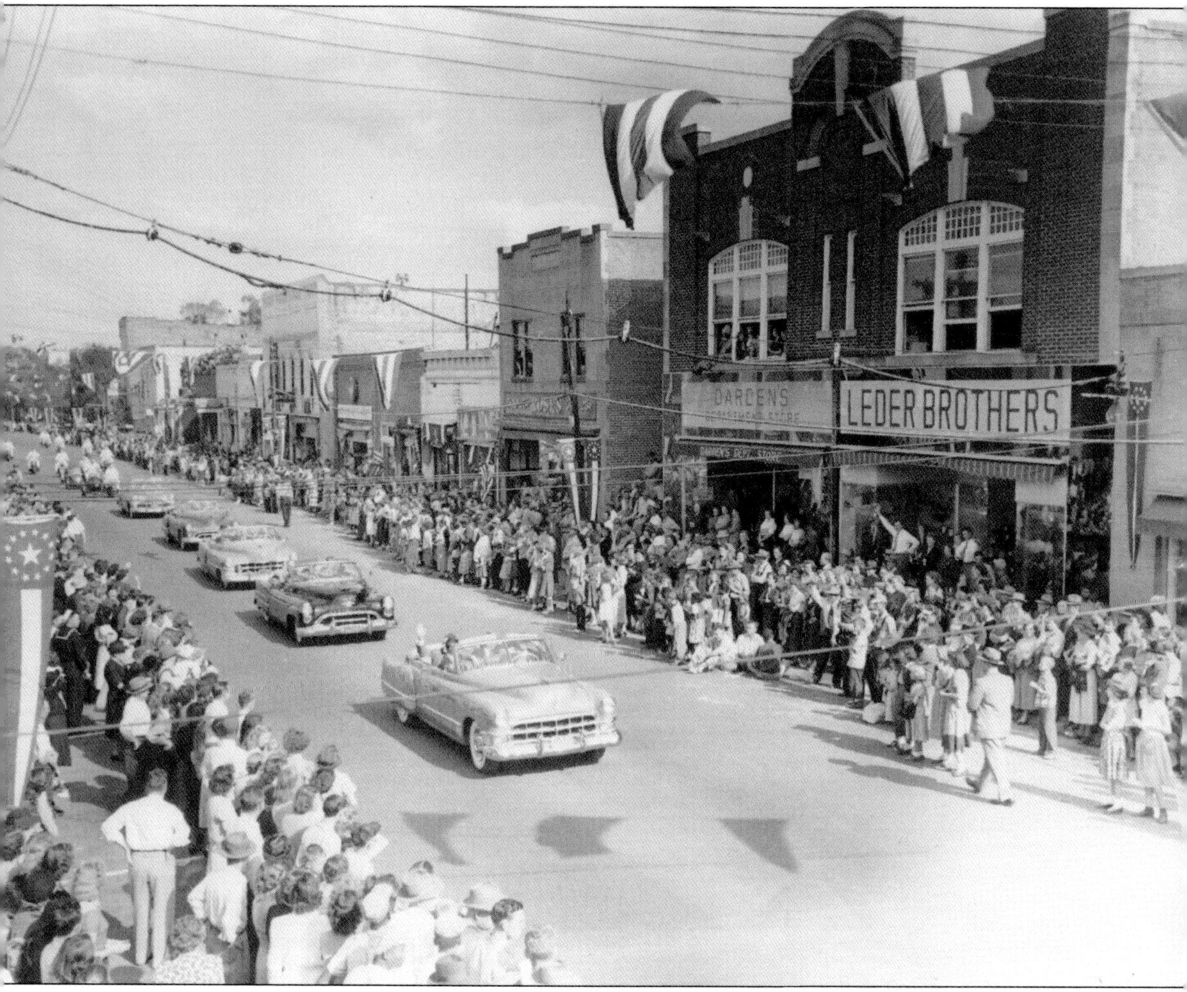

Williamston Harvest Festival Parade, c. 1951–1952. This image is attributed to the Royal Photographic Studio. Identified at right in the photograph as jointly occupied by Darden's Department Store and Leder Brothers is the original Harrison Brothers Store, constructed about 1917. Harrison Brothers was a primary business concern in Williamston from 1901 to 1938. (Courtesy of Jesse Silverthorne.)

Seven

Williamston Along the Ocean Highway

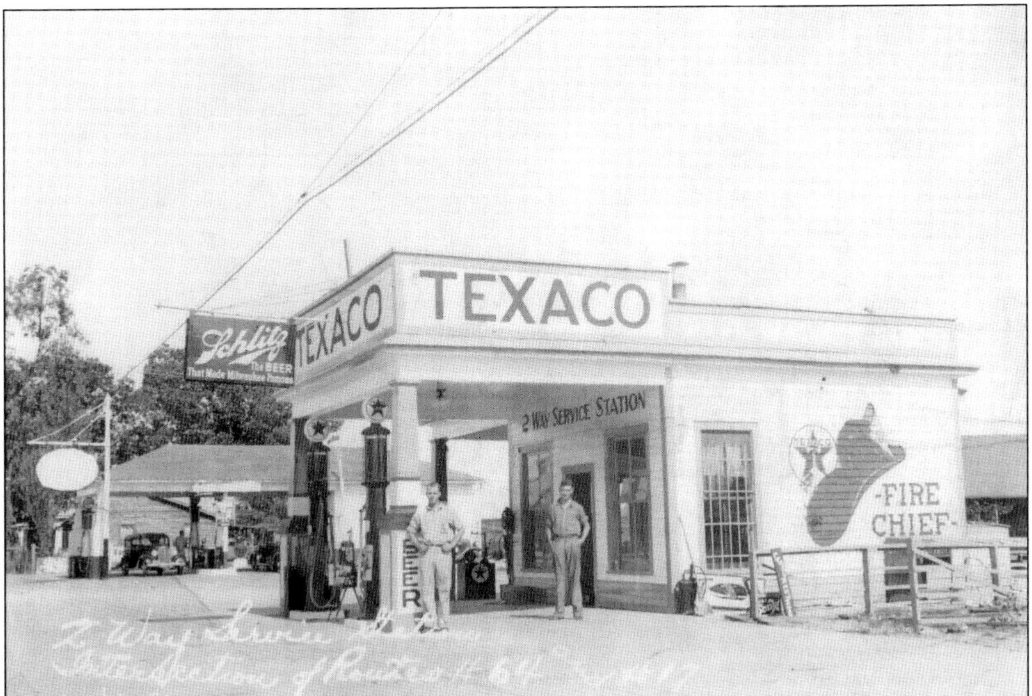

Two-Way Service Station, Late 1930s. This site, at the corner of Jamesville Road and Washington Street, was later the location of Williamston Motor Co. Jasper E. Jones is identified near the entrance. (Courtesy of Martha J. McDonald.)

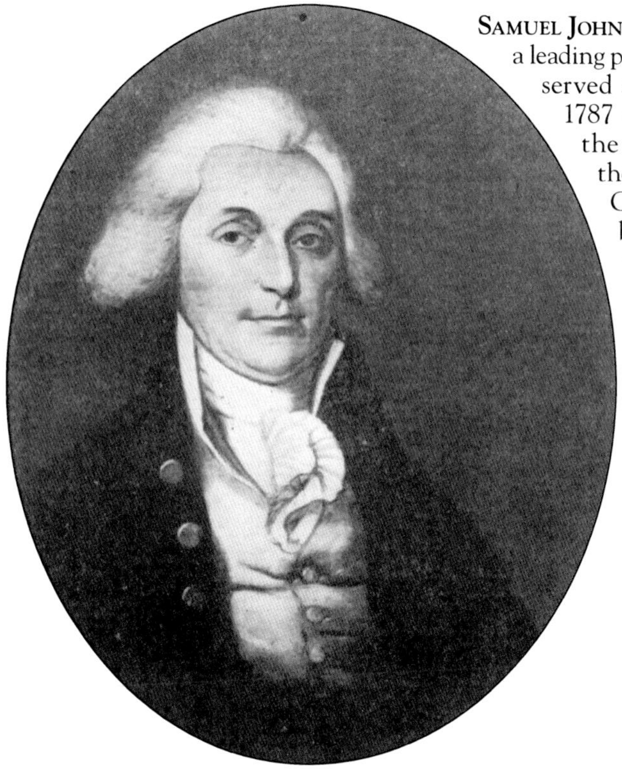

SAMUEL JOHNSTON (1733–1816), C. 1780. Johnston, a leading patriot during the American Revolution, served as governor of North Carolina from 1787 to 1789. He is credited with being the first person elected as president of the United States under the Articles of Confederation. He declined the position but continued involvement in national politics through ratification of the Constitution in 1789. Sometime in the 1780s, Johnston built a home, The Hermitage, in Williamston off present-day Park Street. Ruins of the structure were still visible as late as 1913. (Courtesy of the North Division of Archives and History.)

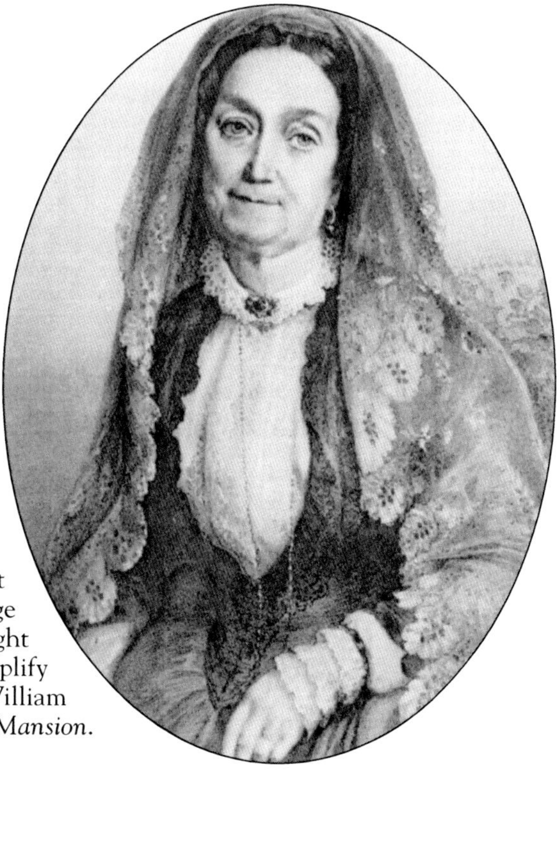

ELIZA BOWEN JUMEL, C. 1840. A notorious prostitute and, later, famed New York socialite, Jumel briefly lived with her family in a rental house across from the present-day courthouse in Williamston in 1798. Married originally to wealthy New York wine merchant Stephen Jumel, she gained access to the court of Napoleon in France. A second marriage to Aaron Burr and the sensational court fight over her will following her 1865 death exemplify her colorful life. This image is taken from William H. Shelton's 1916 book, *The Morris Jumel Mansion*. (Courtesy of the author.)

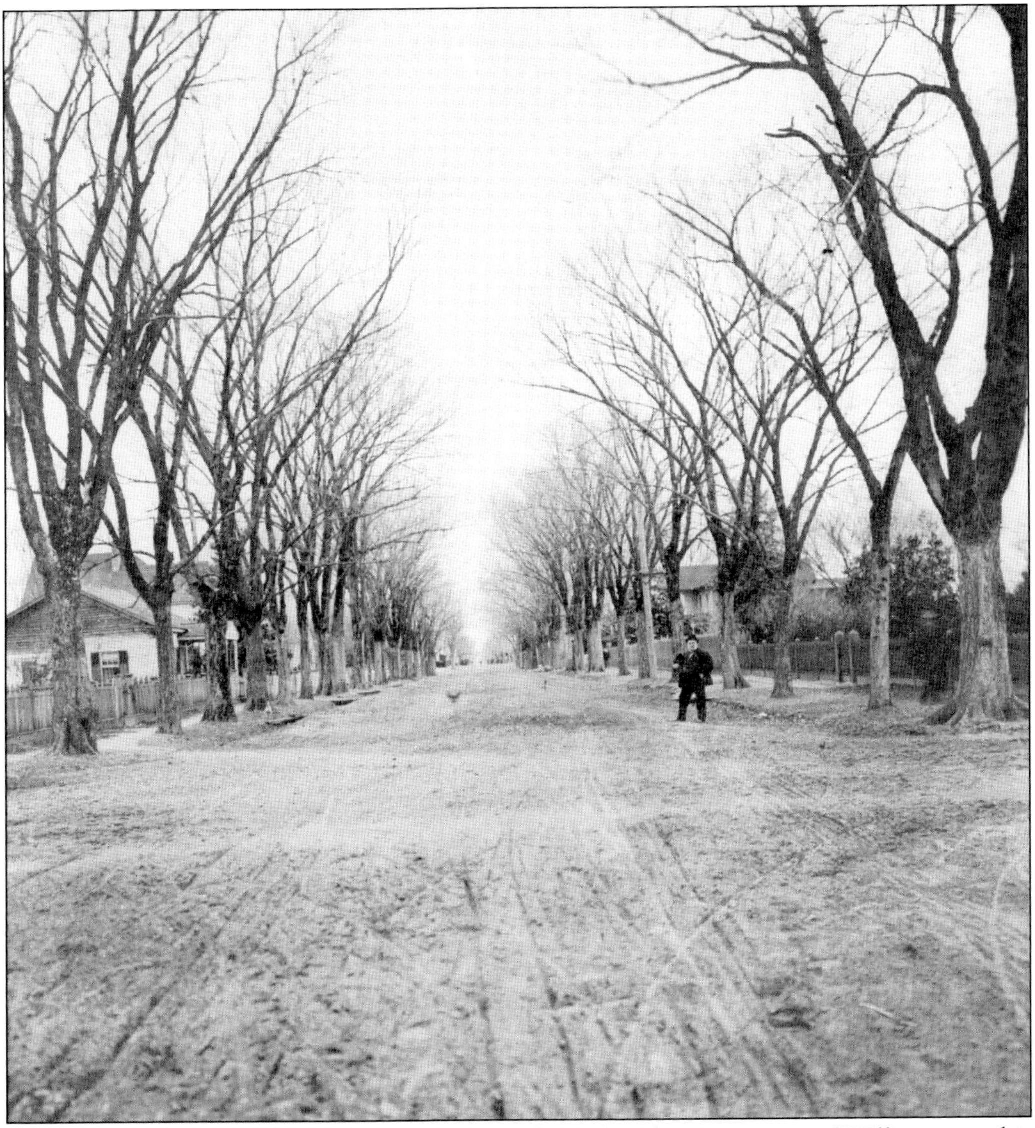

West Main Street, November 1884. One of the earliest known images of Williamston, this albumen photograph with an eastward-facing view was taken by William Garrison Reed, a soldier in the 44th Massachusetts Regiment that briefly occupied the town at two intervals during the Civil War. Reed and his comrades made a return visit in 1884 to record places visited by the 44th for inclusion in a regimental history that was later published in 1887. This photograph is one of several discovered and obtained by the author in recent years. In 1926, Reed donated an album concerning the 1884 visit to the New Bern Public Library. (Courtesy of the author.)

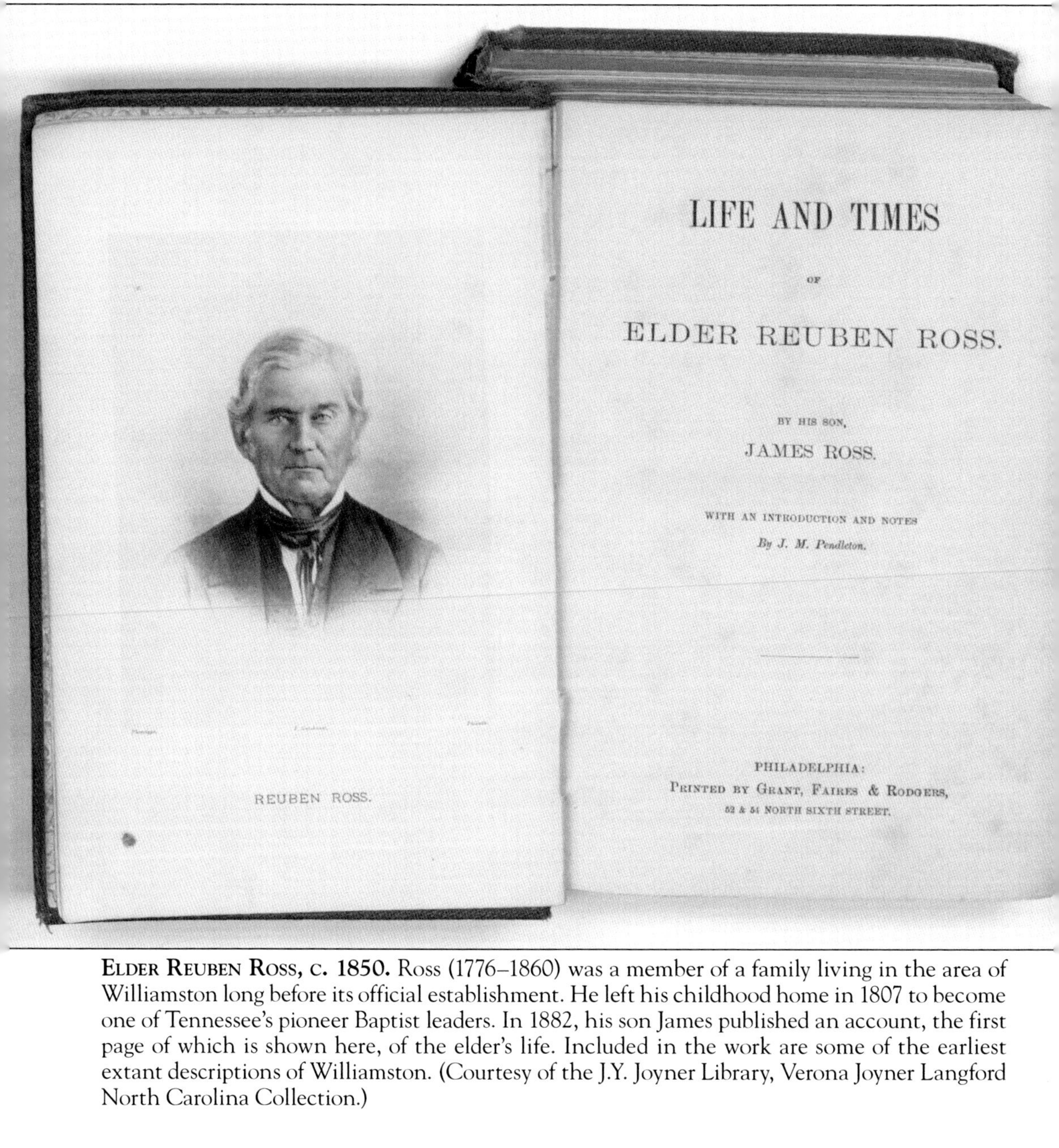

ELDER REUBEN ROSS, C. 1850. Ross (1776–1860) was a member of a family living in the area of Williamston long before its official establishment. He left his childhood home in 1807 to become one of Tennessee's pioneer Baptist leaders. In 1882, his son James published an account, the first page of which is shown here, of the elder's life. Included in the work are some of the earliest extant descriptions of Williamston. (Courtesy of the J.Y. Joyner Library, Verona Joyner Langford North Carolina Collection.)

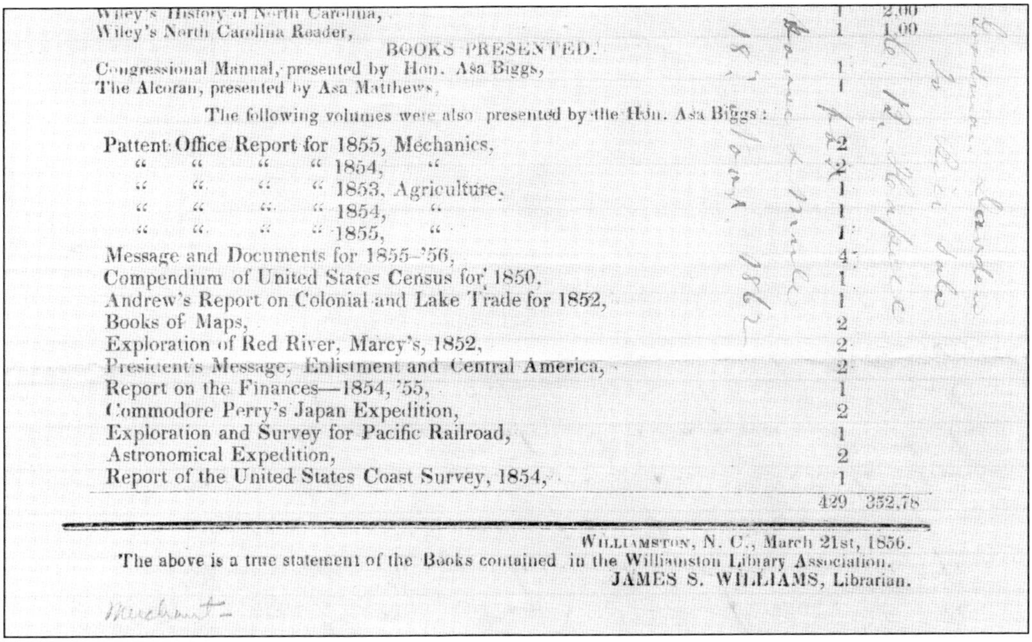

Wiley's History of North Carolina,	1	2.00
Wiley's North Carolina Reader,	1	1.00

BOOKS PRESENTED.

Congressional Manual, presented by Hon. Asa Biggs,	1	
The Alcoran, presented by Asa Matthews,	1	

The following volumes were also presented by the Hon. Asa Biggs:

Pattent Office Report for 1855, Mechanics,	2	
" " " " 1854, "	2	
" " " " 1853, Agriculture,	1	
" " " " 1854, "	1	
" " " " 1855, "	1	
Message and Documents for 1855–'56,	4	
Compendium of United States Census for 1850.	1	
Andrew's Report on Colonial and Lake Trade for 1852,	1	
Books of Maps,	2	
Exploration of Red River, Marcy's, 1852,	2	
President's Message, Enlistment and Central America,	2	
Report on the Finances—1854, '55,	1	
Commodore Perry's Japan Expedition,	2	
Exploration and Survey for Pacific Railroad,	1	
Astronomical Expedition,	2	
Report of the United States Coast Survey, 1854,	1	
	429	352.78

WILLIAMSTON, N. C., March 21st, 1856.
The above is a true statement of the Books contained in the Williamston Library Association.
JAMES S. WILLIAMS, Librarian.

LIBRARY INVENTORY, MARCH 1856. Williamston's first public library was created in the 1850s and was located in the 1835 courthouse. Owing to the Civil War and an 1884 fire that destroyed the building, the institution had only a brief existence. The survival of this small slip of paper owes its existence to the fact that it was later recycled for use as a receipt (reverse side) during the Civil War. (Courtesy of Martin County Historical Society.)

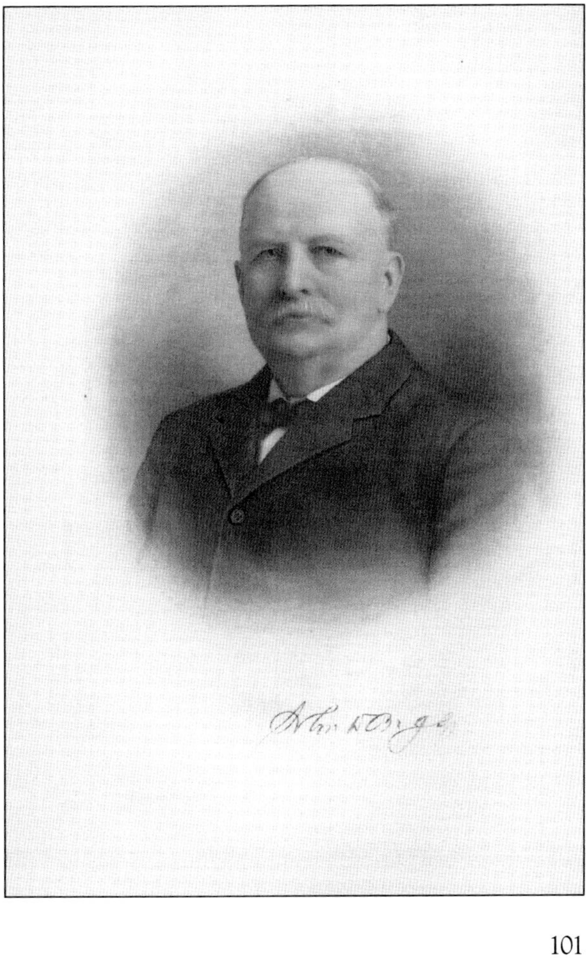

JOHN DAWSON BIGGS, C. 1900. One of Martin County and Williamston's leading merchants during the late 1800s, Biggs (1837–1905) held a partnership and family connection with the Dennis Simmons Lumber Company. This image is included in the 1917 B.F. Johnson biographical series, *Makers of America*. (Courtesy of the author.)

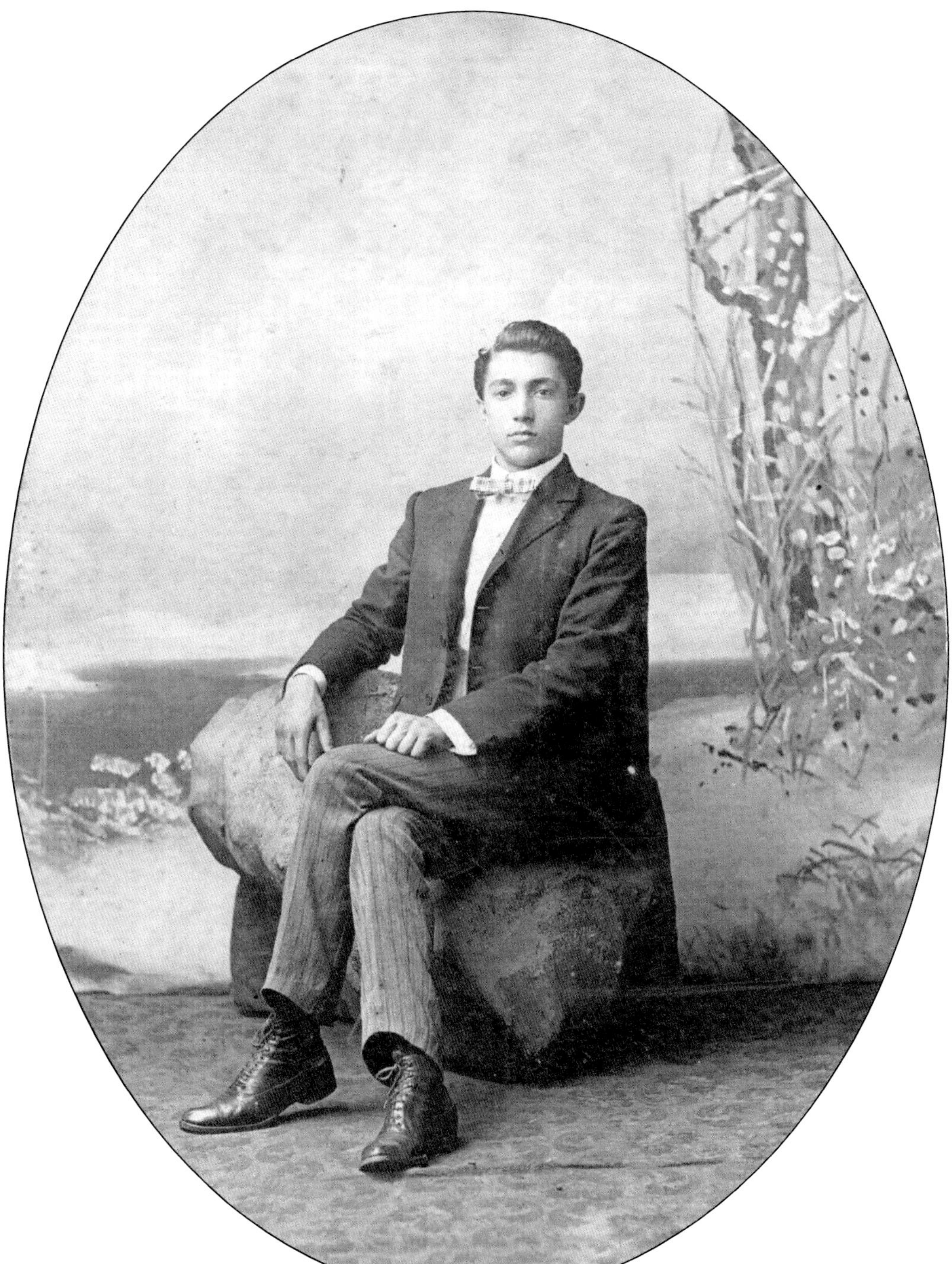

George Hyman Harrison, c. 1900. A native of the Bear Grass community, Harrison (1882–1949) built and organized a number of thriving businesses in Williamston during the early 20th century, including a wholesale grocery firm and oil distributorship. He was also instrumental in the negotiations leading to the location of the North Carolina Pulp and Paper Co. in the lower part of the county. (Courtesy of Martin County Historical Society.)

JAMES GRIST STATON, C. 1900. A progressive farmer and Williamston businessman, Staton (1874–1946) inherited extensive land interests originating from his great-great-grandfather William Biggs I. In 1907, after the deaths of his first wife and their five infant children, he married Fannie B. Chase. Two landmarks in the town of Williamston are credited to him—the Flatiron Building and People's Bank, later known as the Baker and White Professional Building. (Courtesy of Beverly G. Mills.)

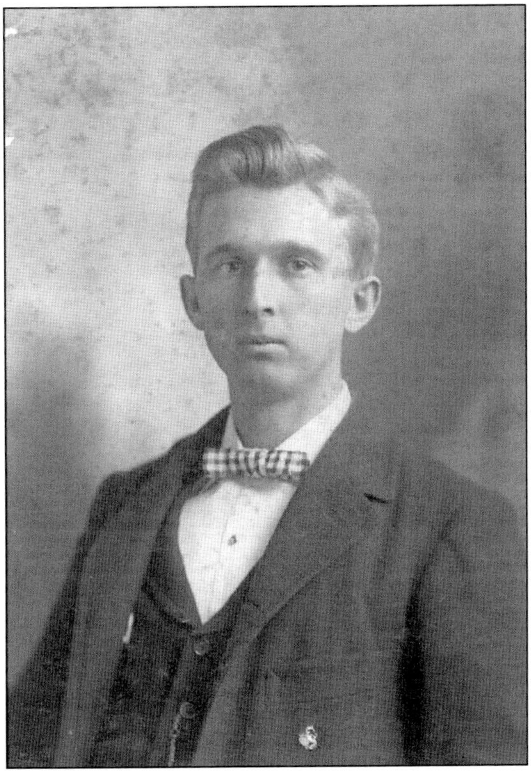

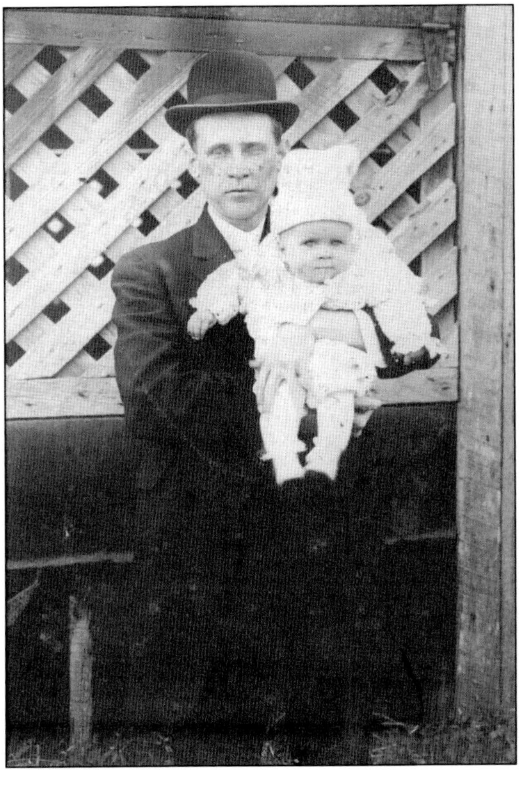

ARCHER R. DUNNING (1877–1932) AND DAUGHTER MARY ALICE, C. 1912. Prominent Williamston attorney A.R. Dunning served as mayor of Robersonville for a time before moving to Williamston around 1910. He married Mary Alice Grimes of Robersonville, and they had one daughter, Mary Alice. The family built and lived in an impressive brick home on the corner of South Haughton and Main Streets in Williamston. (Courtesy of Madge R. Partin, Robersonville Public Library.)

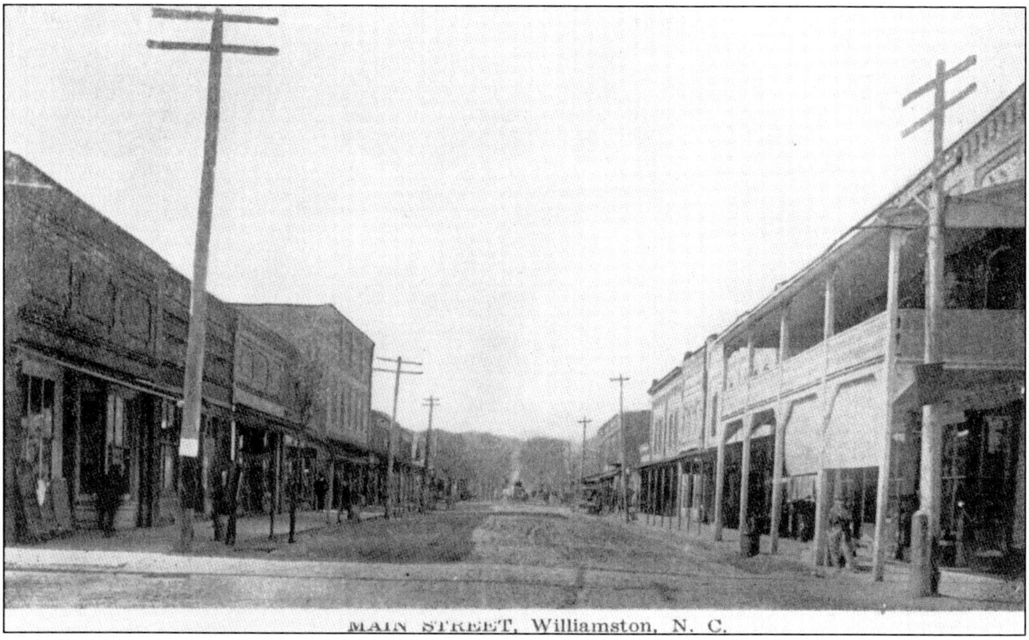

WILLIAMSTON MAIN STREET, c. 1910. In this rare postcard view of Williamston's Main Street, note the second-story porches at right. (Courtesy of the author.)

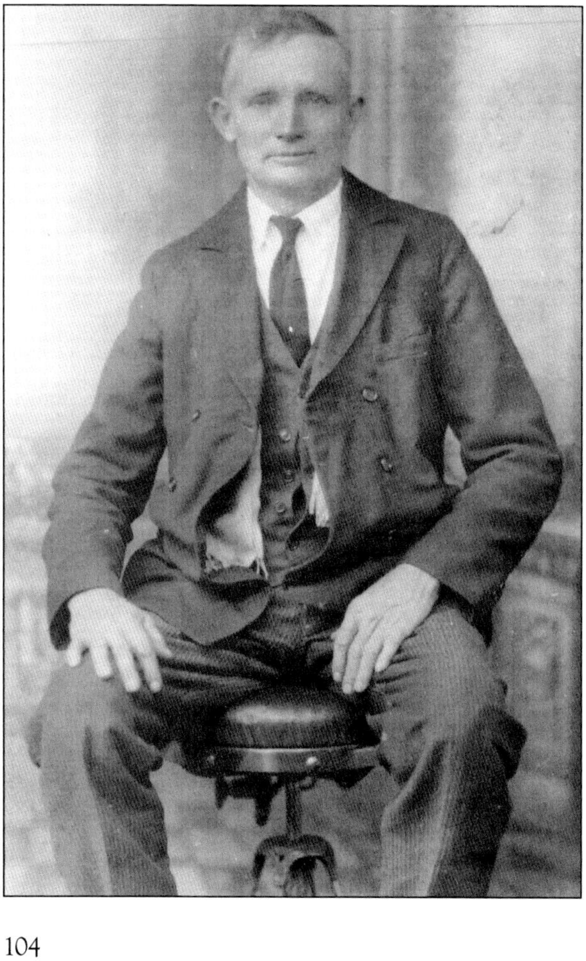

JOHN DAWSON COLTRAIN, c. 1902. A Martin County merchant-farmer from Jamesville, Coltrain (1872–1947) in his youth was the commissary manager for the old Dennis Simmons Lumber Co. In "retirement," he owned and operated a grocery business on North Haughton Street in Williamston. (Courtesy of Angela G. Grady.)

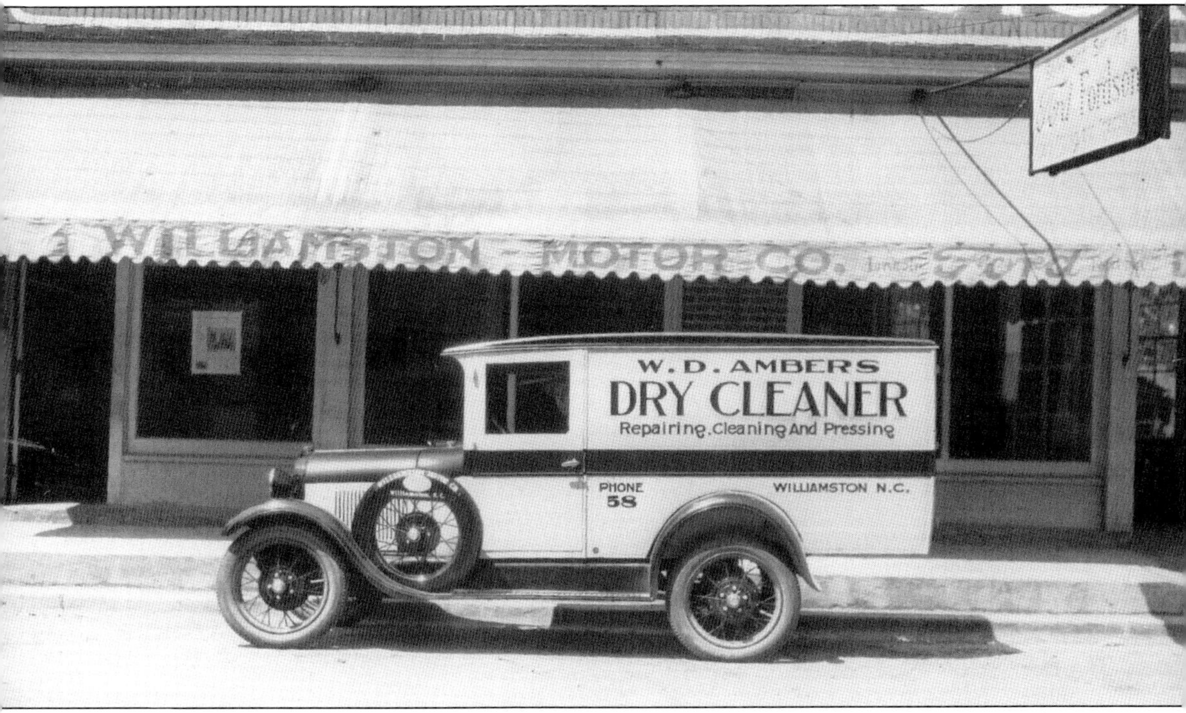

DRY-CLEANING SERVICE VEHICLE, C. 1925. In addition to a dry-cleaning service, W.D. Ambers also ran a soda shop in Williamston, though its location is not certain. (Courtesy of Martin County Historical Society.)

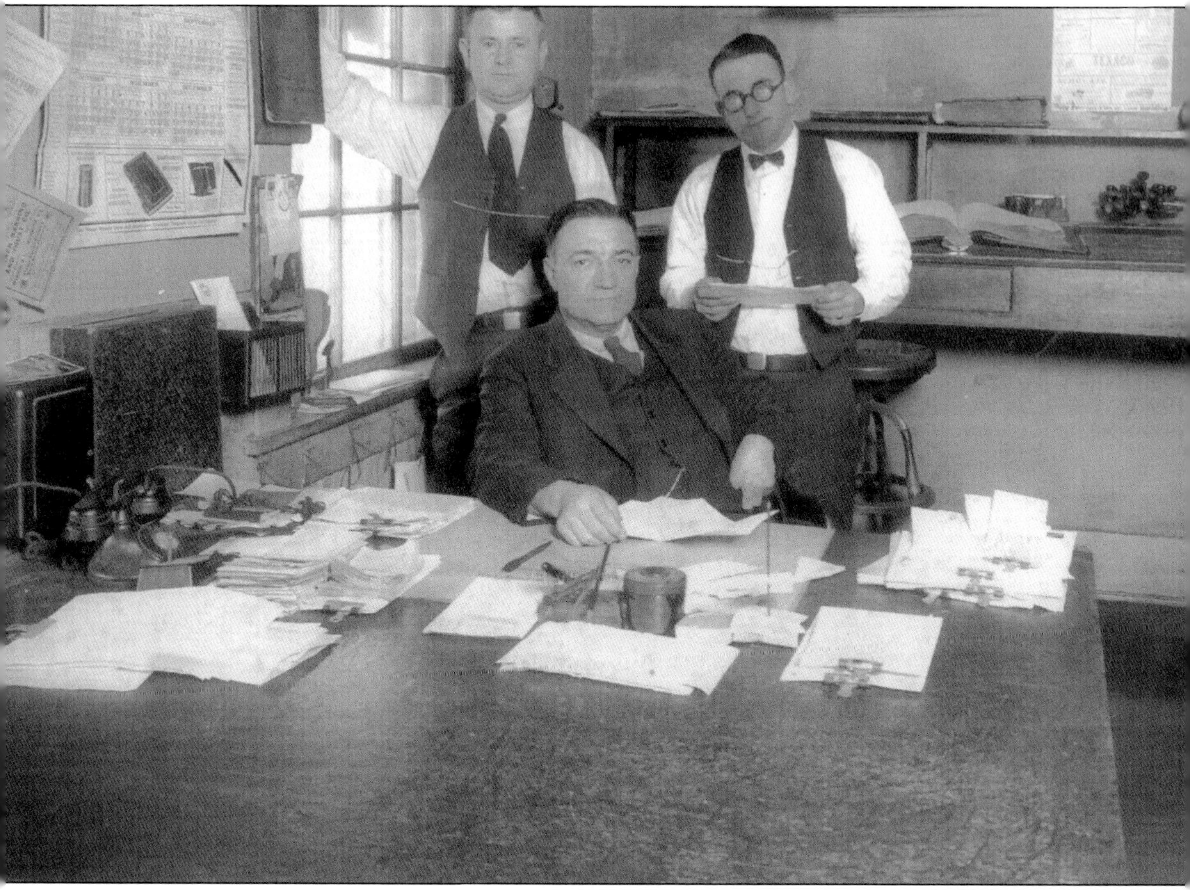

Harrison Wholesale Company Office Staff, 1934. Located on South Haughton Street beside the railroad station, the firm was begun in 1916. Initially dealing in groceries, it soon expanded to include a separate oil-distribution business. George H. Harrison Sr. is seated at center. (Courtesy of Elizabeth T. Brandon.)

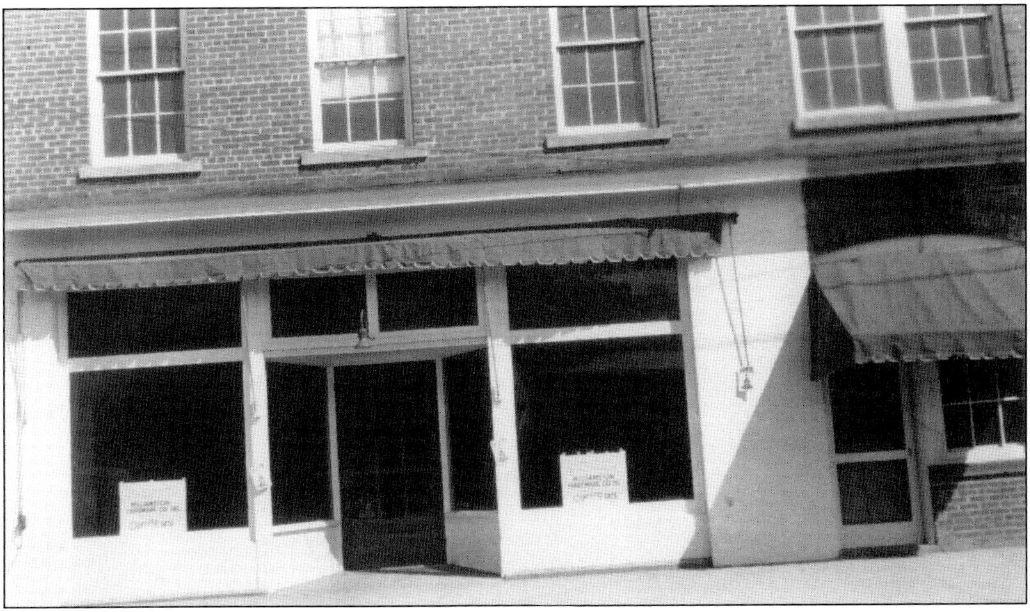

Williamston Hardware, 1935. Located in the Flatiron Building on Washington Street, this business was a fixture in the town for more than 40 years. (Courtesy of Martin County Historical Society.)

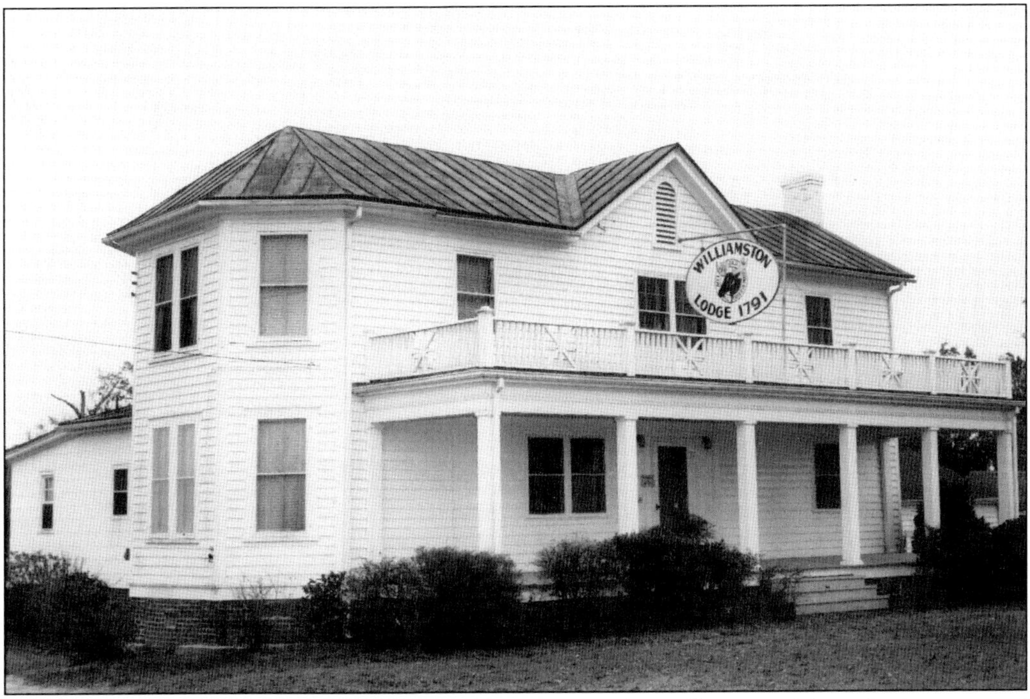

Williamston Moose Lodge, c. 1970. From 1959 to 1986, the Williamston Moose Lodge occupied and made extensive improvements to this building, formerly the home of A.D. and Melva Harris. Prior to the Harrises' ownership, the structure had a long and interesting history as home to the Staton family, and prior to that, William Biggs I, a wealthy landowner with extensive holdings in the area. The image is attributed to B.W. Parker of Robersonville. (Courtesy of the author.)

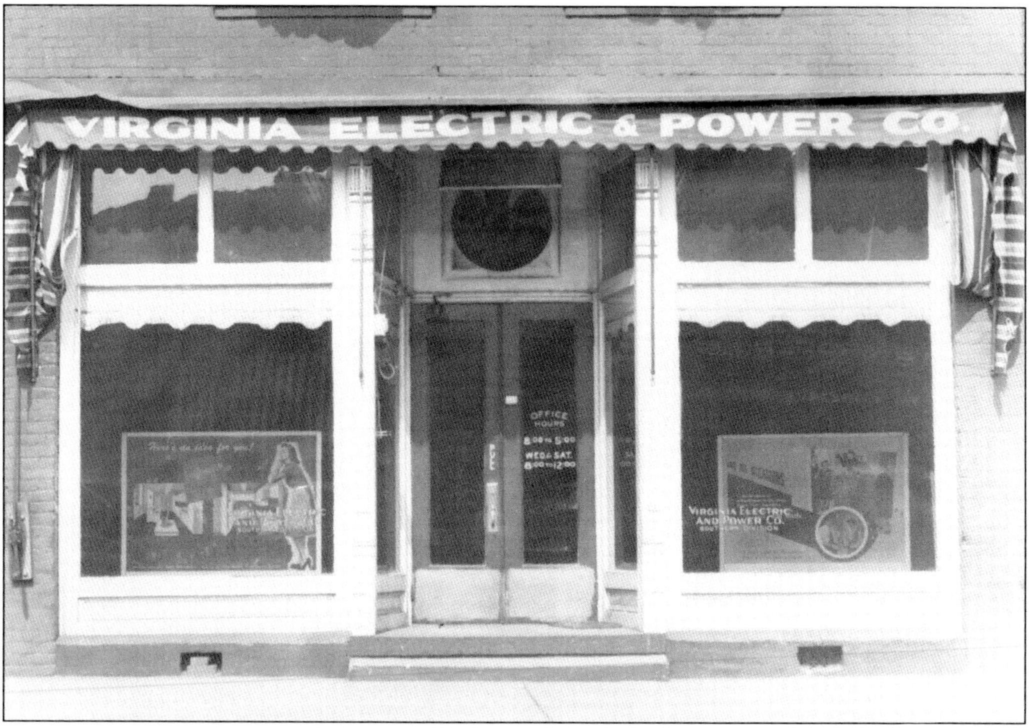

Virginia Electric & Power Co., c, 1935. The company's original office is shown here; in the 1950s, it relocated to a more spacious and modern facility on West Boulevard in Williamston. It is now part of energy giant Dominion Power. (Courtesy of Martin County Historical Society.)

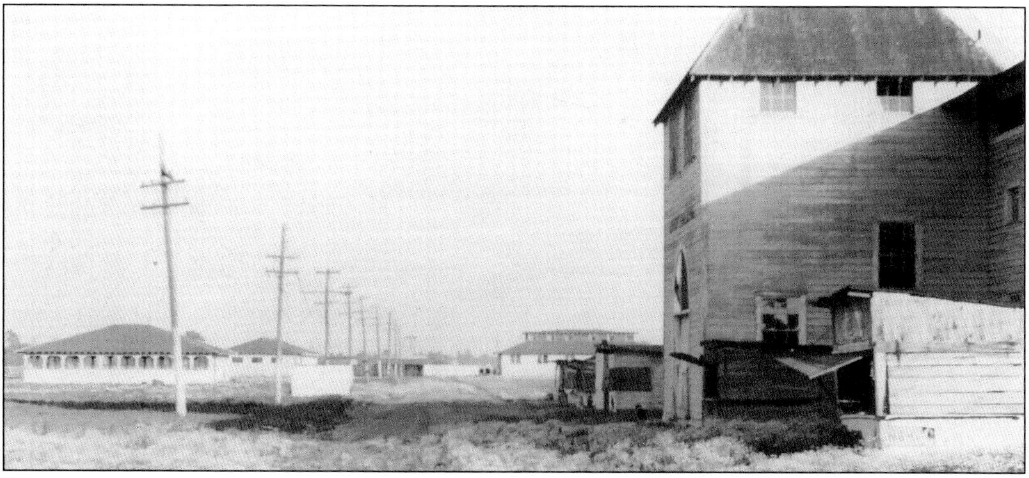

Williamston Fairgrounds, June 9, 1937. At one time, Williamston boasted one of the largest county fair establishments in the state, rivaled only by the state fair in Raleigh. Its heyday was from the 1920s to the 1940s. After World War II, the property began to be subdivided into residential lots that now make up the neighborhood known as West End. (Courtesy of Martin County Historical Society.)

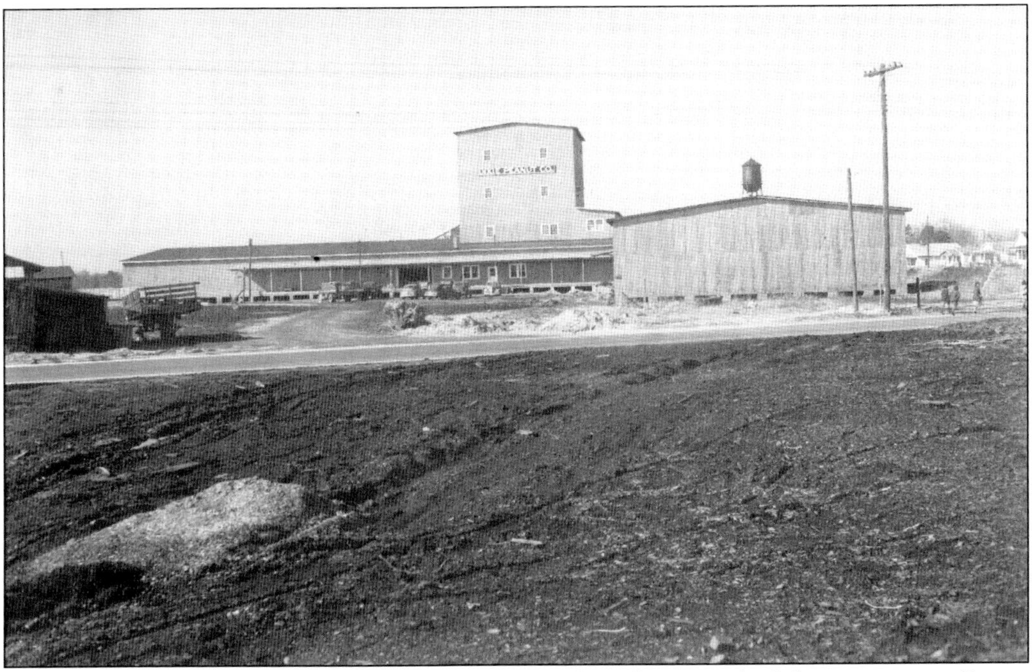

Dixie Peanut Company, c. 1945. During this period, Williamston had the reputation of being the largest "wagon market" for peanuts in the world. The Dixie Peanut Company was located on the west side of Washington Street. (Courtesy of Martin County Historical Society.)

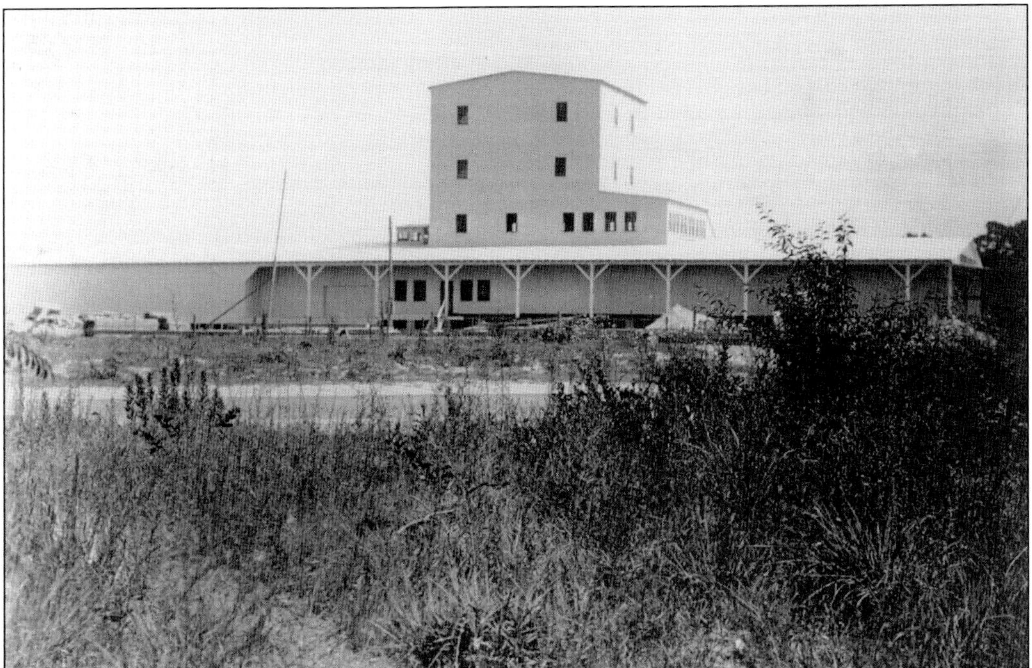

Columbian/Williamston Peanut Company Complex, 1937. Construction of the Columbian Peanut Company (which would later become the Williamston Peanut Company) on the east side of Washington Street started in April 1930. (Courtesy of Martin County Historical Society.)

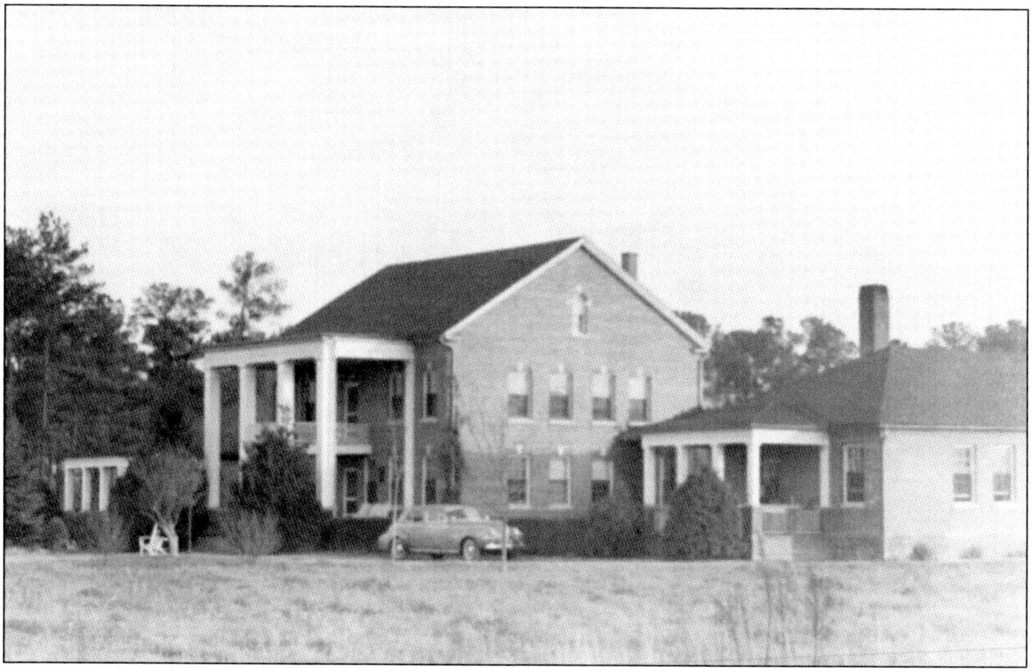

The Martin County Home, c. 1945. Built in 1925 to replace the original Martin County Poorhouse complex serving the area's indigent, elderly population, this facility was demolished in the late 20th century, and the location is now occupied by the Martin County Farmer's Market. (Courtesy of Martin County Historical Society.)

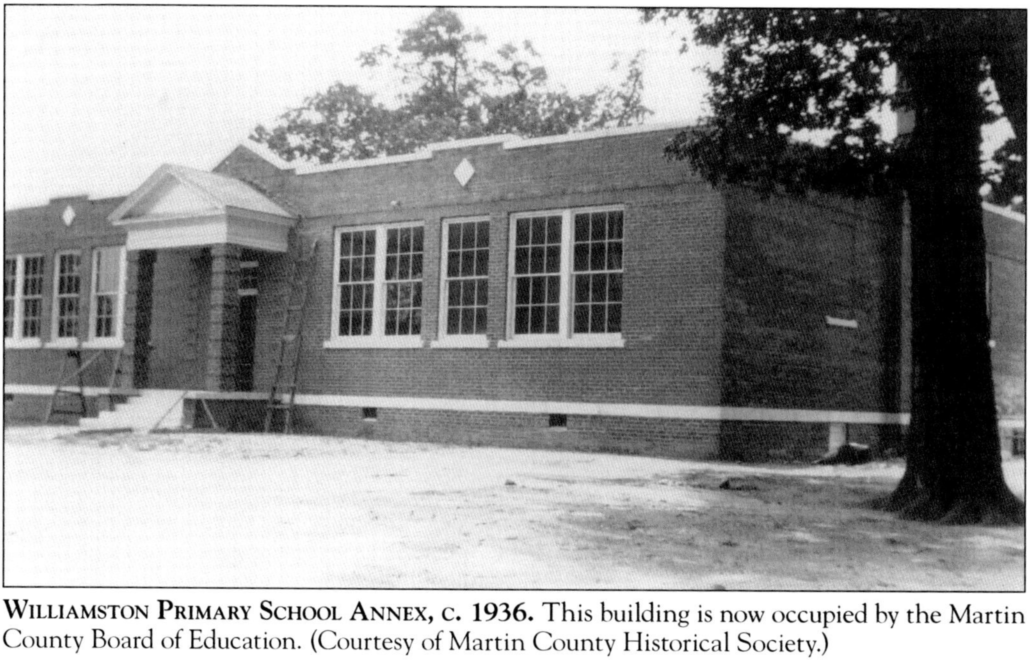

Williamston Primary School Annex, c. 1936. This building is now occupied by the Martin County Board of Education. (Courtesy of Martin County Historical Society.)

James Grist and Fannie Chase Staton, c. 1940. This well-remembered couple, photographed at their home, engaged in extensive farm and commercial interests in Williamston. Each had considerable fortunes from both inheritance and previous marriages. From the fortune of her first husband, Dennis Simmons Biggs, Fannie is credited with giving Williamston's Church of the Advent a new building in 1917 and with the construction of the Tar Heel apartment building on West Main Street in 1920. (Courtesy of Beverly G. Mills.)

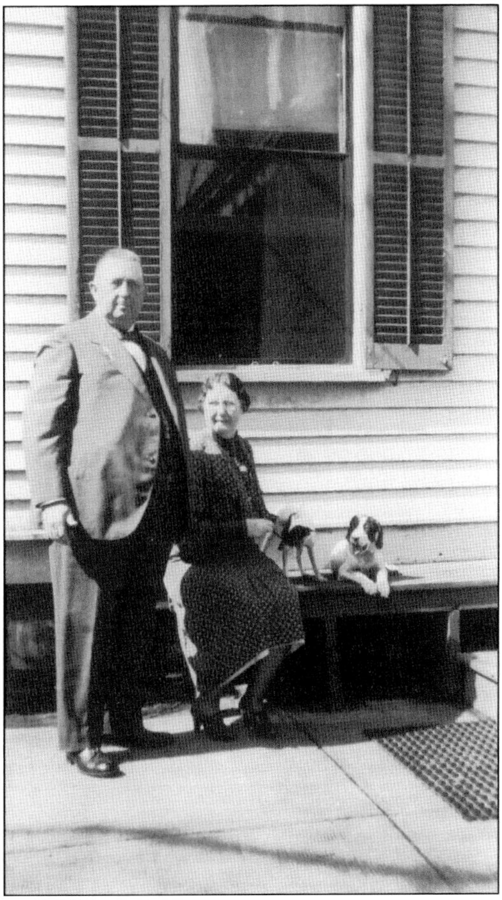

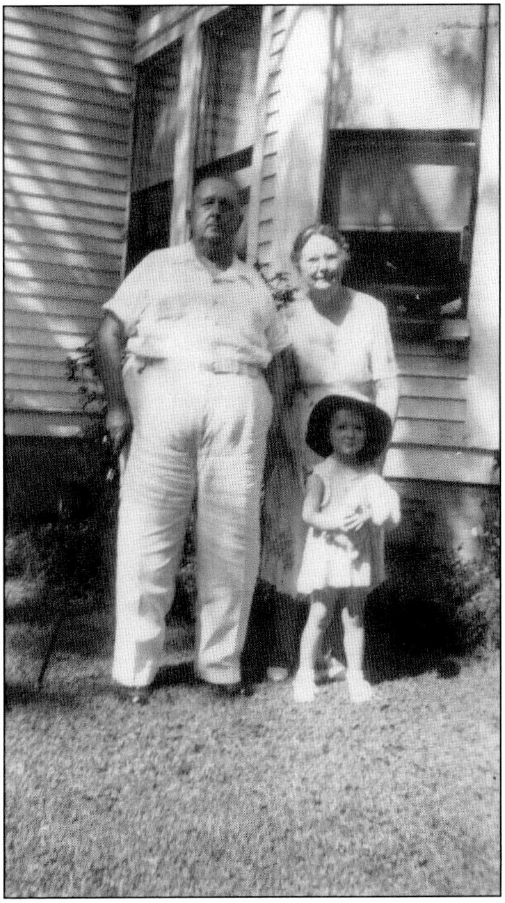

Statons with Niece, c. 1944. Here, the couple is seen with niece Louisa Godwin Celebrezze. James Staton died in 1946, and Fannie, in 1956. Their lovely home on the corner of South Haughton and Main Streets was demolished sometime in 1957 or 1958, and the property was redeveloped for commercial purposes. (Courtesy of Beverly G. Mills.)

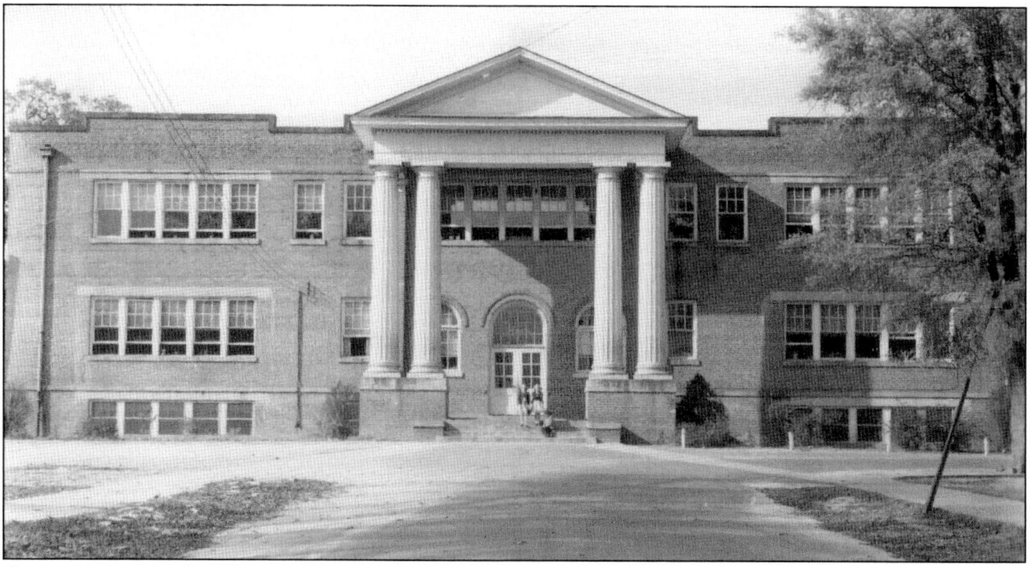

CHURCH STREET GRAMMAR SCHOOL, C. 1945. Built between 1917 and 1918, this structure replaced the old Williamston Academy building, which dated to nearly 100 years before. Until 1929, it served all grades. Use of the school was discontinued in the 1970s, and it was finally demolished in 1990. (Courtesy of Martin County Historical Society.)

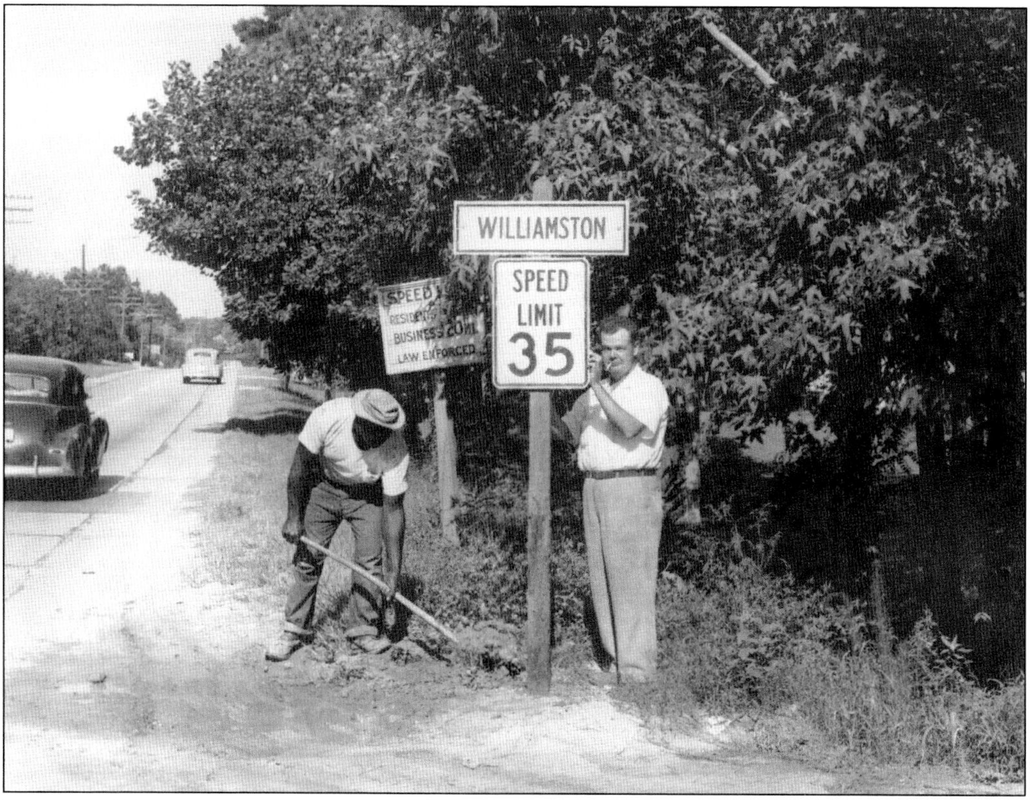

ENTERING WILLIAMSTON, C. 1945. This area of West Main Street is somewhere close to Brown's Community Hospital. (Courtesy of Martin County Historical Society.)

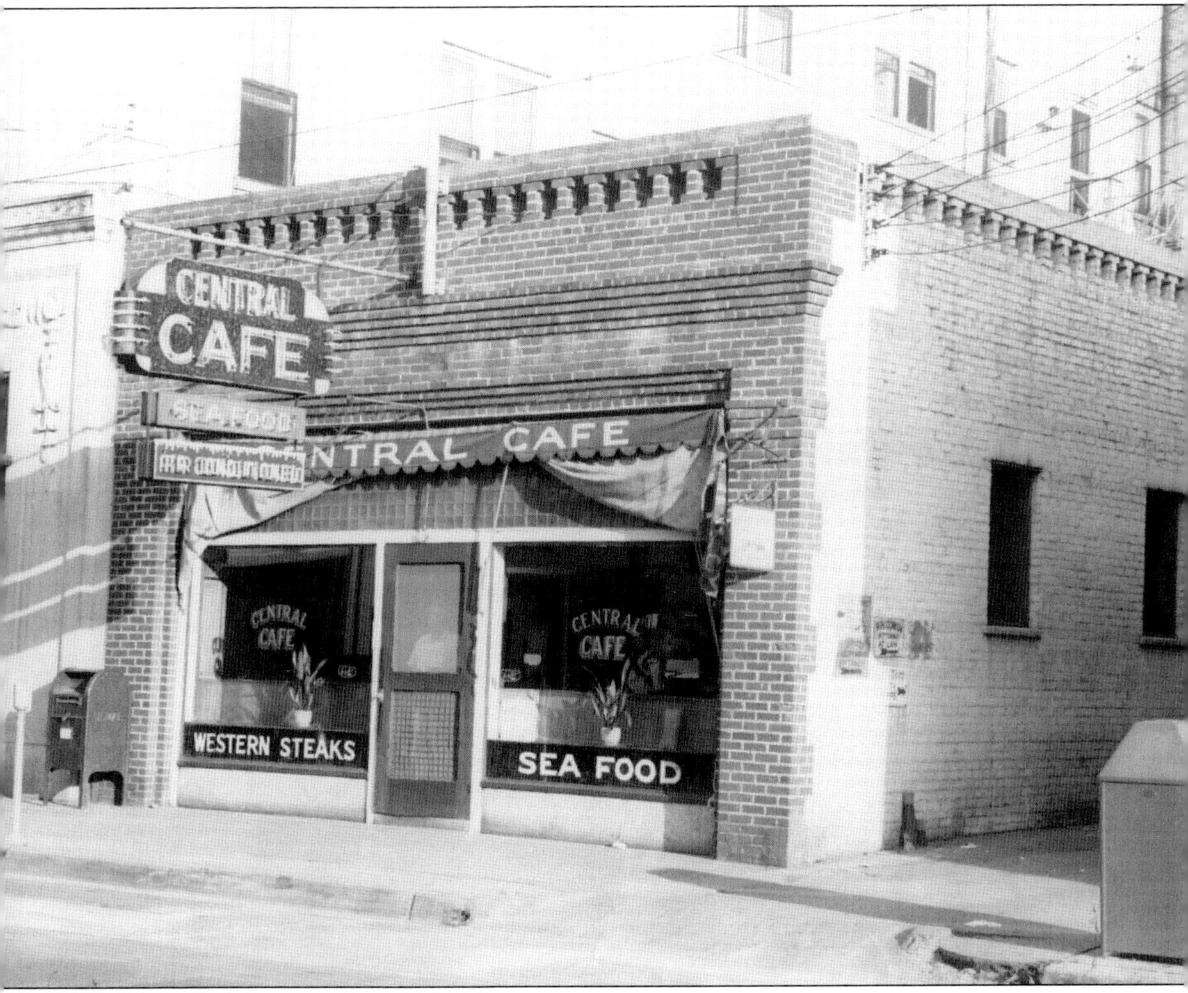

Central Café, c. 1945. Opened in Williamston in 1936, the Central Café (photographed here by Eugene Rise) was owned and operated by George Stetsos and later, Pete Christopher. In 1952, it was purchased by J.S. Whitley, who remodeled it for Pittman's Clothing Store. (Courtesy of Martin County Historical Society.)

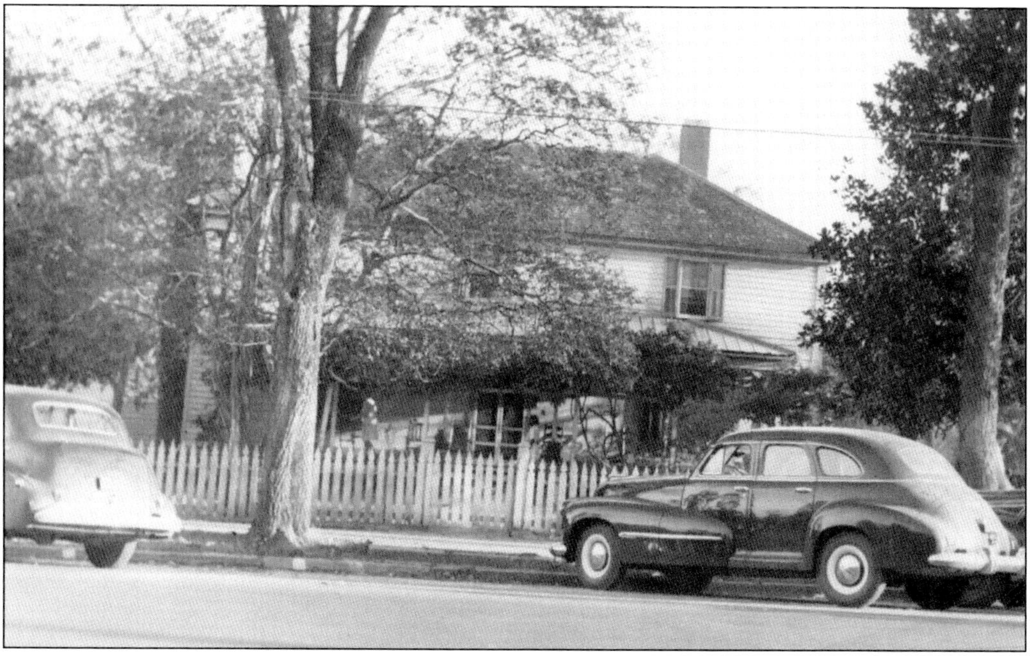

W.K. Parker Home, c. 1945–1950. Not long after this picture was taken, the porch on this East Main Street structure was raised to the height of the second story, as it appears today. Considered one of Williamston oldest houses, the residence was originally constructed around 1810 for Richard Williams, a grandson of Williamston's namesake, Col. William Williams. (Courtesy of Ila F. Parker.)

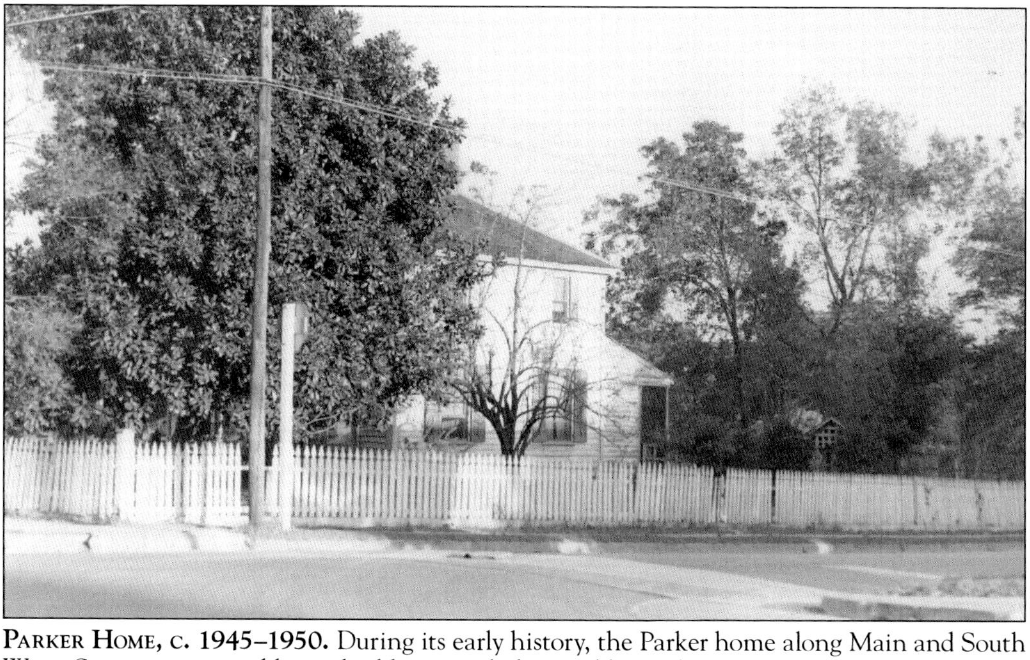

Parker Home, c. 1945–1950. During its early history, the Parker home along Main and South Watts Streets was served by outbuildings, including stables and a carriage house located across Watts Street on the property now occupied by the Williamston Presbyterian Church. (Courtesy of Ila F. Parker.)

W.K. Parker Home, c. 1947. Sometime in the 1840s or 1850s, this house was enlarged from a simple side-hall plan to its present size. The chimney on the left marks the original portion of the house and holds a brick inscribed with the date 1810. (Courtesy of Ila F. Parker.)

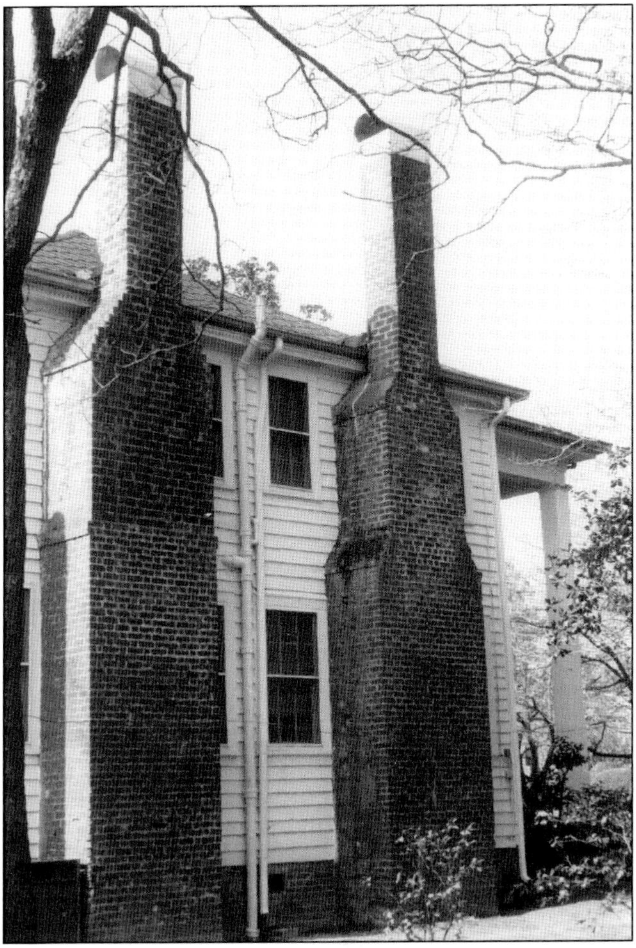

Williamston Prisoner-of-War Camp, c. 1944–1945. German and Italian prisoners housed in the camp, located along East Main Street near the Roanoke River Bridge, were well thought of by the citizens of Martin County. During their stay, the Germans built a life-size nativity scene. It was highly publicized and left as a gift to the town of Williamston after of the war. Sadly, in 1958, it was destroyed when the old Williamston City Hall burned. (Courtesy of the J.Y. Joyner Library, East Carolina Manuscript Collection.)

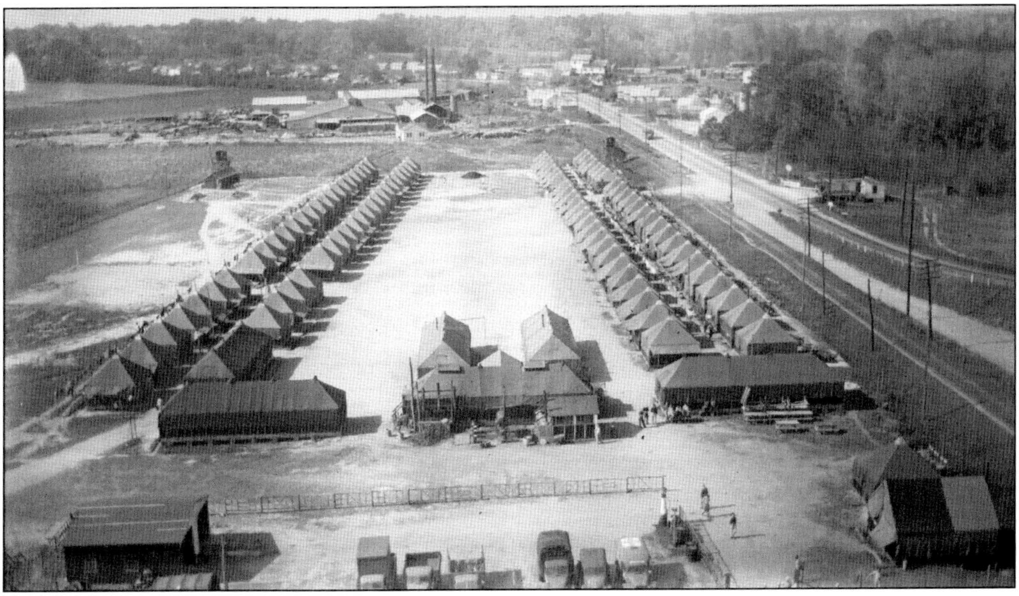

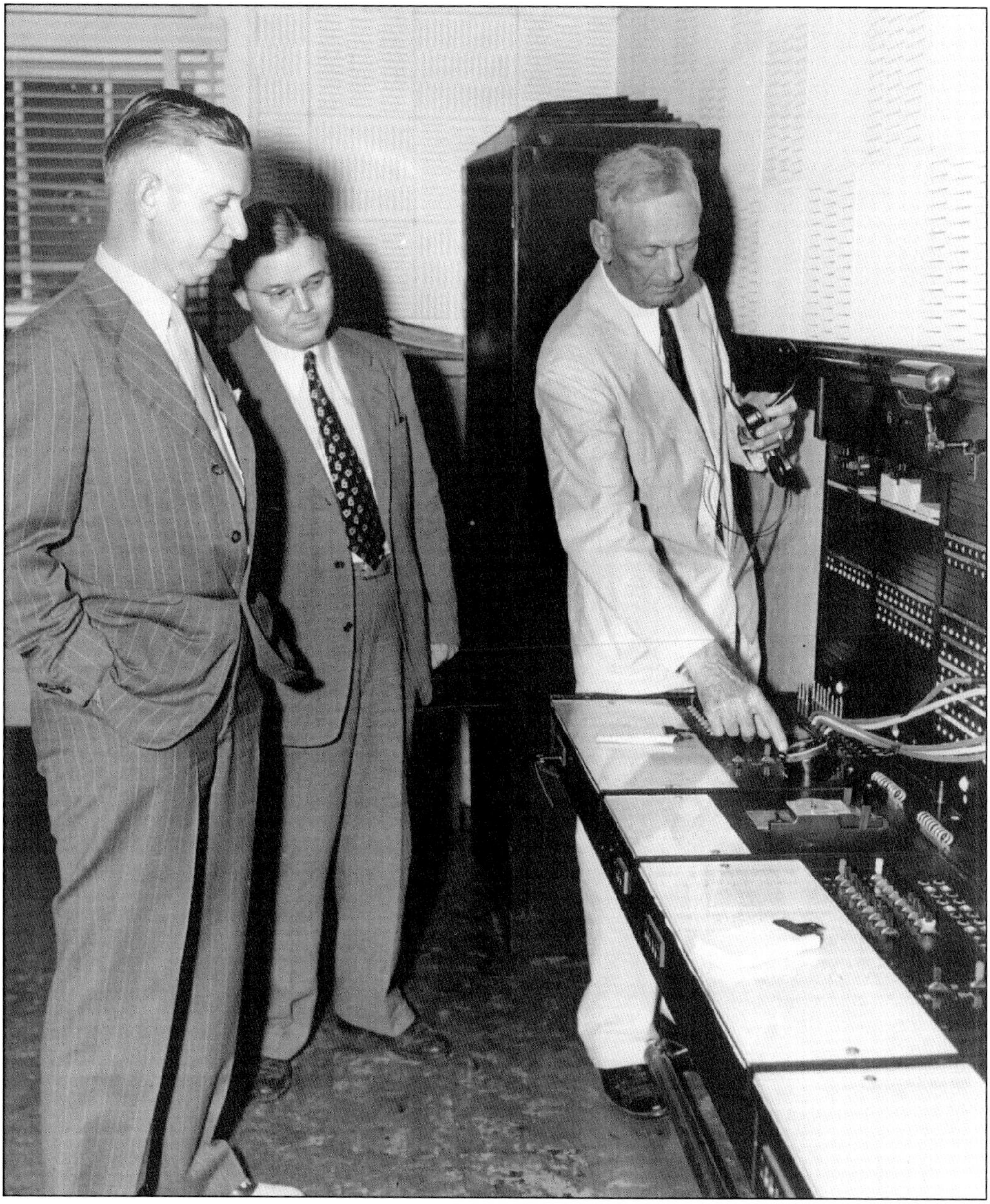

Advances in Telephone Technology, 1947. Williamston men Bill (left) and Francis Manning watch a demonstration given by a representative of Carolina Telephone & Telegraph Co. in Tarboro, North Carolina, concerning the new dial system. The brothers' father had started Williamston's first telephone exchange before selling it to the Tarboro-based company in the 1920s. (Courtesy of Martin County Historical Society.)

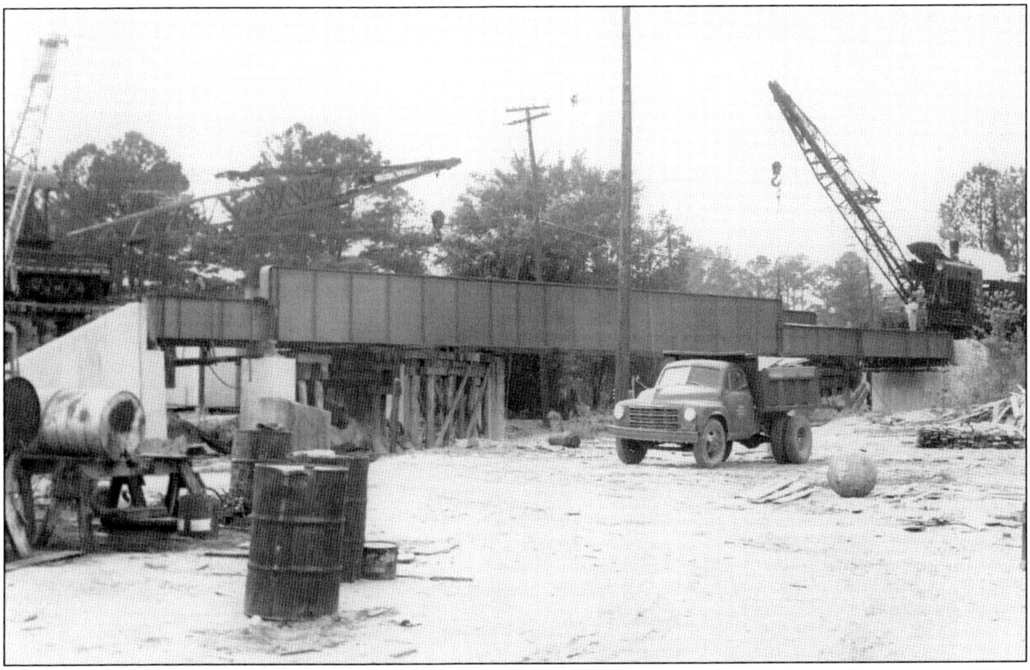

Railroad Overpass Reconstruction, c. 1952. Prior to these improvements, this area on West Main Street was regarded as a great safety hazard for motorists. (Courtesy of Martin County Historical Society.)

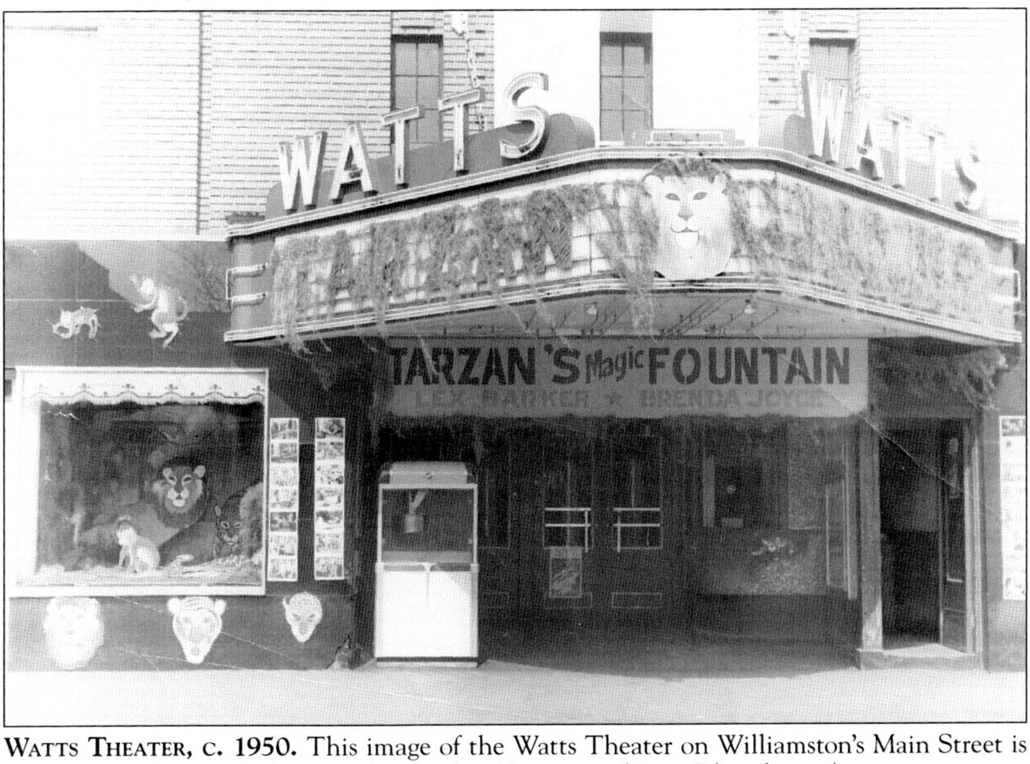

Watts Theater, c. 1950. This image of the Watts Theater on Williamston's Main Street is attributed to the Royal Photographic Studio. (Courtesy of Jesse Silverthorne.)

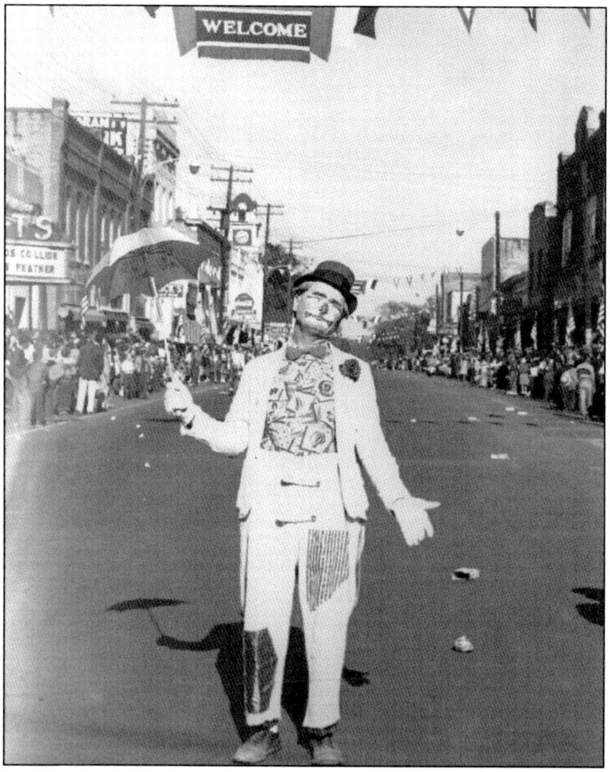

Parade Clown, c. 1951. This unidentified subject is believed to have been photographed by Eugene Rice during the Williamston Harvest Festival parade. (Courtesy of Martin County Historical Society.)

Williamston Harvest Parade Entry, 1952. By the mid-20th century, accidents in North Carolina were becoming a serious problem, necessitating a statewide campaign for public awareness (as demonstrated with this parade entry). (Courtesy of the J.Y. Joyner Library, East Carolina Manuscript Collection.)

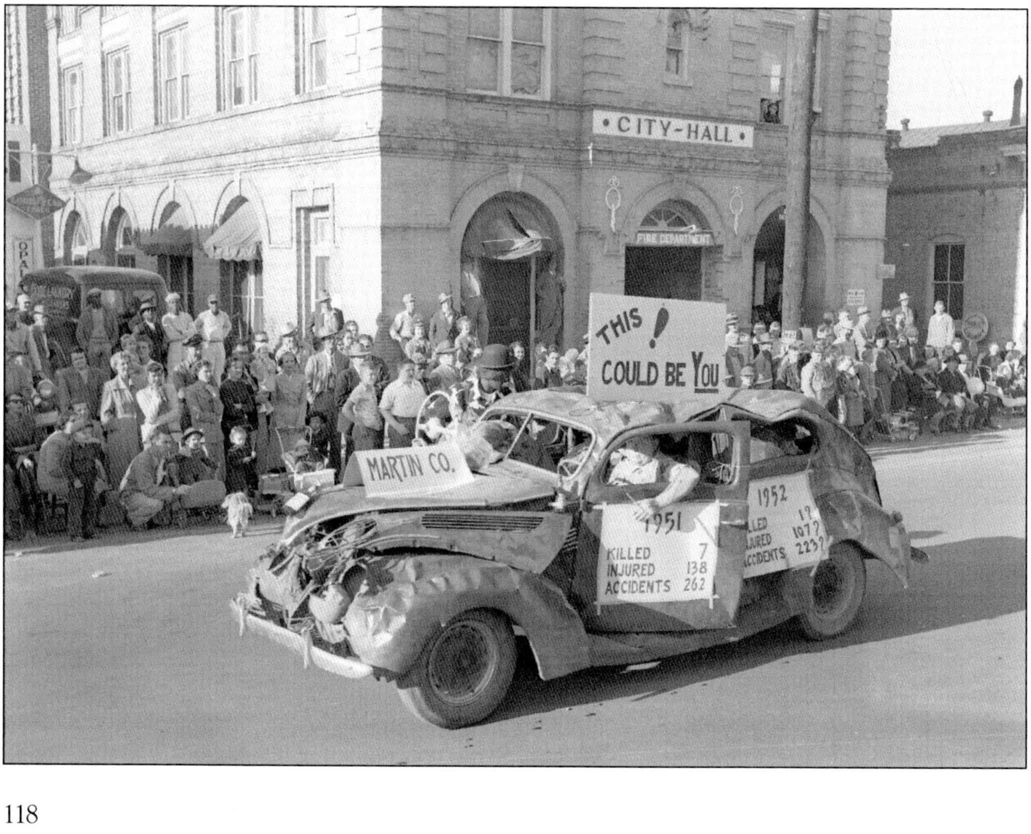

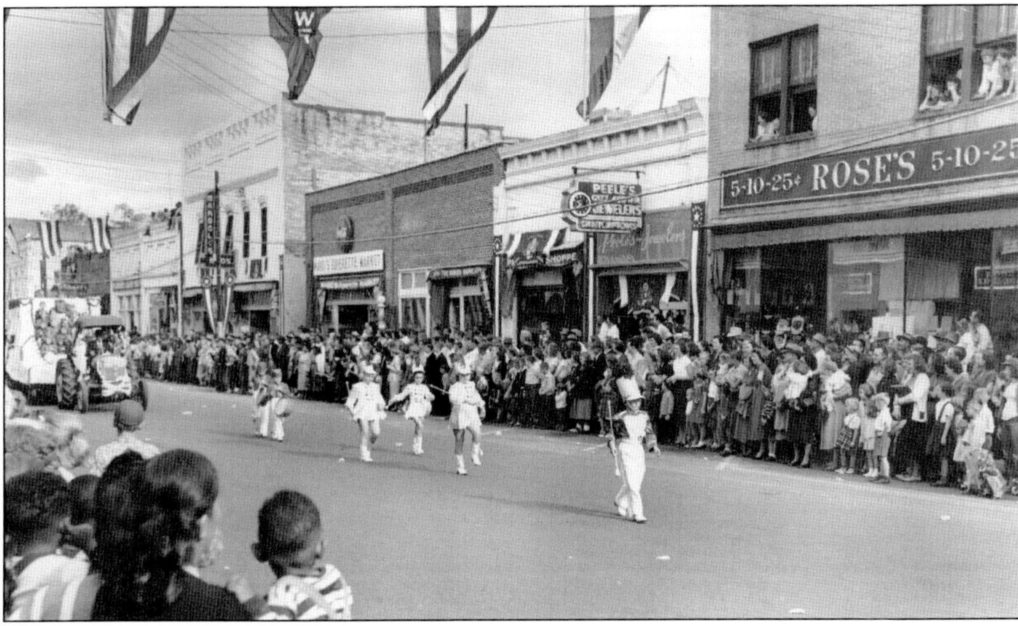

WILLIAMSTON HARVEST PARADE, C. 1951–1952. In the background of this view are several well-remembered retail businesses, including Margolis Brothers (two-story white building at left), Ward's Superette Market, the Pioneer Shop, the Proctor Shoppe, Peele's Jewelers, and Rose's dime store. (Courtesy of Jesse Silverthorne.)

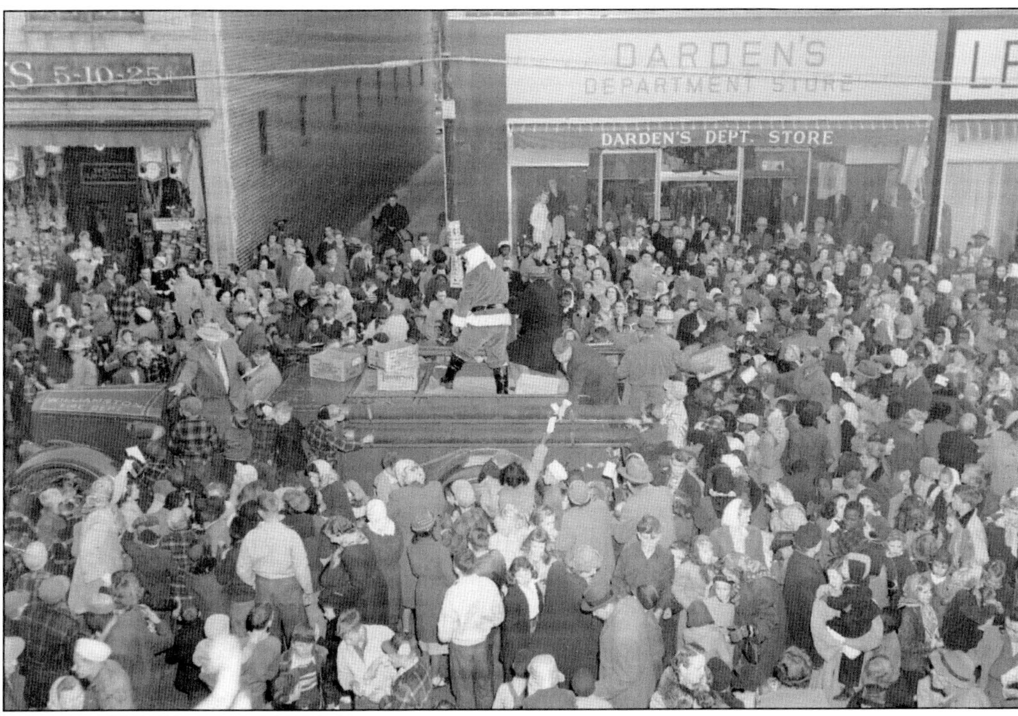

WILLIAMSTON CHRISTMAS PARADE, C. 1951–1952. In Martin County, the appearance of Santa Claus traditionally marked either the end or beginning of a holiday parade. (Courtesy of Jesse Silverthorne.)

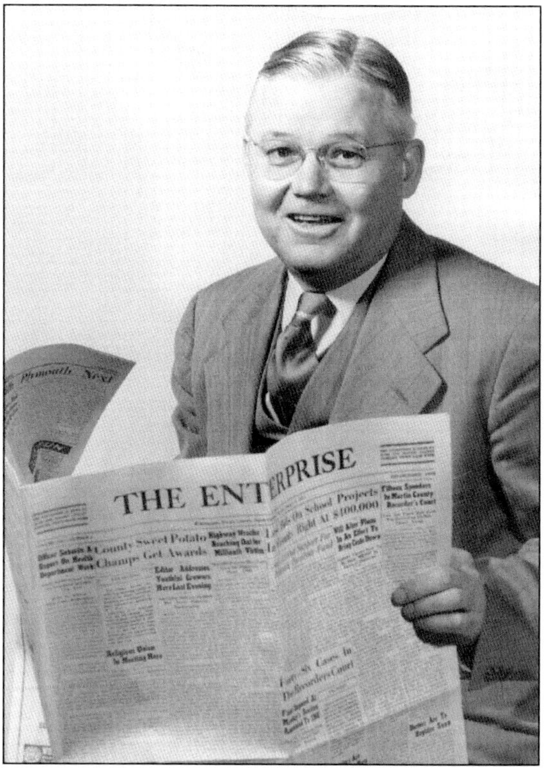

Francis Marion Manning, c. 1950. Son of William Christian and Sarah Roberson Manning, Francis Marion Manning (1903–1982) is best remembered for his longtime role as publisher of Williamston's newspaper, the *Enterprise*. (Courtesy of Martin County Historical Society.)

Worrell Appliance Co., c. 1950–1955. This business is remembered for advertising and selling the earliest television units in Williamston. Its display window with televisions was a popular feature in town before widespread access to personal sets. (Courtesy of Jesse Silverthorne.)

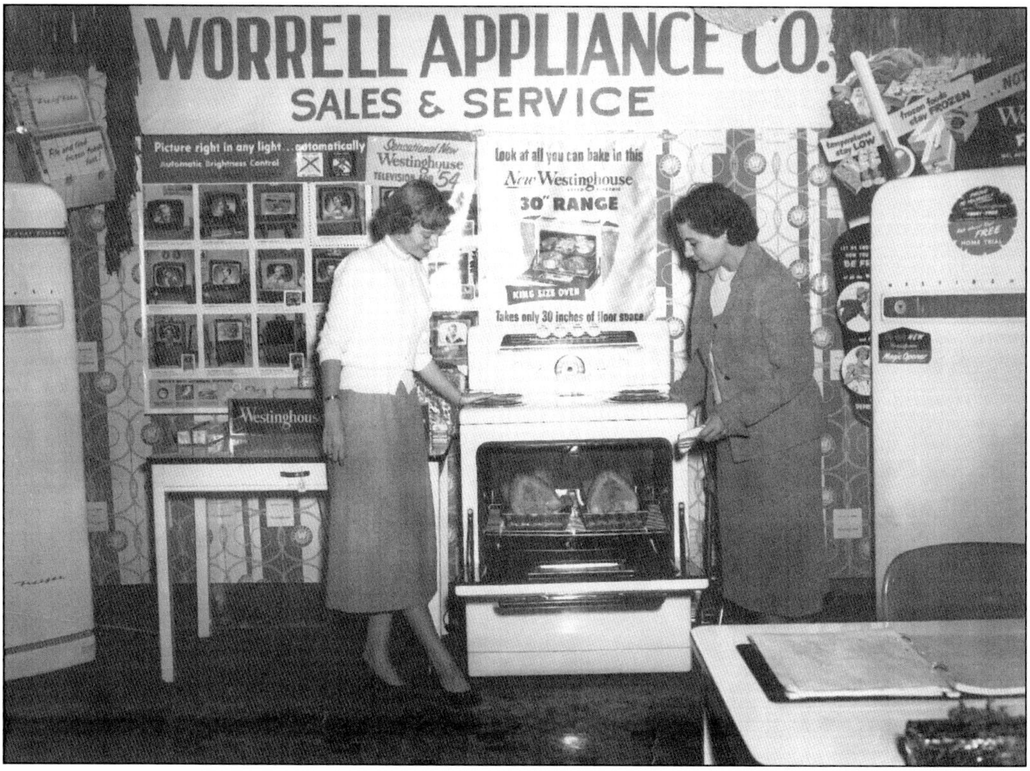

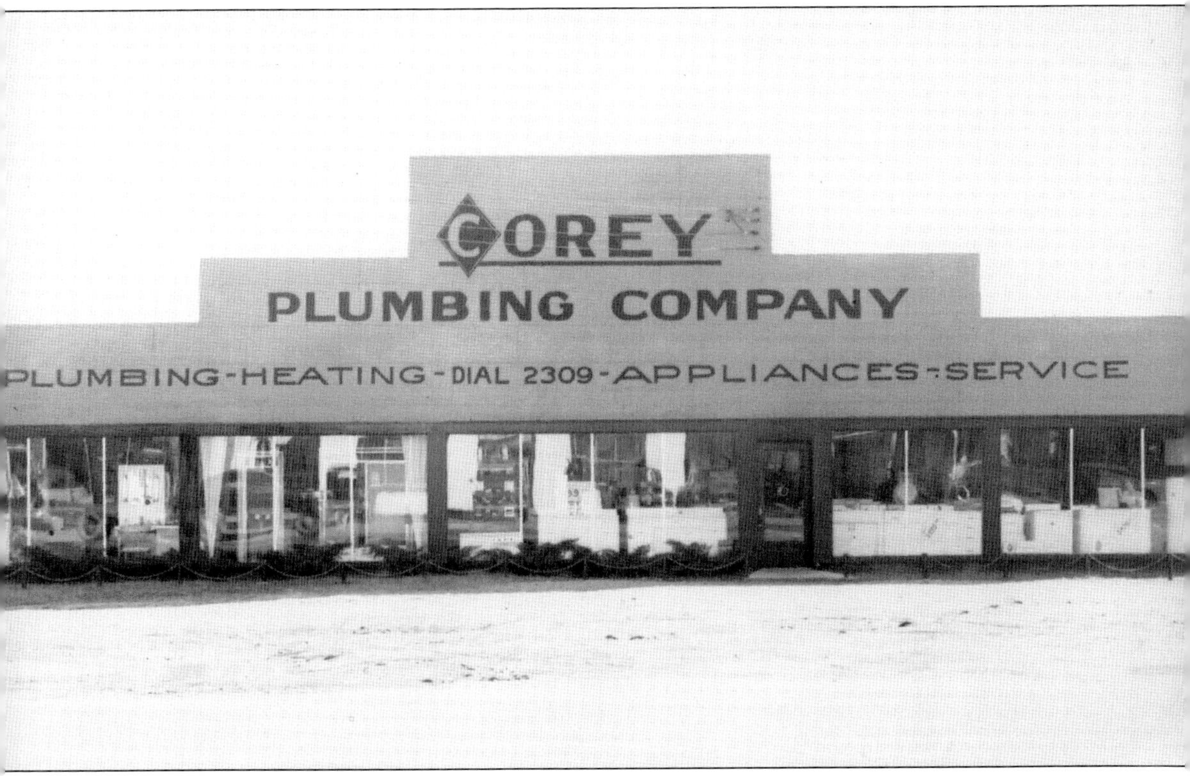

COREY PLUMBING CO., c. 1955. Chartered on April 28, 1948, with George W. Corey, John Gray Corey, and Anne Johns Corey as stockholders, this business had a history spanning just over 60 years in Williamston. (Courtesy of Martin County Historical Society.)

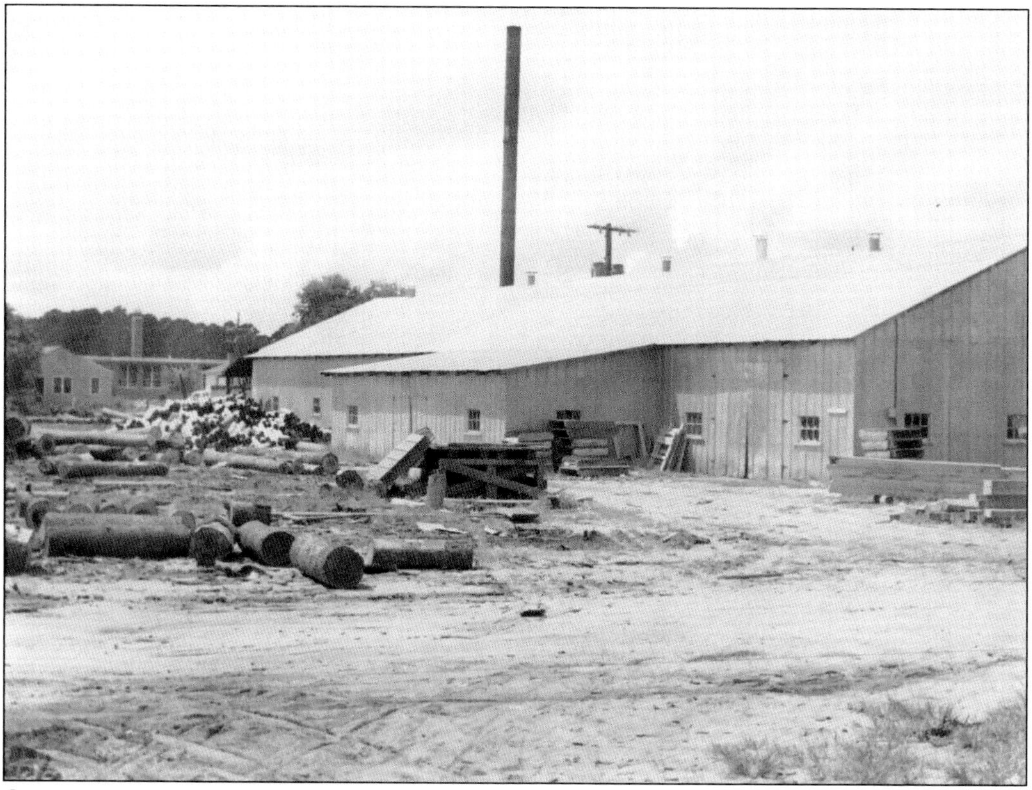

CRITCHER LUMBER MILL, C. 1960. This facility was located in the vicinity of the E.J. Hayes School (Photograph by Eugene Rice, courtesy of Martin County Historical Society.)

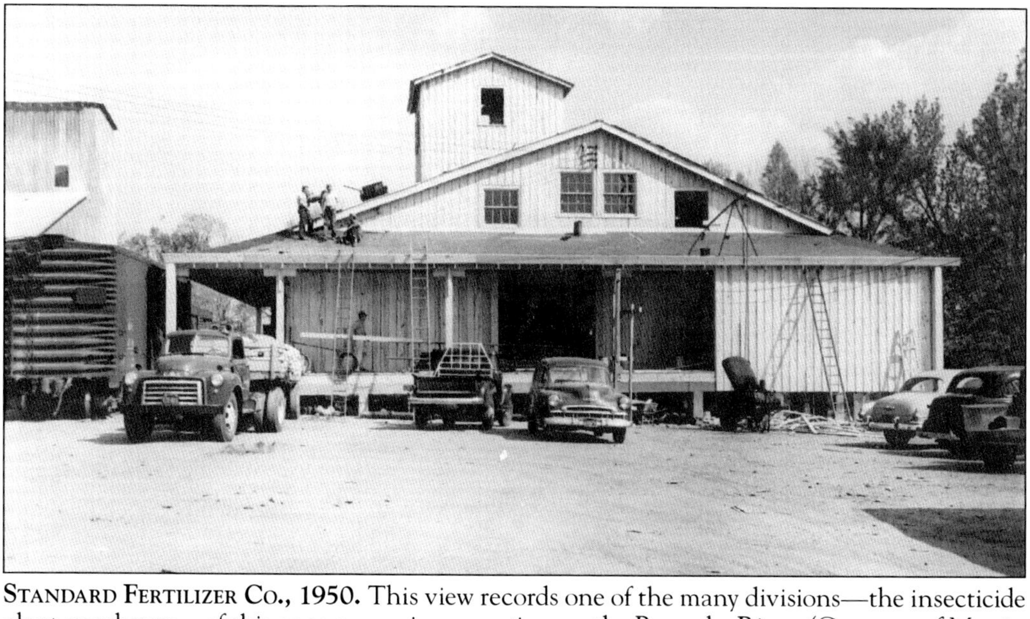

STANDARD FERTILIZER CO., 1950. This view records one of the many divisions—the insecticide plant warehouse—of this once expansive operation on the Roanoke River. (Courtesy of Martin County Historical Society.)

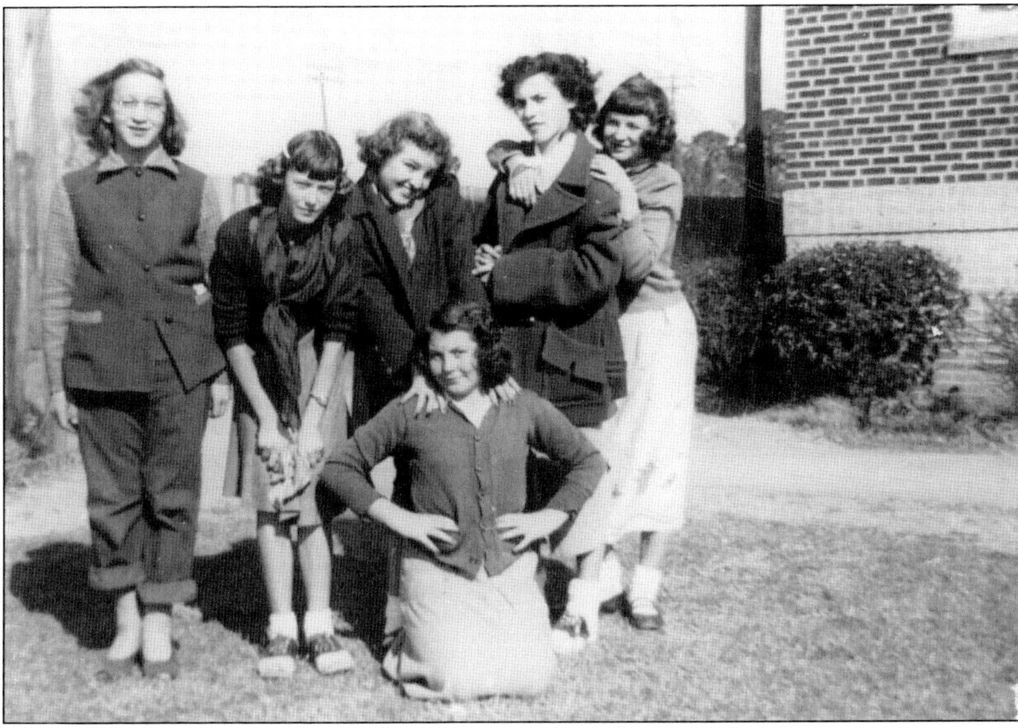

Williamston Seventh Graders, 1951. Students identified from Mrs. Parrott's class are (standing), from left to right, Janie Harrison, Margaret Barber, Pat Coltrain, Helen Christopher, and unidentified; (kneeling) Ethel Bowen. (Courtesy of Ann H. Harrison.)

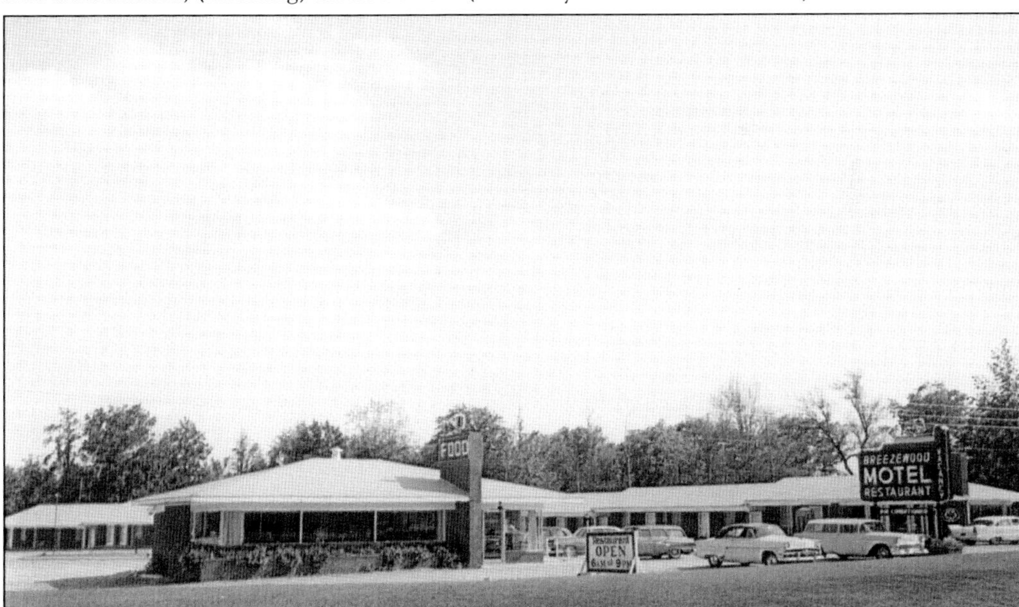

Breezewood Motel and Restaurant, c. 1956. Owned and operated by John T. and Ann Gurkin, the site featured "100% centrally heated and air-conditioned" rooms, "wall to wall carpet and TV," plus "20 Deluxe Units" when it opened in 1956. (Courtesy of the author.)

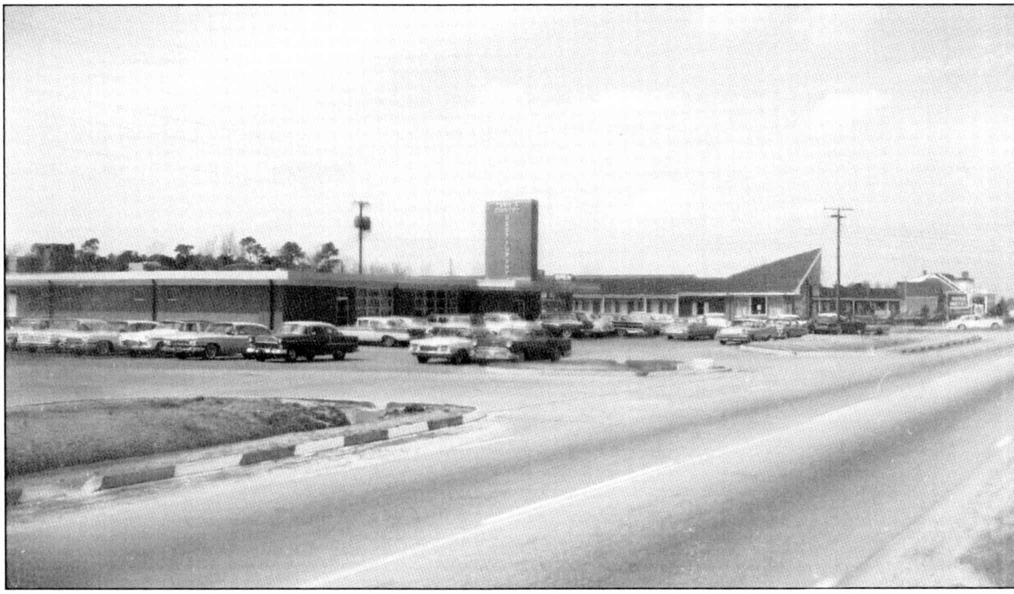

Town and Country Restaurant, c. 1955. Seen here in a Royal Photographic Studio postcard image, this restaurant was a popular and well-known location along the Ocean Highway for over 30 years. A successor restaurant, Cobb's Corner, was later moved to the Williamston Holiday Inn. This building and the adjoining Ross Motel were owned and managed by the W.T. Ross family.

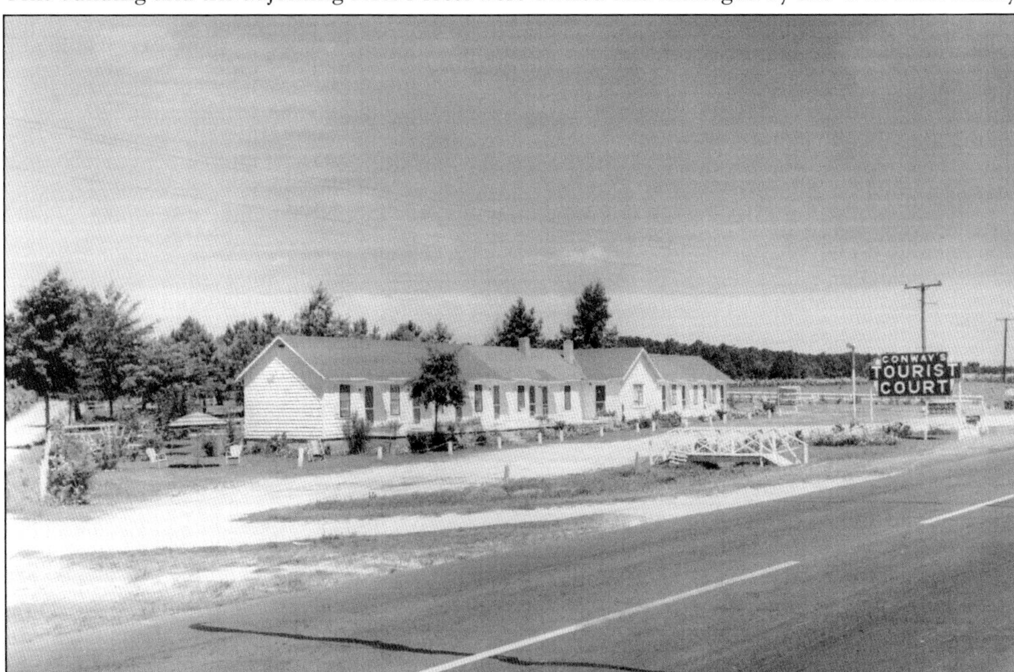

Conway's Motor Court, c. 1950. In addition to this US Highway 17 business, proprietor Barney Lee Conway, originally from Tennessee, was also involved in a number of motel and restaurant ventures along Williamston's outer limits in the 1950s. In 1959, he and his wife, Sallie Gurkin Conway, opened the Redwood Motel and Restaurant on the southwest corner of US Highway 17 and the US 64 Bypass. (Courtesy of Jesse Silverthorne.)

David A. Boyd, January 15, 1959. For many years, Boyd served Williamston as an insurance agent for Life of Virginia. He was active in civic and community affairs until his death in 1980. (Courtesy of Martin County Historical Society.)

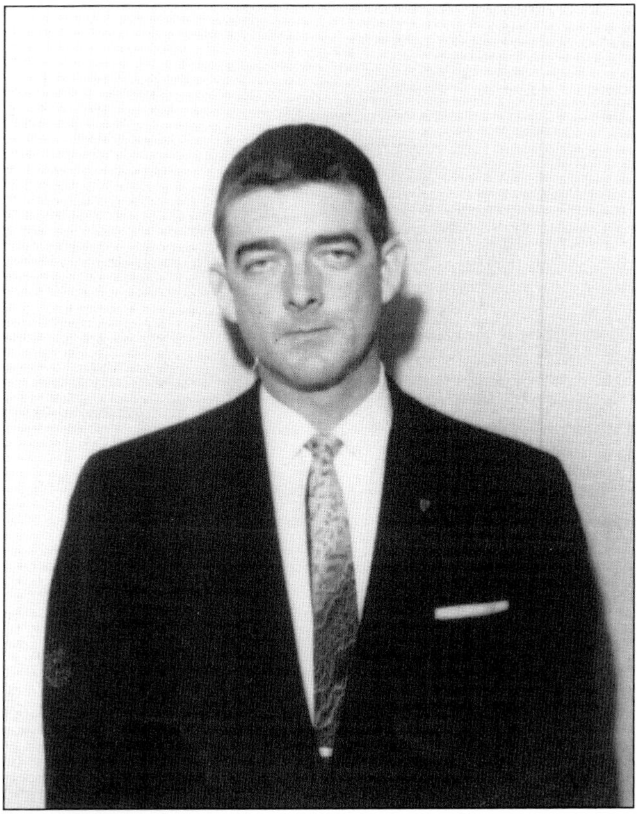

Pal Motor Court, c. 1948. During the 1950s, Williamston emerged as a central terminus for several major highways in North Carolina. The name of this Highway 17 North motor court, Pal, is derived from an abbreviation of the name Patricia Ann Lilley, a daughter of the establishment's owners, James Paul and Blanche Lilley. (Courtesy of Jesse Silverthorne.)

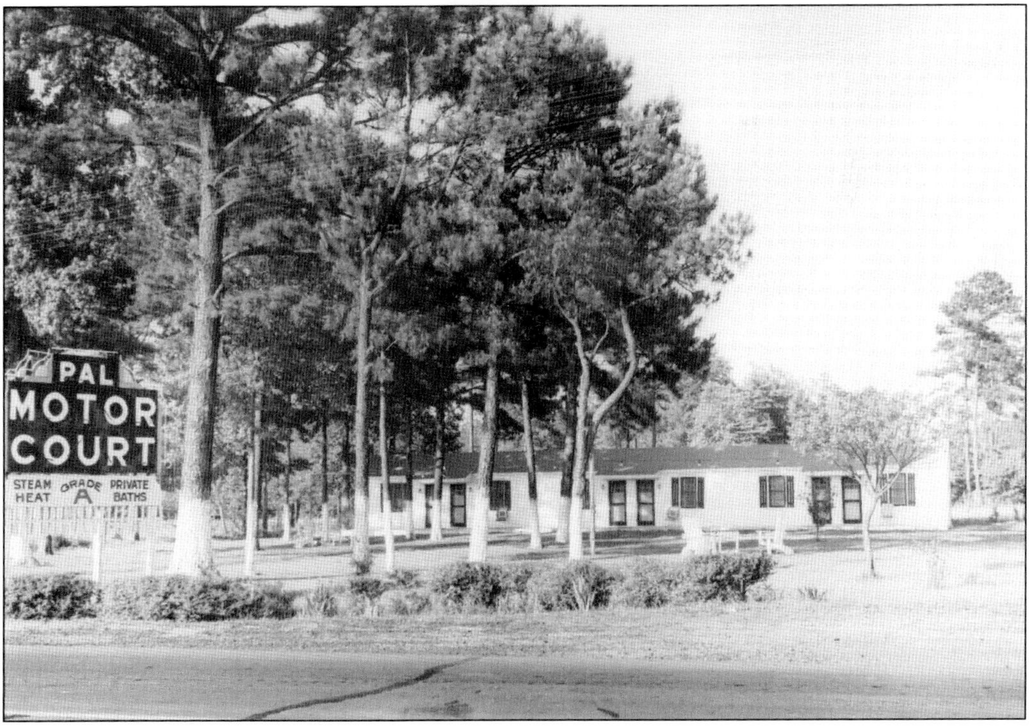

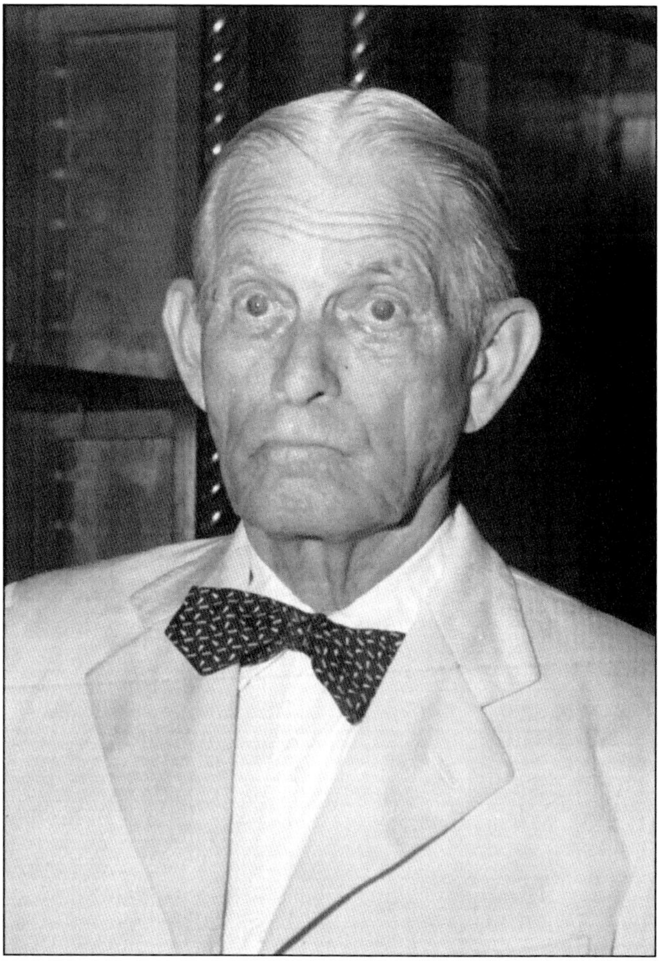

Warren H. Biggs, c. 1960. A longtime county historian and collector of rare books and manuscripts, Biggs (1881–1966) operated Biggs Drug Store, which was begun by his father, S.R. Biggs, in the 1880s.

Members of the Williamston Rescue Squad, June 25, 1964. Pictured standing along Smithwick Street are, from left to right, Ernest Cox, Landy Griffin, Rudolph Saunders, Dr. G.G. Himmelwright, David Davis Jr., and Warren Golf. The Williamston Rescue Squad was organized on May 28, 1960. (Courtesy of Martin County Historical Society.)

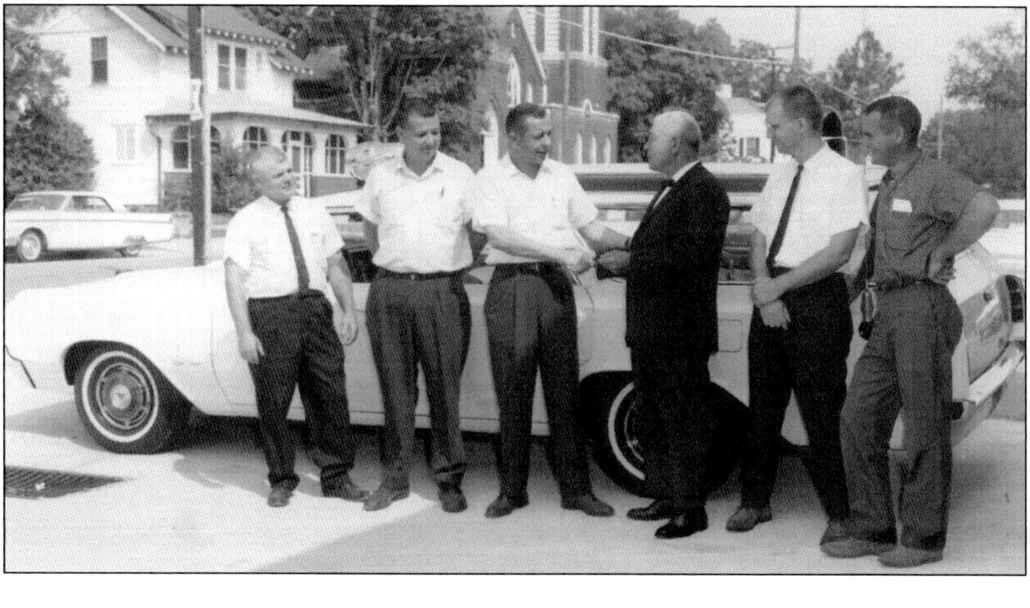

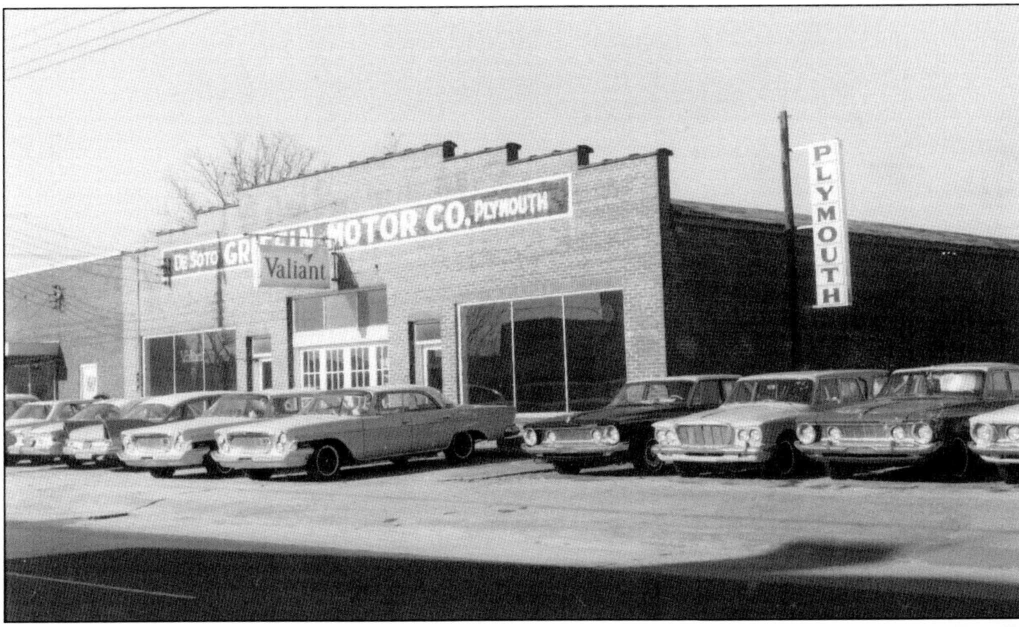

Griffin Motor Company, c. 1962. This automobile dealership on Washington Street officially began business in November 1959. (Courtesy of Martin County Historical Society.)

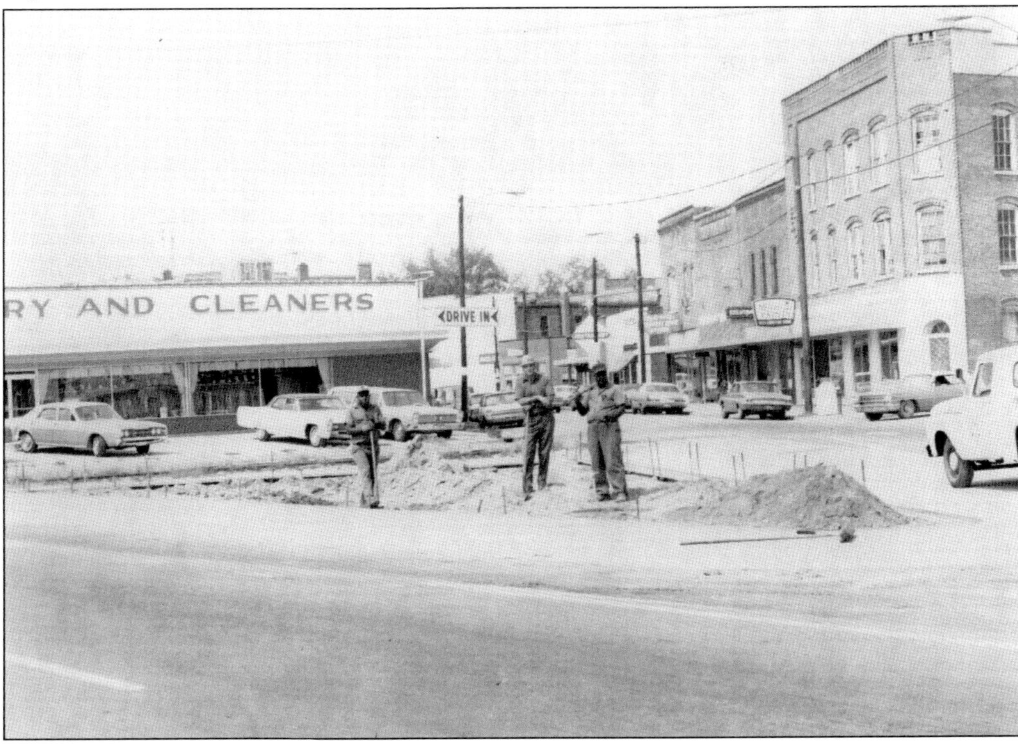

First Municipal Fountain, September 11, 1970. This image records workers preparing to wall in the triangle bordered by Washington, South Haughton, and Railroad Streets, the site of what would become the town's first municipal fountain. (Photograph by Eugene Rice, courtesy of Martin County Historical Society.)

Discover Thousands of Local History Books Featuring Millions of Vintage Images

Arcadia Publishing, the leading local history publisher in the United States, is committed to making history accessible and meaningful through publishing books that celebrate and preserve the heritage of America's people and places.

Find more books like this at
www.arcadiapublishing.com

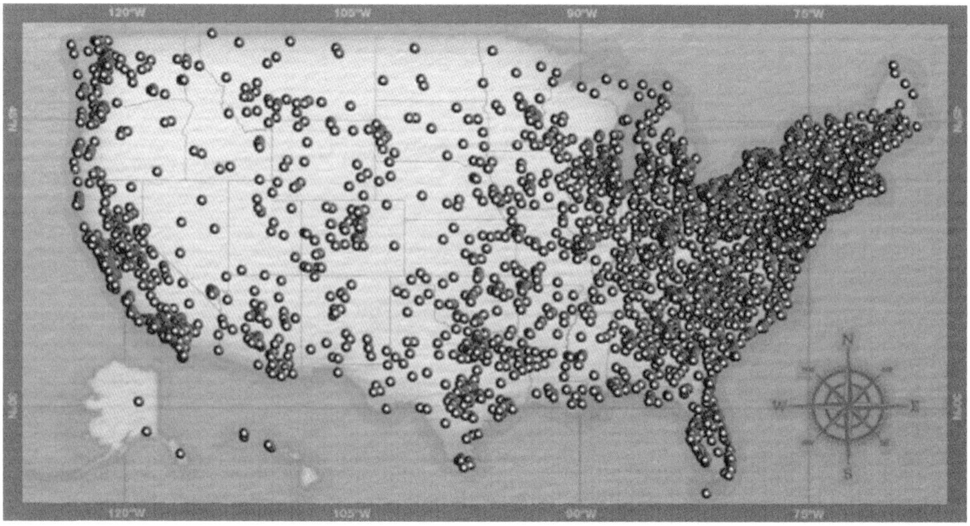

Search for your hometown history, your old stomping grounds, and even your favorite sports team.

Consistent with our mission to preserve history on a local level, this book was printed in South Carolina on American-made paper and manufactured entirely in the United States. Products carrying the accredited Forest Stewardship Council (FSC) label are printed on 100 percent FSC-certified paper.

MADE IN THE USA